State Institutions, Private Incentives, Global Capital

Michigan Studies in International Political Economy

SERIES EDITORS: Edward Mansfield and Lisa Martin

Michael J. Gilligan
Empowering Exporters: Reciprocity, Delegation, and Collective Action in American Trade Policy

Barry Eichengreen and Jeffry Frieden, Editors
Forging an Integrated Europe

Thomas H. Oatley
Monetary Politics: Exchange Rate Cooperation in the European Union

Robert Pahre
Leading Questions: How Hegemony Affects the International Political Economy

Andrew C. Sobel
State Institutions, Private Incentives, Global Capital

State Institutions, Private Incentives, Global Capital

Andrew C. Sobel

Ann Arbor

THE UNIVERSITY OF MICHIGAN PRESS

Copyright © by the University of Michigan 1999
All rights reserved
Published in the United States of America by
The University of Michigan Press
Manufactured in the United States of America
⊗ Printed on acid-free paper
2002   2001   2000   1999   4   3   2   1

A CIP catalog record for this book is available from the British Library.

Library of Congress Cataloging-in-Publication Data

Sobel, Andrew Carl, 1953–
    State institutions, private incentives, global capital / Andrew C.
Sobel.
       p.   cm. — (Michigan studies in international political
economy)
    Includes bibliographical references and index.
    ISBN 0-472-11005-5 (cloth : alk. paper)
    1. Capital movements.   2. Investments, Foreign.   3. Loans,
Foreign.   4. International finance.   I. Title.   II. Series.
HG3891.S67   1999
332'.042—dc21   99-34110
                                                              CIP

To Ken Organski, scholar, teacher, mentor, friend

Contents

Acknowledgments

I began floating trial balloons for this project during the summer of 1994. Peter Lange and Doug McAdam invited a group of young academics to participate in a two-month Summer Institute on International Economy and National Politics at the Center for the Advanced Study of the Behavioral Sciences in Palo Alto. I thank Phil Converse and Bob Scott, the director and associate director at CASBS, for their gracious hospitality and wonderful work environment. The summer proved fruitful in a variety of ways. I found the interactions and activities productive in crystallizing the direction and design of this project. I developed professional and personal relationships with colleagues who have provided critical feedback on this project and will supply productive comments on future research. In addition to Peter Lange and Doug McAdam, I owe thanks to Beth Simmons, Bruce Western, Ilene Grabel, Chris Anderson, Lori Leachman, George DeMartino, Jim McGuire, and David Rowe for their feedback and insights. In particular, Beth Simmons read several versions of the complete manuscript. She provided comments and feedback that went well beyond the call of duty. The manuscript is greatly improved as a consequence.

After the summer in Palo Alto, I spent the academic year as Visiting Fellow at the Wallis Institute of Political Economy at the University of Rochester. Going from summer in Palo Alto to winter in upstate New York seems like a dramatic shift but only in snowfall and temperature. Academically, the intellectual environment for political economy at Rochester was every bit as exciting as at Palo Alto. Daily coffees with David Austen-Smith, Jeff Banks, Larry Rothenberg, and Randy Calvert were a treat. They pushed and prodded me with questions and comments about my project. I learned a great deal about political economy in general and much about my project specifically.

I owe thanks to several anonymous reviewers for their thoughtful comments. I received helpful feedback from workshops and conferences at Rochester, Cornell, Duke, and Columbia. The Center in Political Economy and Center in

Law, Business, and Economics at Washington University in St. Louis provided funding for a small conference. Several graduate assistants contributed time and effort tracking down data, facts, and sources. I recognize Brady Baybeck, Steve Ceccoli, Ron Kruse, and Michelle Lorenzini for their labors. John Sprague, my friend and colleague at Washington University, provided invaluable assistance and guidance as I struggled with the data problems in chapters 6 and 7. I am lucky that John turned his infectious enthusiasm, agile mind, and determination to my puzzles. His insights helped unlock key obstacles to this research. Thanks to Chuck Myers, Colin Day, and the folks at the University of Michigan Press for their continued support and assistance.

Although they are placed at the beginning of a book, composing acknowledgments signals the completion of a manuscript. They demand a celebration. But as I finished this manuscript I heard that Ken Organski had passed away. Ken actively influenced my last book and this one, but he will also influence the next. He offered comments and instructions on my career, research, and writing. He began as teacher and scholar and became a mentor, colleague, and friend. I wish I could celebrate this book with him.

Finally, I thank Pam Lokken for her patience, support, and assistance. She read, reread, and read again drafts of the manuscript. As always, the remaining problems are my responsibility.

CHAPTER 1

Introduction

All politics is local.

—Tip O'Neill (1987)

All politics is local, but all markets are global.

—Senior Economist for Deutsche Bank Capital Markets (1997)

Capital formation, accumulation, and access are essential components of the modern economic food chain. One of the key factors of production, capital transforms scarce resources and labor, fuels economic growth and development, affects a nation's aggregate welfare, and influences nations' and firms' performances in the global political economy. Capital allocation and credit sit at the heart of modern industrial societies (Bryant 1987; Gerschenkron 1962; Kindleberger 1993; Strange 1988; Zysman 1983). Those able or fortunate enough to have access to capital gain advantages on the path to economic growth. As recently as the early 1800s, the functions of saving and investment often occurred within the same household or firm (Kindleberger 1993). Such forms of accumulation fell short of the capital needs of nascent industrial societies.

Merchants, financiers, and public officials invented more effective, and less personal, capital accumulation and allocation mechanisms. These ranged from decentralized markets to centralized state mechanisms. The growth of markets that generate credit and transfer surplus capital from savers to borrowers ranks as a stunning economic achievement. Private actors access such markets to borrow capital for production, investment, and expansion. Public actors seek capital in such markets to fund military needs, social welfare activities of the state, public infrastructure, and other collective goods. On the supply side, savers must decide how to lend their savings.

Today capital markets span national boundaries to connect lenders and borrowers of diverse nationalities. Financial globalization became a buzzword in the 1990s as analysts, pundits, and academics marveled at the expansion of a global financial infrastructure (Kurtzman 1993; McKenzie and Lee 1991; Strange 1986; Wriston 1988). Yet, like Haas's critique of the balance of power (1953), *globalization* takes on so many meanings that the term can mean almost anything to anyone depending upon his or her needs. In this book, I limit the domain of financial globalization to international and foreign debt instruments in medium- to long-term intermediated and disintermediated markets.[1] In these markets, globalization expands borrowing constraints beyond those imposed by the local accumulation, or savings, of capital. Clearly, financial globalization encompasses far more than these markets. Yet, these markets constitute the bulk of a specific type of global capital. They differ from short-term global money markets in that the capital raised in medium- to long-term markets goes predominantly to capital investment rather than hedging currency risk, engaging in currency speculation, or using it as a means of payment in international trade. Medium- to long-term capital investment funds industry infrastructure and production. It helps create products, services, and employment. Capital investment helps define and create the economic infrastructure of nations and firms.

Depictions of financial globalization as a new phenomena ignore history. Vibrant, deep, and liquid global capital markets existed before 1929 and the Great Depression (Zevin 1992). In a financial age characterized by the great British merchant banking houses, dealings in financial markets frequently stretched far beyond national boundaries. Foreign bond issues in New York accounted for 15 to 18 percent of all new issues yearly from 1921 to 1928 (Smith 1989, 23). With the onset of the Depression, global capital markets shrank to minuscule proportions and nearly disappeared from 1929 until the early 1960s. National policymakers reacted to the Depression by erecting barriers to global capital flows and separating national financial markets.[2] Such policy choices defined financial sectors of national political economies for almost forty years. The pulse of international financial markets beat faintly during this span, but then global markets began to reemerge from their long dormancy.

After decades of stagnation, international borrowing accelerated in the 1960s. Within a short frame of ten to twenty years, a trickle of cross-border interactions turned into a flood. In a remarkably rapid transformation, global capital flows and borrowing expanded to levels unseen since before the Depression (Smith 1989, 23; Zevin 1992). International borrowing in long- and medium-term financial instruments has experienced stunningly exponential growth since the 1960s (see fig. 1). International investments of private pension funds in the eleven largest industrial nations grew from $19 billion in 1980, to $83 billion in 1985, to more than $300 billion by 1990 (Smith 1989, 54). During this period, capital emerged as an international commodity as well as a payment tool for international trade.

Financial globalization receives much popular attention, but globalization constitutes only one major aspect of the recent transformation of financial arenas. Market liberalization pushed bankers and financiers toward a greater range of financial services, new strategies to manage risk, and price competition. Innovations in financial instruments and strategies contributed to diversification and heterogeneity in capital markets. Shifts away from intermediated and toward disintermediated capital markets emerges as one of the far-reaching outcomes of liberalization. During the 1980s, more and more capital shifted to disintermediated markets as they began to offer less costly, more stable, and more flexible borrowing and investment arrangements vis-à-vis intermediated markets. As the depth and liquidity of disintermediated markets increased, so did their attractiveness. Patterns of borrowing in global markets reflect this shifting preference for disintermediated instruments over intermediated loans. Liberalization led to increasing complexity and linkages across such markets. Financial infrastructures within nations deepened to accompany the expansion and enrichment of financial interactions between nations (Bryant 1987; McKinnon 1973; Shaw 1973). Capital mobility increased across national boundaries, within nations, and across types of financial markets.

Financial globalization and liberalization constitute some of the most important transformations in social relations during the twentieth century. The revitalization of global finance and development of an increasingly diversified global capital pool redefine how borrowers borrow, investors invest, lenders lend, speculators speculate, regulators regulate, and governments govern in the international political economy. In addition to their historic function of providing means of payment for international trade, global capital markets now play critical roles in promoting economic growth and development, affect notions of representation in society, create linkages across national economies, and offer global economic opportunities to complement those within national boundaries. These monumental shifts fuel interdependence and alter notions of ownership, risk, investment, time, geography, and the nation-state.

Financial globalization and market liberalization present policymakers, investors, and borrowers with an expanding menu of opportunities, pitfalls, and dilemmas as financial flows transmit benefits and risks across borders. Firms, governments, financial institutions, and individuals employ new instru-

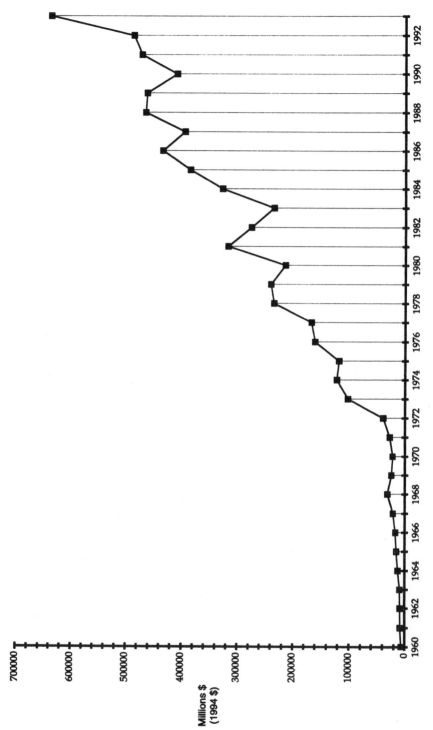

Fig. I. International borrowing

ments to unbundle risk, redistribute risk, and select among the risks that they bear. Global markets provide governments with the means of avoiding politically costly tax increases, programmatic cuts, inflation and seignorage, and the discipline of domestic interest rate swings.[3] But global markets also convey dislocations that strain national political economies, generate dilemmas for policymakers, discipline policymakers, and constrain their autonomy. Public and private decision makers must now consider the impact of global markets on their decisions. Regulators and policymakers operate in environments where cross-border private capital flows can defeat or support policy intentions. Traders in financial markets literally "vote" on public policies. James Carville, President Clinton's 1992 campaign manager, noted the ability of capital markets to constrain policies, impose discipline, and punish:

> I used to think that if there was reincarnation, I wanted to come back as the president or the pope. But now I want to be the bond market: you can intimidate everybody. (*Economist,* October 7, 1995, survey insert, 3)

Former U.S. Secretary of Labor Robert Reich echoed this sentiment in his account of his experiences as a member of President Clinton's National Economic Council (1997). Reich claims that the Clinton administration was acutely, if not exclusively, attentive to the reactions of Wall Street to policy choices. If policymakers pay disproportionate attention to the expectations and reactions of capital markets, then this can distort political representation and color the policy preferences of political actors. Who votes in capital markets more than likely differs from who votes in a democratic election. The threshold for participation in capital markets differs from the threshold for participation in democratic elections. Movements in price mechanisms of capital markets do convey information to politicians and policymakers, but the voting population in such markets is skewed toward wealthy elites and investment professionals. Financial globalization further distorts the notion of representation if other nations' financial elites help precipitate capital market movements that influence national politicians and policymakers.

Financial globalization and liberalization promote interdependence, which may challenge the sacred cow of Westphalian sovereignty, a pillar of the nation-state system. Some view the latitude of national policymakers to address constituent demands as withering away in the face of advancing economic integration and globalization (Barber 1996; Eichengreen 1994; Freeman 1992; Goodman and Pauly 1993; Rodrik 1997; Wriston 1988). Others view globalization of material relations and growing interdependence as complicating the tasks of national policymakers but not obviating their responsibilities and activities (Keo-hane and Nye 1977; Pauly 1997). In this environment, nations become more sensitive and vulnerable to global material relations, but state policymakers use their tools to intermediate these effects upon the domestic arena. This produces different national faces of globalization (Alt et al. 1996; Frieden 1991; Frieden and Rogowski 1996; Garrett and Lange 1995; Keohane and Milner 1996; Milner 1997; Rogowski 1989).

Clearly, the changes wrought by globalization of finance, trade, production, and information alter the context for national policymakers. State policymak-ers react to pressures unleashed by growing interdependence, but their choices also prove critical to transforming the global context and creating such inter-dependent linkages. Interdependence limits state actors but also empowers state actors by expanding the impact of state policies and institutions beyond do-mestic arenas. Without effective centralized enforcement mechanisms in the global arena, interdependent economic relations rest upon decentralized na-tional regulatory infrastructures (Kapstein 1994). These decentralized national infrastructures regulate economic activity, assign property rights, guarantee contracts, provide adjudication mechanisms, enforce agreements, and affect ex-pectations across national boundaries and time. Our increasingly refined and subtle understanding of global capital prohibits a simple assessment of the na-ture of the state in this changing context. State policymakers discover their glasses half full and half empty.

Does the rise of global capital markets reduce the role of national markets and financial mechanisms? With global integration of previously distinct na-tional markets, the price mechanism should operate across boundaries and pro-duce convergence in financial products and costs across markets. Yet a variety of distinct global and national capital markets persist, replete with differences in capital costs (Sobel 1994). These differences appear extremely robust. Signif-icant discontinuities persist in the emerging global capital pool, and local mar-kets appear extremely healthy. Globalization remains far from complete and in fact is only in its infancy as a process. Frankel (1992), Feldstein and Horioka (1980), Goldstein and Mussa (1993), Sobel (1994), and Taylor (1997) have noted that the vast majority of capital exchange continues to occur in national markets between lenders and borrowers of the same nationality. A home bias persists despite the appeal of global diversification and the popular rhetoric sur-rounding financial globalization. Just to maintain perspective on this phenom-enon labeled globalization, global capital markets remain proportionately mar-ginal in comparison to national markets, yet they are expanding faster than national markets and are increasingly important to an expanding global economy.

Debating and exploring the future implications of globalization is tempting, but I find understanding the current terrain and processes producing that terrain foundational to any speculation about the future. In this book, I try to provide a solid foundation by clarifying how these markets have changed, the magnitude of the changes, who the shifts affect, and the causal role of national political arenas in explaining those outcomes. Other factors feed the transformation of global finance and affect international investment and borrowing. Economics, industrial organization, and cultural, social, and community characteristics influence international investment and borrowing. As a political scientist, I focus upon how national public policies and institutions help account for the global outcomes of financial globalization, liberalization, and variations in those outcomes.

Specifically, I look at the role of the regulatory and participatory state in affecting the incentives and activities of private sector market actors. Invariably, any account of financial globalization must include the activities of private sector actors. Global capital markets depend on private actors for their existence. Private organizations produce and manage the vast majority of financial instruments and trading mechanisms in these markets. Almost all the capital in those markets comes from surpluses accumulated by private actors and a huge portion of the exchanges in these markets occur between private actors. But private actors operate in contexts defined and bounded by public activities, which affect private incentives and behavior. The interaction of public and private arenas underpins the reemergence of global finance. I examine three aspects of this phenomenal shift in the international political economy: (1) the reawakening of these markets, their extraordinary transformation since the early 1960s, and the role of politics in that metamorphosis; (2) systematic differences in access for borrowers in this rapidly transforming and expanding global capital pool; and (3) the effects of political factors in producing differential access to the global capital pool.

Reawakening

I begin with the extraordinary transformation of these markets since the early 1960s. Many accounts emphasize the primacy of technology, international competition, and market pressures in producing this transformation (Wriston 1988). Assigning primary causation to systemic factors such as technological change and international competitive pressures poses problems for understanding financial globalization. As noted earlier, financial globalization was well under way by the turn of the century. Globalization slowed and actually reversed directions following the Depression. Global capital markets lost liquidity and volume. They disappeared as major factors in the global political economy until their reawakening almost forty years later. Yet technology did not retrench in 1929 only to reverse direction again in the late 1960s. Nor did participants in the global economy lose competitive zeal during the interim only to regain their competitive instincts in the 1960s. These pressures continued in domestic capital markets even as they faded from global markets. Domestic capital markets incorporated technological innovations and reflected competitive pressures during the stagnation of global capital markets.

Nevertheless, many explanations for financial globalization continue to assign responsibility to factors exogenous to the state such as technological change and international competitive pressures. Such rationales frequently recur in regulatory debates over reforming the banking system, repealing the Glass-Steagall Act of 1934, and the adjustment of capital adequacy measures. Resorting to arguments that raise the specter of technological change and declining international competitiveness offers powerful tools for those attempting to reconfigure national regulatory structures. These perspectives implicitly view all states and markets as embedded in similar global circumstances. They ignore local factors, the state, and politics. Economic and technological pressures play important roles in transforming global finance, but politics deserves its due. I take a different tack and consider the contribution of shifts in national policies and political institutions to financial globalization. Global economic outcomes are rooted in local processes.

National policies and institutions delineate what North describes as the "rules of the game" (1990). The state helps define the context of social and economic interactions. National regulatory arenas affect the incentives of private market actors. Regulatory boundaries create rewards and penalties and thus incentives to maintain or adapt behavior within those boundaries. The demise of major industrialized nations' capital controls and other public policy shifts liberalized financial markets and created new avenues for those experiencing surpluses and shortages of capital. Private market actors took advantage of newly defined financial services arenas and lower national barriers. Bankers, institutional investors, and market entrepreneurs harnessed communication and information technologies in a changing regulatory environment. Private reactions to shifts in public institutions and policies interacted with technological innovations to unleash financial innovation and competitive market pressures, reduce discontinuities across national markets, open national doorways to capital flows, and awaken global financial markets from their slumber (Helleiner 1994; Pauly 1988; Sobel 1994, 1995).

Policy and institutional shifts in major states unleashed market processes that affect all states and markets. Key nations' endogenous changes spilled over to produce fundamental shifts in the international political economy and generate exogenous pressures upon other nations' public and private policymakers. What began as endogenous to several became exogenous to others and perhaps to all. In a dynamic world, endogenous policy and institutional choices can generate changes in the global context that return as exogenous pressures. International pressures are now part of all policymakers' concerns, albeit to differing degrees, whether big or small state. Yet a key insight remains. Local choices spawn global outcomes. Activities in the political sphere led to four key shifts that radically transformed the international environment: (1) capital's increasing international mobility, (2) increasing securitization and disintermediation,[4] (3) emergence of intangibles as commodities, and (4) changes in the socialist command economies.

First, political choices such as the American implementation of policies intended to act as capital controls in the 1960s; abandonment of the Smithsonian Agreement and adoption of flexible exchange rates; the end of the faux U.S. capital controls of the early 1970s; the demise of other nations' currency controls and foreign exchange restrictions during the 1970s and 1980s; and regulatory changes that liberalized national financial markets during the 1970s and 1980s proved pivotal in altering capital's international mobility. Regulatory policy and institutional shifts reduced disincentives for moving or raising capital abroad, enlarged global financing options for borrowers, allowed investors to balance risk and rate of return internationally, and generated international pressures on capital pricing.

Second, government policy and institutional shifts liberalized markets in addition to lowering national barriers to capital movements. Regulatory changes and macroeconomic conditions during the 1970s and 1980s fed a movement toward securitization. Regulatory liberalization altered the environment sufficiently to provide financial firms with incentives to invent securitized instruments and investment strategies (Sobel 1994). Financiers developed new instruments and strategies to meet client needs, handle risks, and advance their own positions. Preferences over the duration and terms of borrowing pushed borrowers toward securitization. Securitized instruments offered borrowers more flexible financing at lower and more predictable rates. New securitized instruments and the deepening of existing markets reinforced greater disintermediation. Capital grew more heterogeneous and mobile across types of financial markets to complement its new international mobility.

Third, choices in the American political arena opened doors to dramatically new financial instruments. In the early 1970s, Congress defined intangibles such as financial instruments as commodities. Financial options and futures tied to instruments in other financial markets quickly began trading after the regulatory revisions. Financial derivatives are pegged to equities, bonds, or baskets of securities in other markets. This links the fortunes of one market to another and deepens the financial infrastructure of an economy. Defining intangibles as commodities created the opportunity for these new markets. The decision in 1973 to move from a fixed to a floating exchange rate regime generated a demand for such markets. Floating exchange rates exposed those involved in international trade and investment to exchange rate risks. Financial futures provided a means for hedging that risk. The definition of intangibles as commodities by Congress complemented the institutional shift in the international monetary regime. By 1993, such derivative markets surpassed $5 trillion in value, and they passed the $8 trillion level by 1995.

Fourth, détente, the dismantling of the Soviet Union and its sphere, and economic liberalization in the People's Republic of China brought new borrowers to the global markets. During the Cold War, these states accumulated capital almost independent of Western capital markets and the international financial mechanisms created at Bretton Woods. Détente and the resulting thaw in relations marked a major shift in political-economic relations between East and West. Glasnost, perestroika, the demise of communist governments throughout Eastern Europe, and the ensuing disintegration of the Soviet Union stunningly transformed the political landscape of the late twentieth century. Borrowers from these states approach global capital markets with ravenous appetites for capital to reform their economic infrastructures. Borrowers from developing nations fear these new borrowers may compete for the same pool of capital and crowd out investment in other areas. In chapter 4, I focus on these political economies and their involvement in global capital markets.

Who Borrows in Global Capital Markets

Capital's enhanced international mobility and heterogeneity produce overall welfare gains. Financial globalization and liberalization may help all borrowers in absolute terms, but is financial globalization global? Does globalization systematically favor some borrowers more than others? Eyeballing financial tombstones in the business newspapers suggests an abundance of issues from borrow-

FT / ISMA International Bond Service

Listed are the latest international bonds for which there is an adequate secondary market.

U.S. DOLLAR STRAIGHTS
Abbey Natl Treasury
ABN Amro Bank
African Dev Bk
Alberta Province
Argentina
Asian Dev Bank
Austria
Baden-Wuertt L-Fin
Bancomext
Bank Ned Gemeenten
Bayer Vereinsbk
Belgium
British Columbia
British Gas
British Telecom
Canada
Cheung Kong Fin
China
Credit Foncier
East Japan Railway
EIB
Ex-Im Bank Japan
Exxon Capital
Fed Home Loan
Federal Natl Mort
Finland
Ford Motor Credit
General Mills
INI Finance
Inter-Amer Dev
Inter-Amer Dev
Intl Finance
Italy
Italy
Japan Dev Bk
Korea Elec Power
Matsushita Elec
Mexico
Minfin Russia
Ontario
Ontario
Oster Kontrollbank
Portugal
Quebec Hydro
SAS
Spain
Sweden
Tennessee Valley
Tennessee Valley
Tokyo Elec Power
Toyota Motor Credit
United Kingdom
United Kingdom
Walt Disney
World Bank
World Bank

DEUTSCHE MARK STRAIGHTS
Austria
Baden-Wuertt L-Finance
Bayerische LB
Credit Foncier
Depfa Finance
Deutsche Bk Fin
Deutsche Finance
EEC
EIB
Finland
Helaba Intl
KFW Intl Finance

LKB Baden-Wuertt
Ontario
Spain
Volkswagen Intl Fin
World Bank
World Bank
World Bank

SWISS FRANC STRAIGHTS
Asian Dev Bank
Austria
Denmark
EIB
EIB
Finland
Helaba Finance
Iceland
Inter Amer Dev
Ontario
Quebec Hydro
SNCF
Sweden
World Bank
World Bank

YEN STRAIGHTS
Belgium
EIB
Ex-Im Bank Japan
Fed Nat Mort
Inter Amer Dev
Italy
Italy
Japan Dev Bk
Japan Dev Bk
SNCF
Spain
Sweden
World Bank

OTHER STRAIGHTS
EBRD
World Bank
Austria
PTT Nederland
Bell Canada
British Columbia
Canada Mtg & Hsg
Elec de France
KW Int Fin
Nippon Tel Tel
Ontario
Ontario Hydro
Ontario Hydro
Oster Kontrollbank
Quebec Hydro
Quebec Prov
Council Europe
Credit Foncier
Denmark
EC
EIB
Finland
Italy
Italy
United Kingdom
ADC
Comm Bk Australia
EIB
Nat Australia Bank
NSW Treasury Zero

R & I Bank
State Bk
Sth Aust Govt Fin
World Bank
Abbey Natl Treasury
British Land
Denmark
Depfa Finance
EIB
Finland
Glaxo Wellcome
HSCB Holdings
Italy
Japan Dev Bk
Land Secs
Ontario
Powergen
Sevem Trent
Tokyo Elec Power
TCNZ Fin
World Bank
Credit Local
Denmark
Elec de France

FLOATING RATE NOTES
Abbey Natl Treasury
Argentaria Global
Cades
Canada
CCCE
Commerzbk
Credit Immobilier
Credit Lyonnais
Fed Nat Mort
Finland
Halifax
IMI Bank Intl
Italy
Italy
LKB Baden-Wuert Fin
Lloyds Bank Perp
Malaysia
Nova Scotia
Ontario
Portugal
Quebec Hydro
Renfe
Spain
State Bk Victoria
Sweden
United Kingdom

CONVERTIBLE BONDS
Allied-Lyons
Fuji Intl Finance
Gold Kalgoorlie
Grand Metropolitan
Hong Kong Land
Land Secs
Lasmo
MBL Intl Fin
Mitsui Bank
Sainsbury
Sandoz Capital
Sappi BM Finance
Sapporo
Sumitomo Bank
Sun Alliance
Transatlantic Hldgs
Yamanouchi Ph

Fig. 2. International bond market table (Adapted from *Financial Times*, various issues.)

ers in developed nations and an absence of issues from borrowers in developing and transitional political economies. International bond market tables in the *Financial Times* (see fig. 2) list issues in which an active secondary market exists. Issues from borrowers in developed nations dominate these tables, with only an occasional listing of an issue from a developing or transitional economy.

Globalization describes a highly selective, rather than global, phenomenon. Perhaps globalization is a misnomer, as it is predominantly an Organization of Economic Cooperation and Development (OECD) phenomenon. Shifts in global finance disproportionately favor those from developed economies. Only borrowers and investors from OECD economies appear capable of taking advantage of shifts in global financial relations. Borrowers from developing economies historically encountered higher barriers to capital than borrowers from developed economies, but the recent shifts accentuate this dilemma. Borrowers from the former command economies of the Soviet and Chinese spheres of influence also face substantially higher hurdles to global capital access than do those from the OECD states. Developing economies and transitional economies from the former communist sphere fall increasingly further behind in their relative access to global capital. The relative disparities in access increase as borrowers move from more rigid intermediated financial instruments to more flexible disintermediated strategies.

Borrowers from developed states have greater access to international markets *and* to a wider range of options among instruments and strategies in those markets. This finding is robust regardless of one's conception of distributional fairness and justice. Whether one uses an egalitarian standard of distributional fairness based upon equal per person shares of the global capital pool or an effort standard of distributional justice based upon economic contribution to the global economy the distribution of global capital resources falls heavily in favor of those from OECD nations. This systematic bias appears to be increasing with the advance of globalization. Such distributional effects within and across nations pose significant normative and positive dilemmas for public and private policymakers as they struggle to cooperate and compete in an increasingly global economy.

Local Politics and Differences in Access

What accounts for differential access to global capital? Why do investors choose to loan their surplus disproportionately to some categories of borrowers versus others? Systemic explanations suggest that such differences arise from the distribution of power and hierarchy (realist and neorealist explanations), dominance of the weak and poor by the rich and powerful (Marxist and dependency explanations), or the degree of integration into the global political economy (interdependence and neoliberal explanations). Each of these explanations has some appeal, but they are woefully inadequate and insufficient. They fail to account for important variations in access within categories of borrowers, the inability of borrowers from the nations most vulnerable to the global economy to access capital, changes in access over time for borrowers from particular nations, and the type of markets in which each category of borrowers finds greatest success.

Some developing economies successfully and repeatedly gain access to global capital, but others not. Many economies from the former Soviet-Chinese sphere of influence have proven less successful in accessing global capital since the disintegration of the Soviet Union and the communist bloc than when they were actively challenging the U.S. hierarchy in the global political economy. Conceivably, asymmetrical outcomes result from centralized manipulation and discrimination by bankers, industrialists, and political leaders. Yet the most skewed outcomes occur in the most decentralized global markets, where literally thousands of decisions made by institutional and other investors produce market outcomes. Developing borrowers achieve the greatest success in accessing the most centralized global markets—those most open to manipulation. In terms of degree of exposure to the global economy for predicting success in obtaining global capital, these are endogenous to each other and the direction of causality is hopelessly confounded. More important, borrowers experiencing the least success in obtaining global capital come from those nations most vulnerable to the currents of the global economy (Keohane and Nye 1977). The most successful borrowers come from states that in absolute terms are heavily engaged in global economic interactions but in relative terms are often less sensitive and vulnerable than those far less successful in accessing global capital.

Reducing the focus to investment decisions pierces the schizophrenia that plagues systemic explanations and provides a microfoundation for understanding global borrowing patterns. Investors, whether institutional managers or individuals, make choices in private markets. Ultimately, investors weigh the safety of their investments against expected rates of return. They evaluate default, inflation, and price stability risks that threaten their investments. Investors try to estimate and price their degree of risk by probing the history and capabilities of individual borrowers and by assessing the investment context. Cross-border investment adds exchange rate risk to investors' concerns. Investors struggle with their decisions in incomplete and asymmetric information environments replete with varying degrees of uncertainty about the investment context and prospective borrowers.

Market exchange faces severe handicaps in expanding beyond face-to-face interactions in such environments without some means, private or public, of limiting informational concerns and fears about risk and uncertainty in the environment (Milgrom, North, and Weingast 1990). Incomplete information environments inevitably produce some market failure, defined as suboptimal outcomes, but extremely dysfunctional information environments can lead to complete breakdown in market exchange when investors choose not to play (Akerlof 1970; Kreps 1990; Spence 1974). Lenders confront such challenging information problems when evaluating prospective borrowers within their same political jurisdictions, but investing across multiple political jurisdictions compounds these problems.

A number of factors at this level of analysis helps explain national variations in access by addressing informational handicaps, limiting risk and uncertainty in local environments, or clarifying why investors find particular investments attractive despite risk and uncertainty in local environments. "Home bias" by OECD investors, name recognition of prospective borrowers that favors multinational firms in global capital markets, investor preferences over economic sectors, cultural affinity, the domestic market potential of prospective borrowers, and a variety of other behavioral factors influence investor choice. Private agreements, private institutions, public policies, and public institutions supply other strategies and pathways that also address investors' dilemmas.

I focus upon the influence of national policies and institutions upon investor choice. Specifically, I examine the effects of two components of the public arena, the regulatory and participatory states, upon investor behavior. Time and space complicate extensive economic interactions. Investment decisions remain fundamentally economic choices, but public policies and institutions can reduce or exacerbate the risks and uncertainties of exchange over distance and time. Modern economies rest upon public policies and institutions that define property rights and contracting procedures, affect common knowledge, provide complaint and adjudication procedures, enforce contracts, promote compliance, determine monetary policy, underpin national symbols such as currencies, and affect expectations. These institutions affect expectations among interacting parties (Calvert 1992; Knight 1992; North 1990; Schotter 1981) and are characteristics of the regulatory state.

The participatory state defines who participates, the nature of that participation, and who has what rights along what dimensions. I originally thought the regulatory and participatory components of the state might operate at cross-purposes in attracting international capital. Contributors to the growing body of literature on the relationship between democracy and economic growth disagree. Some theoretical and empirical studies find a positive relationship between democracy and economic growth, others find a negative relationship, and still others find no relationship. I briefly discuss these studies and findings in chapter 7. After controlling for developed versus developing nations, I conclude that democracies prove more successful in obtaining global capital. I find that both regulatory and participatory states affect access to global capital but by different paths. The regulatory state affects access through evaluations of country credit risk. It is endogenous, embedded, to those evaluations. The participatory state operates exogenously to evaluations of country credit risk. It has an independent effect.

Governments vary in their provision of regulatory and participatory goods. Governments are supreme authorities within their geographic boundaries, but they are not impartial overseers of public rules and institutions, nor are they disinterested parties to exchange. Some governments succumb to myopic temptations that prove dysfunctional for market exchange and long-term social welfare. They seize undue rents, deny rents to parties engaged in exchange, redistribute rents unfairly among private parties, behave inconsistently, and threaten individuals' property rights over their endeavors. Such government activity undermines incentives to participate in exchange. Considering the vulnerability of politicians to short-term pressures, it is surprising that governments resist such temptations at all.[5]

Yet many governments do limit themselves and build arrangements conducive to stable market exchange.[6] Institutions offer one strategy by which governments commit themselves to such limits, to honoring their agreements and societal bargains, and to enforcing the bargains made between private actors within a state's jurisdiction. Such public institutions and policies are self-enforcing or self-restraining (North and Weingast 1989; Weingast 1995). The absence or dysfunction of such reinforcing social constructions—humanly devised scaffolding—limits exchange to small-scale local interactions.

As investors consider opportunities across national borders, they search for information that enables them to assess and price the risks to their investments from the microconditions of individual borrowers and the macroinvestment context. Investment opportunities that span distinct political jurisdictions add complexity to already challenging information problems, complicate contractual arrangements, and compound enforcement dilemmas. Government policies and institutions provide information about investment climates. They act as signals, explicitly or implicitly, to investors about the safety of their investments from political manipulation. They help constrain uncertainty and stabilize investors' perceptions of risks from the investing environment—good or bad. They act as selective incentives—positive or negative—to the investor. If government policies and institutions succeed in allaying investor concerns about the investment context, they act as positive selective incentives or insurance mechanisms for investors. Variations across nations' institutions can dramatically affect investors' expectations of risk and uncertainty.

The Data

The data come from a variety of sources. I have included much of the data in appendix B. I omit some data from the appendix due to their proprietary nature. This is noted here and again in the appendix. The *OECD Financial Statistics Monthly* supplies the data on international borrowing. Originally released only in the monthly publication, the OECD now offers these data as part of a historical series on diskette. The data on international borrowing consist of international and foreign debt instruments in medium- to long-term intermediated and disintermediated markets. These include international bond issues, traditional foreign issues of bonds, special placement bonds, international medium- and long-term bank loans, foreign medium- and long-term bank loans, and other international facilities. They include publicized transactions, transactions with maturities greater than a year, and commitments to loan money regardless of whether the loans actually occur, and they may include some double counting if one reason for borrowing is to back up other means of financing. They do not include private placements, nor do they include money market and short-term transactions, which often increase with market tensions. I do not include private placements, as they are by definition private and are not reported to public agencies. The size of this market is difficult to gauge without public disclosure. The OECD ignores domestic transactions that may be used by a firm for overseas enterprises. I avoid international equity offerings. These will become increasingly interesting in the future, but to date they constitute only a tiny part of global capital markets.

I converted the data on international borrowing into 1994 dollars to ease comparison. Gaps occur early in the series—in the 1960s—when international markets were small. Categorization and counting rules changed over the years. Oil-exporting states were a separate category for 1979–86. Some oil exporters were not included, and other exporters were switched midstream. Israel switched from being an "unattributable" to a "developing" nation in 1978. The OECD lumps the Peoples Republic of China in the developing rather than the

Eastern European category, which includes the other socialist economies. European-based international organizations were lumped with OECD nations. I adjusted categories as well as possible to maintain consistency over the series. See the *Methodological Supplement to the OECD Financial Statistics Monthly* for more information.

Data on country credit risk come from *Euromoney* and *Institutional Investor*. These are trade publications that appeal to investment professionals. They regularly publish surveys evaluating country credit risk. These furnish investors with information about contextual risk to their investments. Professional investors use such information as they ponder investment choices across national boundaries. I discuss these surveys and their composition in greater detail in chapter 6. I use the survey results as an indicator of the economic climate or contextual risk for investment in nations.

Next I use the *Euromoney* and *Institutional Investor* surveys to construct a measure of uncertainty about investment contexts. In a world with complete and accurate information, the *Euromoney* and *Institutional Investor* surveys should converge even when they are constructed using different techniques. The surveys should arrive at the same conclusion except for some minimal measurement error and the fundamental uncertainty that underpins risk. Failing to converge in a complete information environment means that one of the surveys is clearly wrong. This will be revealed relatively quickly in the marketplace. In such a world, the incorrect survey would either correct its methodology or find itself without a market. Investors would refrain from purchasing the risk analyses of a survey that deviates from known information.

The *Euromoney* and *Institutional Investor* surveys overlap to a large extent, which suggests a large amount of agreement among investment professionals concerning different national contexts. Yet a significant amount of disagreement remains between the two surveys. Those differences persist and are robust over time. A market exists for both surveys. This can only occur under conditions of incomplete information. International investors operate in incomplete and complicated information environments, not environments of full information. I take the differences across the two surveys as indicators of uncertainty over investment context.

I use Freedom House data to construct measures for the participatory state. Freedom House began a Comparative Survey of Freedom in the 1970s, which became an annual evaluation of political and civil liberties. The Comparative Study of Freedom is divided into two categories, political rights and civil liberties. It offers a metric by which we can compare political and civil liberties of individuals across nations and time. Political scientists may be wary of the

Freedom House Surveys for fear of some systematic bias in the measurement instrument. I checked the Freedom House measures against Polity III, a data set constructed by researchers at the University of Colorado-Boulder and released by the Inter-University Consortium of Political and Social Research at the University of Michigan in Ann Arbor. Table 1 shows an extremely high correlation across measures in the two data sets. A systematic bias may plague the Freedom House measure, but the same bias burdens the Polity III data set, which political scientists generally find more comfortable. In research design terms, the Freedom House and Polity III instruments measure the same phenomena. They are both reliable instruments, but if one is not a valid measure then the other is similarly contaminated. These data are included in appendix B.

I employ the International Country Risk Guide (ICRG) to construct an indicator for the regulatory state. The Center for Institutional Reform and the Informal Sector (IRIS) at the University of Maryland produced the ICRG. IRIS researchers used data originally collected by Political Risk Services at Syracuse University. The ICRG data set includes a set of variables that reflect upon the institutional environment of the state. Coverage begins in 1982 and includes more than one hundred countries. I discuss these variables and their transformation into an indicator of the regulatory state in chapter 7. These variables and their transformations are excluded from appendix B due to the proprietary rights reserved by the owner, but they are available through Political Risk Services at a nominal cost.

I use a variety of descriptive, exploratory, and analytical statistical tools to examine the data. Many of the analyses are straightforward and easily accessible. Unfortunately, the structure of the data employed in the analyses of chapters 6 and 7 imposes a significant challenge. The initial analyses in those chapters reveal a perversely odd structure in the data that precludes statistical manipulation and inference based upon assumptions of normal distribution. The data are violently skewed, truncated, heteroskadastic, and extremely resistant to transformation into a more manageable distribution. The structure of the data insures that a linear model violates all the key assumptions necessary to draw statistical inferences based upon a Gaussian distribution. In this case, a

TABLE 1.   Correlation Coefficients for Freedom House and Polity III Indices

	Autocracy	Democracy
Autocracy	—	
Democracy	−.930	—
Freedom House	.854	−.890

linear model severely underestimates effects and sells my argument short, but a linear model could also overestimate effects with such an abnormal distribution of the data. Essentially, a linear model operating under such conditions raises the specter of garbage in, garbage out. Considering the level of aggregation and sources of data, this problem could easily plague many data analyses in international and comparative political economy. This serves as a good reminder and strong warning to examine the distribution of the dependent variable and the residuals.

The data problems force an approach and attack on the data that I think is relatively novel in political science. I use exploratory and visualization techniques available in S-Plus, a data analysis package invented at Bell Labs during the 1970s, to manipulate and gain leverage on the data. I employ a two-step modeling strategy with more creative and robust techniques to deal with the perverse structure of the data. The improvement in results over the linear specification are staggering. The nonparametric distribution of the data hid important information about the state of the world and was extremely reluctant to give up such information to normal inferential techniques. Due to the novelty of the analyses in chapters 6 and 7, I take the reader step by step through the analyses, beginning with the normal linear model and its difficulties.

Conclusion

In the pages ahead, I explore amazing changes in global financial relations and the effects of activities in national political arenas upon those changes. Although they are economic phenomena, choices in national political arenas underpin the movement toward financial globalization and help account for important and sometimes troubling variations in globalization. Globalization remains in its infancy, a work in progress. Connecting such large global outcomes to local choices and actions highlights the nexus of political and economic contexts. The next chapter provides the theoretical underpinnings for this study. As all outcomes in global markets begin as choices by individual investors and borrowers, I start from their perspectives and describe their decision environments and calculations. I consider how state policies and institutions affect their calculations by altering their range of options, modifying their incentives, changing their cost-benefit calculations, and influencing their notions of risk and uncertainty. This provides a microfoundation for global behavior and, to paraphrase Walter Bagehot, the editor of the *Economist* in the late 1800s, lets the daylight in upon the magic.

CHAPTER 2

Borrowers, Investors, and National Institutions

During the last great age of international finance, before the Great Depression, one nation's firms floated obligations on other nations' markets or borrowed from overseas banks. Representatives of J. P. Morgan, Barings, Rothschild, S. G. Warburg, and other major financial institutions traveled or maintained limited office facilities overseas to conduct their cross-national dealings. International activities by bankers and financiers slowed dramatically from the 1930s to the 1960s, even regressed. The 1970s and 1980s witnessed a resurgence in global finance and a transformation of financial relations. Capital markets grew increasingly global and differentiated. Today, foreign borrowers access capital through other nations' markets as before, but the euro markets emerged as truly international markets. Financial service institutions have replaced the traveling financier of yesteryear, with overseas offices replete with specialized routines and structures. International finance departments grew at disproportionate rates during the 1980s. Traditional banker-client relations broke down and grew more mobile as clients sought deals based upon price competition instead of traditional financial service firm-industry relations.[1] Changes in institutional investing brought new investors to the markets as individuals bought shares in institutional investors (such as mutual funds or pension plans) in increasingly larger numbers. A "home bias" exists in the portfolios of most institutional investors, but the managers of these funds increasingly look for opportunities across national borders as a strategy for diversification and increasing returns.

Financial globalization describes an outcome as well as a process. In global capital markets, the interactions and activities of individual borrowers and investors produce the observed outcomes. These markets aggregate individual-level activities that occur within firms, economic sectors, societies, nations, and markets. Global market outcomes have local roots. These foundations of the

21

global outcomes that we observe and label as globalization rest within domestic political economies. They vary from society to society, nation to nation, sector to sector, and firm to firm. Understanding global market outcomes, and variations in those outcomes, requires unpacking the motivations behind the choices of market actors and understanding the boundaries within which such choices are made.

Political, economic, and social factors influence choices of capital market participants. Clearly, economic considerations dominate the transfer of surplus capital from savers (investors) to borrowers in capital markets. The objective of transferring such surplus is first and foremost economic gain. Micro- and macroeconomic factors affecting risk and rate of return are of primary interest to investors as they evaluate their options. This research recognizes the importance of economic considerations but seeks to expand the focus to consider the role of national political factors in accounting for financial globalization and variations across nations in their integration into global markets. The political and economic are not competing explanations from this perspective but different components of an explanation. Politics operates endogenously and exogenously to the economic considerations that drive investor behavior. In this chapter, I describe the process by which investors transfer their surplus savings to borrowers, the context of such interactions, and the potential role of the political sphere in affecting those dealings.

Disintermediation: A Borrower's Perspective

Some borrowers in the international political economy enjoy the good fortune of a wide range of financing strategies that spans intermediated and disintermediated markets. Other borrowers face a more limited menu in their search for capital. For those with the greatest freedom of choice, disintermediated markets generally offer the lowest costs and greatest flexibility. Many understand how one obtains a loan from a commercial lending institution (an intermediated loan). Often this knowledge derives from personal experiences such as obtaining a mortgage, a home equity loan, an automobile loan, or a student loan. Intermediated lending for big projects may differ in complexity, strategic maneuvering, and the degree of flexibility in negotiations between lending institution and borrower, yet the basic process remains similar to that of an individual borrowing from an intermediated lending institution.[2]

Disintermediated borrowing presents a very different story, so I focus here upon how borrowers access disintermediated markets. Most individuals never borrow, at least consciously, in a disintermediated financial market.[3] Many individual investors increasingly participate in global disintermediated markets, but they usually do so through institutional investors, which employ trained staffs and fund managers. Few individuals knowingly participate in an international initial public offering (IPO), yet corporate and public borrowers increasingly prefer the sale of debt and equity in disintermediated markets.

The disintermediated instruments bought and sold in capital markets, debt or equity, may be traced back to IPOs in a primary market.[4] In these markets, public and private regulators, issuers, underwriters and members of a selling group, and end purchasers participate in elaborate interactions that determine whether capital is transferred from those with a surplus to those confronting a shortage, the quantity transferred, its price, and the distribution of earnings and costs. In disintermediated markets, borrowers are usually corporations, government agencies, or international organizations. They seek new project funding or refinancing for past liabilities. Underwriters and members of a selling or placement group, a syndicate, are financial institutions that serve as go-betweens. They represent the issuer of a security to the purchasing public and channel funds from the purchasing public to the issuer. Syndicates usually consist of investment or commercial banks that perform investment banking functions.[5] A syndicate takes the IPO of an issuer and offers it to the investing public. The purchasers of an IPO are investors. In global markets, they are usually institutional investors such as mutual funds, pensions, banks, insurance companies, or any large institution that invests in securities. Individuals can purchase IPOs in such markets, but they constitute a very small part of the market. Most individuals participate in an IPO through an institutional investor, which pools the resources of individuals.

Why raise capital through an IPO in a disintermediated capital market instead of borrowing in intermediated capital markets? Capital costs and availability structure a borrower's options among financing instruments. Borrowing in disintermediated markets became more popular due to their growing depth and liquidity, differences across markets in the costs of borrowing, the size of borrowings, and the duration of obligations.

Traditionally, the bulk of commercial banks' earnings comes from the difference between what they pay depositors in interest on their deposits and the interest banks charge for loaning those deposits to borrowers.[6] Commercial lenders compete on price. But national regulatory standards, international agreements among national regulatory authorities, and national central banks impose constraints on such competition. National regulations, and now international agreement, mandate that banks in all the major financial centers withhold some of their deposits and maintain at minimum a specified level of capital reserves as determined by the quantity of total deposits and the risk category of each outstanding loan (Kapstein 1989; Simmons 1996). These are called reserve requirements. Such regulations seek to ensure short-term liquidity to meet depositors' demand withdrawals and protect against financial crises and market failures. This makes some deposits nonperforming and limits the capital that intermediated institutions can commit to borrowers—imposing a supply constraint.

The organization of state financial regulators varies across nations, but all industrialized nations have some form of a central bank (Goodhart 1988; Henning 1994). Central banks act as central depositories for private banks and clearinghouses for transactions between banks. Their positions in national banking systems award them responsibilities in managing national monetary systems and influence over the cost of capital in intermediated lending markets (Goodhart 1988). As bankers to banks, they provide liquidity to national banking systems to cover short-term spikes in depositor demands and establish interest rates at which banking institutions borrow to cover short-term capital requirements. Central bankers' choices of monetary policy, monetary reserves, reserve requirements for private financial institutions, and interbank lending rates affect the lower boundaries of what commercial bankers can charge borrowers for capital—imposing price constraints and affecting the incentives of borrowers. Disintermediated markets do not have artificial floors generated by government policies. What the market will bear produces the final costs of capital in disintermediated markets. If commercial loans grow more expensive, then IPOs in the disintermediated markets may become increasingly attractive.

In disintermediated markets, borrowers often employ the services of underwriters who purchase the entire offering from an issuer and then place (market) that issue with the investing public. Underwriters compete for issues. Underwriters' earnings come from the "spread" between what they pay the issuer and the price the investing public pays to the underwriter for the issue. Narrower spreads translate into cheaper capital for issuers, as they capture most of the capital the investor transfers to own the financial instrument. The underwriter's profit margin per unit of the issue declines. Underwriters price their offers by trying to estimate the demand for an issue and the likelihood (risk) that the issue will clear the market at the expected price. They fear being caught holding shares of an IPO due to insufficient interest and consequently prefer to increase the spread by lowering their bids. This reduces their risk. Yet price competition among underwriters pressures them to narrow the spread as they price their bid. The better the reputation of an issuer the greater the expectation that the issue will clear the market at or above the predicted price and consequently the stiffer the competition to underwrite the issue. Intense competition among under-writers to participate in an IPO actually generates risk for the underwriter as the spread narrows, reducing the leeway for miscalculating the market price of an offering.

Increased price competition and the growing size of corporate and govern-ment borrowings contributed to an expansion of disintermediation and secu-ritization. The leveraged buyout boom, government deficit spending, mergers and acquisitions, foreign direct investment, the construction of new production facilities, and the retooling and upgrading of old plants required huge sums of capital. In many cases, a borrower's capital appetite exceeded the capabilities of individual commercial banks; it often surpassed the capabilities of a consortium of commercial lending institutions. Large borrowers were literally forced into the disintermediated markets. New borrowers, such as start-up firms, often found risk-averse commercial lenders unwilling to place depositors' capital at risk in an unproven venture. These firms turned to disintermediated and ven-ture capital markets.

Borrowers' preferences to stretch their obligations over longer periods of time also favor the disintermediated markets. Commercial lenders worry about the effects of inflation and changing interest rates upon their loans. They hesi-tate to commit to fixed rate loans for extended periods. Floating rate loans con-strain such concerns if the changes in the floating rates are manageable for borrowers. The Third World debt crisis highlighted the pernicious effects of in-flation and monetary instability upon floating rate loans. Borrowers became re-luctant to commit to floating rate notes. Disintermediated markets supplied a mechanism for resolving these seemingly incompatible time preferences be-tween borrowers and lenders. Borrowers can extend the duration of their fi-nancial obligations, and at the same time investors can use secondary markets in securitized instruments to shorten the time horizons of their investments and gain liquidity.[7] The costs of capital, its availability, the size of borrowers' capital needs, and the duration of borrowing contributed to the shift toward securiti-zation of capital needs.

Bringing an Issue to Market

The process of issuing and placing an IPO involves numerous steps,[8] which I collapse into four stages: (1) bargaining between the issuer and the primary (lead) underwriter, (2) bargaining between the market's regulators and the is-suer and the primary underwriter over disclosure of information,[9] (3) bargain-ing between the primary underwriter and other members of the underwriting syndicate and selling group, and (4) bargaining between the syndicate and the buying public. The four stages occur sequentially. One stage affects and constrains behavior in the other stages, both forward and backward. Bargaining in the early stages constrains the choices and negotiations that follow—a form of path dependence (Arthur 1990; North 1990)—but expectations about the future constrain earlier stages.

A borrower begins the search for capital by considering financing options. A borrower questions the amount of capital to be raised, its cost, the length of the obligation, the flexibility of terms, debt versus equity, what information must be disclosed, the advantages or disadvantages of different markets, and the likelihood of obtaining capital given the answers to such questions. If the borrower has access to disintermediated and intermediated capital markets and decides to pursue disintermediated financing, then that borrower approaches financial institutions that provide investment banking services (stage 1). Specifically, a borrower seeks firms that underwrite and manage IPOs.

The choice of where to issue a security, the motivation behind the issue, nuances of national regulations, and the issuer's identity influence the choice of a financial institution to "lead manage" an offering. Lead managers put an offering together by negotiating terms with the issuer, filing appropriate disclosure statements and abiding by issuing regulations, building a syndicate to finance and sell the issue, setting the price of an offering, allocating shares of the issue to syndicate members, and managing the sale of the securities to the investing public. A nation's regulatory framework determines which institutions can offer such services. In some nations, such as the United States and Japan, regulatory arrangements separate investment and commercial banking services by financial institution. In other nations, such as Germany and France, universal banks provide an entire range of commercial and investment financial services under one roof. If a borrower leans toward the euro markets, the range of choices among financial firms may change again. Whether an issuer is a government agency or a private corporation also affects the range of choices. In nations that enforce separation between investment and commercial banking, laws may prohibit commercial banks from underwriting corporate securities but allow those same institutions to underwrite government securities.

Despite such complexity of choice, the options remain very limited. An issuer selects a lead manager based upon the skills of a firm but also by reputation—often using price competition to select among firms that rate highly on skill and reputation.[10] The choice of a lead manager signals investors about an issue and its likely success. Respected underwriters and managers provide a stamp of approval to an issue, as they have voted with their feet and put real resources at risk. Only a small number of financial firms enjoy reputational auras that span the boundaries of distinct geographical markets. Eyeballing the financial tombstones in the financial press reveals that the same firms appear repeatedly as lead underwriters.[11] A hierarchy exists among financial institutions that offer investment banking services (Sobel 1994, chap. 4 and app. C).

Recognizing that only select members of the financial community possess the stature and skills to usher a successful offering through the international markets, a borrower begins negotiating with those members. Issuers and investment bankers engage in a complicated dance. Both parties face risks. Negotiations affect who bears what portion of the risk and the distribution of rewards. Negotiations follow one of two paths. The traditional route involves one-on-one negotiation between an issuer and its longtime investment banker. Before the 1960s, almost all issues followed this path. A second and increasingly prevalent path involves competitive bidding among investment banks to manage an issue.

The likelihood that investment bankers will engage in competitive bidding for the right to conduct an offering corresponds positively with the quality and reputation of the issuer. Intense competition among investment bankers to manage an issue indicates that they will accept more of the risk in placing that issue. Aggressive price competition to manage an issue may result in a narrower spread with less room for miscalculation. Investment bankers believe that investors will quickly purchase offerings from firms like IBM, Daimler-Benz, AT&T, Sony, United Technologies, and NEC and that they can estimate at what price. Active secondary markets exist in such firms' securities, which help investment bankers price new offerings with confidence. Investment bankers generally bid very aggressively for such offerings—obtaining a smaller profit margin but with greater predictability. This enables such issuers to obtain capital at the lowest cost.

In such cases, investment bankers often buy the securities from the issuer and resell them to the investing public. A financial firm that commits money to purchasing an offering for resale is called an "underwriter." Purchasing an issue up front is called a "firm" commitment by an underwriter. The issuer receives its capital as the underwriter buys the risk of an offering from the issuer. Expecting specific market demand for the issue and a positive spread between the buying and selling price, the underwriter accepts the placement risks. Bankers can miscalculate in their aggressive bidding and price a deal too tightly. In such cases, the underwriter bears the costs of miscalculating.

Issuers without established market reputations are more likely to take the one-on-one negotiated path. These issuers lack sufficiently solid reputations to generate competition among investment bankers to manage and underwrite their offerings. Greater uncertainty prevails about whether an issue will clear the market and at its estimated price, posing greater risks for underwriters. Underwriters resist making a "firm" commitment or buying the deal up front. They prefer to let the risk remain with the issuer. Issuers negotiate with investment bankers over terms but retain most of the risks. No longer acting as underwriters, financial firms negotiate a "best efforts" deal, wherein firms make their "best efforts" to sell the security. The financial firm earns commissions from sales of the offering rather than profiting from the difference in spread. The issuer receives capital after the issue is sold to the investing public.

Rules and regulations institutionalize much of the interaction between regulators and issuers (stage 2). Regulations establish what information must be revealed. Roosevelt's call for "letting in the light of day on issues of securities, foreign and domestic, which are offered for sale to the investing public" (1938, 653) recognized the perverse effects of unequal access to information that contributed to the 1929 crash. The resulting reforms emphasized the importance of market transparency. The U.S. Securities Act of 1933 and the Securities Exchange Act of 1934 required an issuer to disclose more complete information about the issue, the legal status of the issuer, the size of the offering, contractual arrangements between the underwriter and the issuer, costs of the issue, plans for the capital, the issuer's financial condition, outstanding liabilities and lawsuits, officers of the issuing firm, and more. Policymakers hoped that fair access to information would restore investors' confidence. Disclosure and accounting requirements differ by nation and market, but the trend since the 1930s has uniformly been toward more market transparency. Japanese, British, Italian, French, and Canadian reforms in the 1980s and 1990s require more public disclosure and impose harsher penalties upon the misuse of private information.

Investors can access disclosure reports to evaluate an issue. This uses market forces to discipline investors and issuers but with an ultimate threat of government sanction if issuers violate disclosure rules. With full disclosure, investors can only blame themselves for investment outcomes. Even with disclosure regulation, issuers and underwriters have incentives to depict their issues in the best possible light and possess some latitude in revealing information. Issuers and underwriters recognize that disclosure statements help sell issues. They endeavor to file a disclosure report that puts an issuer in the best possible light while remaining within the regulatory boundaries. Many aspects of a business are ambiguous, hard to quantify, and open to interpretation.[12] Assessing issuers' plans proves difficult by definition, as these have yet to be implemented. Full information about the issuer-underwriter relationship is often incomplete, as arrangements are seldom finalized at the time of the disclosure filing.

Regulators and market overseers must accept or reject the disclosure report of an issuer. Regulators may reject the statement or request more information before accepting it. Once accepted, the disclosure statement becomes the prospectus, which the underwriting syndicate uses to market the security to investors. Acceptance or rejection of a disclosure report only certifies whether the issuer and underwriter reported the appropriate information. Accepting a disclosure statement does not ensure the success of an issue or of the endeavor seeking capital, nor does rejecting the statement support the opposite conclusion. In many markets, private ratings agencies evaluate issuers and their offerings.[13] Such agencies examine disclosure reports and other information about issuers and underwriters before they issue their ratings. Investors use these as credit ratings to assess the risk of an issue. A disclosure report, usually one that has been accepted by a regulatory authority, is essential to a good rating for an issue, which proves invaluable in attracting investors.

> Regulators of emerging markets view credit ratings as an effective way of tackling problems of transparency in their jurisdictions. (*Financial Times*, November 2, 1994, 19)

As the size of an issue or its risk increases, lead managers and underwriters attempt to spread the risks of underwriting (stage 3). Lead managers diversify underwriting burdens and risks by forming alliances with other underwriters and investment banking operations. Alliances among underwriters and investment banking operations constitute financial syndicates. A syndicate consists of all the institutions that participate in the underwriting and selling of a particular offering. Syndication is a mechanism for risk and burden sharing. These alliances limit an individual institution's exposure on any particular issue and help sell an issue in a process called placing the issue with the investing public. The members share an interest in reducing their risk exposure but with possibly divergent interpretations about how best to divide the risks and gains of the underwriting. Lead managers resolve this tension between individual and collective action. They establish responsibilities, shares, and a hierarchy among the members of a syndicate.[14] An announcement of the offering, a tombstone, appears in the financial pages the day an offering hits the market, which lists all the members of the syndicate and their roles.

Syndicates are formed for a specific issue and break up when it is complete (successful or not). Despite the temporary nature of each alliance, syndicate members frequently find themselves allying with the same firms. Firms establish working relationships with each other and develop informal ties. But each deal is negotiated separately among members of a syndicate, and syndicates almost always gain and lose members from previous incarnations. Some under-writers and investment banking operations possess greater placement power than others. Placement power describes a financial firm's access to the investing public. It results from building a reputation and networks among the investing public. Such networks allow investment advisers at financial institutions to call customers with whom they have established a relationship and sell an issue quickly. Lead managers seek to include institutions with placement power when putting together an alliance to market an IPO. This helps account for the pres-ence of Swiss banks, with their access to a large number of private accounts, in many underwritings.

An underwriter bids for a share of an issue, but this does not ensure that the firm obtains the share it prefers. Lead managers negotiate with the other underwriters in their syndicate over the price and shares of an offering. The re-sulting agreements allocate underwriting shares and the distribution of bene-fits, or losses, from an issue. An underwriter may receive a smaller share of an issue than preferred or be pressured to accept a larger share than desired. The potential gains are more than just monetary. They include prestige and position within the investment banking community. Successful underwritings advertise the quality of lead managers and underwriters, which affects their bargaining position vis-à-vis other issuers and investment banks in the future.

Even low-risk issues present lead managers and underwriters with prob-lems. Pressures to participate in such issues can lead underwriters to shrink the spread between the price they pay to purchase the issue and the price the under-writer receives from the investing public upon resale. Underwriters face a risk of pricing their deal too tightly. They clamor to participate in "good" issues. Lead managers try to restrict the number of underwriters in such a syndicate, as too many will diminish the payoffs for all of those participating.[15]

Firms may participate in a syndicate without lead managing or under-writing. They can act as sales representatives of an offering without committing capital up front. These firms' earnings come from their sales efforts, whereas lead managers and underwriters earn money from the sales of an offering re-gardless of who sells the shares. A firm may reject buying the deal up front when it estimates that an issue's prospects are too risky. Or a lead manager may limit the number of underwriters to protect share size but allow other firms to join the selling group.

Syndicate members bargain over sales to institutions, which firms to in-clude in the selling group, and the responsibilities of the lead manager in case of an unexpected market response. The lead manager commits to contingencies in case an issue's price falls or climbs beyond agreed limits in the secondary market during the issue. A manager may commit to enter the secondary market, making purchases or sales, to stabilize the price. A manager may commit to withdrawing the IPO from the market if the price drops too far or offering the investing public shares that were reserved for private portfolios if demand exceeds expectations.[16]

After the lead manager and the syndicate members negotiate the terms of the offering, they formalize the agreement. At this point, the underwriting syndicate formalizes an agreement with the issuer. The agreement among the underwriters constrains the agreement between the syndicate and the issuer. Depending upon national regulation, a formalized version of this agreement may be filed with regulatory or market authorities, and it then becomes available to the public. This provides the investing public with access to the initial disclosure statement, the final prospectus, and the agreement between the syndicate and the issuer.

With negotiations between the syndicate and the issuer concluded, the internal dynamics of the syndicate resolved, and the regulatory reporting and filing requirements met; the syndicate begins marketing the offering (stage 4). Sales staffs contact investors with information about the IPO. Institutional investors tend to dominate the pool initially contacted. Each agent of the syndicate accesses his or her connections to institutional investors and other market participants. If investors respond eagerly, the market clears quickly. Extremely high demand can present problems, but syndicates usually welcome such difficulties. If members of a syndicate sell their shares easily, they may pressure the lead manager for more shares, but the lead manager may have fully allocated the issue. In such cases, a lead manager might offer to buy shares of the security that the issuer withheld from the syndicate. Weak interest proves far less welcome. If price drops, underwriters stand to lose substantial sums, as they purchase their shares up front with the expectation that the offering will sell to the investing public at a price above their initial investment.

If the price looks as if it will drop, the underwriting syndicate may enter the market as a purchaser to stabilize it. Usually this is the lead manager's responsibility. In most nations, members of the underwriting syndicate cannot offer more than the going price. This would be considered market manipulation, an attempt to inflate the offering's price to increase profits. But syndicate members can enter buy orders at a price equal to or below the market price. By placing a "standing" order in the market to buy shares at the market price, or just below it, the syndicate can keep the price of the security from falling too far—thus stabilizing the market and constraining risk. If this fails, a syndicate can withdraw the offering, perhaps to wait until conditions improve. This is far easier in cases in which the financial institutions involved in the offering did not purchase the issue up front.

Once a syndicate places the offering with investors, the members complete their final accounting and regulatory filings and then disband. The shares of the IPO now become part of a secondary market. Trades in the secondary market do not translate into new capital for the issuer. The issuer only accesses capital from investors through the primary market. Trading in secondary markets exchanges the property rights of the issue's obligations among investors.

Through the Lender's Lens

Even after going through all the appropriate steps, an IPO still needs buyers to be successful. An issue can fail even if a borrower, and the borrower's agents, take all the appropriate steps in bringing the issue to market. The same is true in intermediated capital markets. Instability in the markets, bad timing, rumors, economic conditions, politics, and many other factors affect the prospects for borrowing capital. Borrowing capital for any project requires investors willing to lend their capital. Investors share one distinct quality: they enjoy capital surpluses and seek to increase this surplus through investment. Their choices affect the supply and price of capital for any particular venture.

Investment involves far more than simply tossing capital at random investment opportunities. Investors consider options, evaluate prospects, investigate, and try to make informed judgments that balance risk and the rate of return. They worry most about the likelihood of recouping their investments and earning profits from them. They care about factors that affect borrowers' willingness and ability to meet their obligations. They select opportunities, which they expect will generate positive returns, and they usually encounter a surplus of such opportunities.[17]

Due to shifts since the 1960s, investors now operate in environments less constrained by capital controls and national barriers. The lowering of national boundaries to capital flows, liberalization of financial markets, and technological advances expand international capital mobility and enrich investment environments. Physical location and geography in this deregulated, liberalized, and technologically enhanced environment present fewer obstacles to investors. Yet the very openness of national economies and the expansion of cross-border opportunities imposes new demands upon investors.

National differences remain strong and vibrant despite the rhetoric of globalization and convergence (Goldstein and Mussa 1993; Sobel 1994; Taylor 1997). Diverse and rich historical experiences contribute to variations in investment contexts. Domestic market size, local economic and political conditions, language, and other indigenous social and cultural factors condition investment climates and impact the conduct of economic enterprise. Cross-border investment encompasses mutually exclusive political and regulatory jurisdictions. Differences appear in institutional arrangements such as legal systems, accounting standards, disclosure requirements, information systems, and reporting techniques. Such discontinuities across national markets, which inhibit the consolidation of many diverse markets into a single global market and generate the very conditions that make international portfolio and risk diversification attractive to investors, pose nontrivial problems for assessing opportunities across national boundaries. Even under the most transparent of circumstances, differences in such frameworks impose risks and informational demands upon investors that differ from those in their home markets.

Risk, Information, and Uncertainty

Information and risk sit at the heart of all investment decisions, affecting the incentives and calculations of investors. Investors operate in complex information environments as they evaluate their investment opportunities. They try to assess and price default, inflation, and price volatility risks that can threaten their investments (Cooper and Fraser 1993, 34). Default risk is the likelihood that borrowers will not fulfill their obligations. Inflation risk is the threat to investment due to declining purchasing power over time. The value of an investment is undermined over time if the benefits derived will not purchase as much in the future as they do today. Price volatility risk is the threat that the price of a financial asset will change to the investor's detriment. Investors use a variety of tools and strategies to pierce the information haze and constrain these risks. Research is the primary tool they use to push back the information boundaries,[18] but they also use strategies such as portfolio diversification and hedging to manage their risks.[19] Pooling risk across a group of lenders or a portfolio of investments constitutes a central tendency approach to investment—averaging risk across numerous investments.

Investors consider a variety of factors when evaluating these risks. Microeconomic conditions of borrowers and their macroeconomic context affect these different components of risk. From a microperspective, a borrower's diligence, skills, strategies, creativity, history of enterprise, and reputation affect the likelihood of success and the expected rate of return. Success also depends upon macroeconomic factors that affect individual enterprises but lay outside the immediate influence of those enterprises. Inflation, unemployment, consumer confidence, overseas events, current accounts, and government deficits contribute to macroeconomic conditions. These contextual effects interact with individual borrowers, sometimes undermining economic endeavors that would be successful under different conditions.

With complete information, investors can decide whether to lend their capital and price their loans with fairly accurate expectations about risk and rate of return (see fig. 3, left column). They add a risk premium on top of the expected rate of return that reflects the risks inherent to an endeavor. Higher expected risks pay a larger risk premium to lenders. But even with complete information lenders confront limitations in predicting the future. Fundamental uncertainty plagues investors and borrowers.[20] It is an attribute of the economic environment, which generates investment risk even under optimum information conditions. Investors and borrowers cannot predict with certainty what their economic activities will yield despite complete information. The success of a borrower's enterprise depends upon the borrower but also upon context and the choices of others in a market. One cannot predict with absolute certainty outcomes of opaque selection mechanisms such as markets, even if one knows the preferences of all the individual participants. If one could, then a centralized allocation mechanism could replace the market and produce market outcomes.

Unfortunately, investors rarely if ever make choices with complete information about the state of the world. Investors function in incomplete and asymmetric information environments. Absent a completely transparent borrowing environment, borrowers know more about their situations than potential investors do. This increases the likelihood of miscalculating risk and rates of return. Investors evaluate opportunities and their risks with limited information under conditions of uncertainty (fig. 3, right column). Uncertainty is the ambiguity investors face in evaluating opportunities. Investors fear that incomplete and asymmetric information conceals threats to their capital. After all, no investor consciously makes bad investments, but poor investment results show investors their limitations in incomplete and asymmetric information environments. Consequently, investors make choices contingent upon their knowledge and expectations about borrowers, the investment context, *and* their uncertainty about both. With relatively stable or "accurate" estimates of risk, investors can still make informed choices and price their risk appropriately. If uncertainty becomes great enough, it introduces doubts about expectations, undermines investors' confidence in their abilities to assess risk, confounds their capacities to price their capital, and affects their willingness to lend.

Uncertainty can produce additional costs for borrowers. This uncertainty

INFORMATION ENVIRONMENT

RISK	Complete	Incomplete
Good	Loans without penalty Appropriate risk premium No uncertainty premium	Adverse selection Too high risk premium Too high uncertainty premium
Bad	Little borrowing Appropriate risk premium No uncertainty premium	Market for lemons Too low risk premium Too low uncertainty premium

Fig. 3.   Lending outcomes and pricing risk with complete and incomplete information

premium is distinct from the risk premium. Under conditions of complete information, the uncertainty premium goes to zero, but with incomplete information investors find pricing rate of return and risk more equivocal. They may charge a higher price to cover their uncertainty. Cumulatively, the expected rate of return, the risk premium, and the uncertainty premium constitute the cost of capital for borrowers.

Uncertainty influences investors by several routes. First, incomplete information and the resulting ambiguity create doubts about the accuracy of risk estimates and expand the variance around those estimates.[21] Investors are less confident about whether a borrower falls within a narrow range of risk—high or low. This increased variance affects capital access primarily through an uncertainty premium. Diversified investment strategies can produce unbiased portfolios of risk across a pool of investments despite expanded variances around individual estimates but only absent any systematic components in the incomplete information (i.e., threats to estimating risk are randomly distributed). There is no reason to believe that the latter condition holds. Borrowers know more about their cases than investors do, and they have incentives to manipulate the information environment. Asymmetric information increases the likelihood of systematic bias and threatens the central tendency assumption that underpins diversified investment strategies.

Second, uncertainty introduces bias into investors' estimates of risk.

Whereas increased variance affects capital costs primarily through surcharges on the uncertainty premium, a shift in the best guess estimate of risk due to bias also affects the risk premium. This can result in a higher or lower risk premium being assessed, which means that uncertainty imposes costs through the risk and uncertainty premiums. In both cases, biased estimates and increased variance, investors are less confident of their risk evaluations, which motivates them to adjust their overall price for capital. If the willingness to loan capital to a venture declines due to uncertainty, then at the very least the cost of capital increases for that borrower. In the worst case, capital becomes too expensive or unavailable.

Investing under such conditions raises the possibility of adverse selection, that is, selecting the bad risk over the good risk or assessing an inappropriate risk premium (Akerlof 1970; Banks 1991; Kreps 1990; Rothschild and Stiglitz 1976; Spence 1974). As uncertainty introduces bias into risk estimates and expands the variance around those estimates, investors attempt to penalize only bad risks. But some good risks may find capital more restrictive than they would if investors could accurately distinguish between good and poor risks. Similarly perverse, some poor risks may obtain capital they would otherwise find unavailable or at costs lower than warranted by their "real" capacities. This constitutes a pooling equilibrium—the right-hand column in figure 3. Good and bad risks look similar and are difficult to separate.

Investors face the problem of destroying a pooling equilibrium to create a separating equilibrium in which they can identify good from bad risks. Distinguishing good from bad risks under conditions of uncertainty proves difficult even when borrowers provide good information sincerely, but asymmetries in information between borrowers and lenders compound this dilemma when strategic borrowers manipulate information to improve their appeal. All borrowers claim that they deserve high credit ratings. Yet defaults and underperforming investments suggest that some borrowers are either badly informed or strategic about their cases.

If uncertainty becomes great enough, undesirable collective outcomes such as capital flight and excessive market failure can occur, and these penalize even unambiguous good risks.[22] At the very moment when good risks should find themselves more appealing to investors, many discover their access shrinking as they face difficulties in separating themselves from bad risks. Gresham's Law formalized this dilemma by stating that bad money drives out good.[23] Bad risks crowd good risks out of highly uncertain markets, pushing capital toward markets and borrowers that offer more complete information. Akerlof labeled this dilemma of adverse selection a "market for lemons" (1970).

Perhaps adverse selection burdens individual but not institutional investors.[24] Institutional investors typically enjoy far more extensive information and research capabilities than individual investors do. They employ sophisticated hedging, diversification, and trading strategies that are seldom available to individual investors—except through an institutional investor such as a mutual fund, pension plan, or insurance annuity. Such research capabilities and trading strategies are sophisticated attempts to insulate institutional portfolios from the uncertainties that generate conditions conducive to adverse selection. Research constitutes an effort to uncover the true state of the world and reduce the likelihood of incorrectly assessing borrowers. Sophisticated trading strategies admit to expectations of being incorrect and attempt to constrain such problems by dispersing their effects.

The resources and strategies available to institutional investors do provide them with greater capacities to avoid adverse selection than individual investors possess, but those same capabilities enable institutional investors to operate in environments (such as the international market) where information problems are inherently more formidable. Institutional investors do not escape the uncertainties and risks that plague individuals. The financial world provides stunning evidence that institutional investors make mistakes and can be fooled despite sophisticated tools to assess and constrain risk. Financial institutions, not individuals, sat at the center of major financial crises during the 1980s—the 1987 stock market crash, the U.S. savings and loan crisis, the Lloyds crisis, and the Third World debt crisis.

Investors can pursue several paths in uncertain environments that affect borrowing costs and capital availability. Choice of strategies depends partly upon the risk-averse or risk-acceptant nature of the investor. First, unsure about the quality of some borrowers, lenders can spread their risk and increase the price of their capital across all categories of borrowers. Attempting to ensure their rate of return and compensate for some losses in their portfolios, lenders tax all categories of borrowers. This constitutes an uncertainty premium added to the default, inflation, and price volatility risk premiums. The tax can vary by category of borrower (i.e., capital costs more for higher perceived risks), but good risks within each category pay higher premiums than would have been necessary with complete information. Despite an added uncertainty premium, some less worthy risks within each category receive capital at prices lower than would be predicted under full information.

Second, lenders can exit one market for another. Capital flight from one nation to another, movement from one financial market to another independent of national boundaries, and movement from one borrower to another all constitute exit options. Exit can reduce the relative supply of capital in specific markets, or for specific categories of borrowers, regardless of the "true" risk of particular borrowers. This results in relatively constrained and more expensive access for some good borrowers in those markets.

Third, lenders can exit and hoard their capital, effectively withdrawing it from investment circulation. Hoarding constitutes a different form of exit than flight to other markets. Hoarding reduces the supply of capital available to borrowers overall and raises costs for all borrowers regardless of market. Modern investors rarely withdraw from capital markets and hide all their capital in the proverbial mattress. Instead they shift capital from one market to another, perhaps placing it in low-risk, low-earning vehicles such as money market accounts or low-interest deposit instruments. The shortage of capital drives its price up in those markets experiencing flight. Hoarding penalizes good risks with higher costs—particularly those good risks difficult to distinguish from bad.

In all three cases, good risks that are shrouded in uncertainty face growing obstacles to capital as investor discomfort grows. As investors try to avoid bad risks, they inadvertently penalize some good ones. These good risks confront tighter capital, or pay more than is warranted to obtain it, than they would if investors could distinguish between good and bad risks with greater certainty. The difficulty in distinguishing good from bad risks also means that some bad risks will be mistaken for good ones, obtaining more capital and at a lower cost than they would receive if the lenders had more complete information. If this results in reinforcing investor discomfort, it compounds the problem for good risks that are hard to discern. This constitutes a dilemma of adverse selection in a world of uncertainty.

State Institutions, Risk, Uncertainty, and Incentives

> Institutions cannot absolutely prevent an undesirable outcome, nor ensure a desirable one, but the way that they allocate decision making authority within the public sector makes some policy outcomes more probable and others less likely. (Cukierman, Webb, and Neyapti 1992, 353)

Evaluating default, inflation, and price volatility risks under conditions of incomplete and asymmetric information involves public and private components. The public component consists of political capabilities, policies, institutions, and mechanisms that can protect or damage investors' interests. Government activities have a significant impact, directly and indirectly, upon the costs of doing business, the incentives of private investors, and the information environment in which investors operate. Changes in government policies can alter costs and benefits of the status quo, shift the costs of "doing business as usual," open the door to reevaluating investment strategies, and generate incentives for private actors to innovate or adjust strategies.

State activities and institutions affect transparency in the investment environment, stability in local economic conditions, notions of private property, monetary policies, tax liabilities, labor policies, securities and banking regulations, contracting procedures, adjudication mechanisms, and enforcement tools. Numerous other state characteristics and activities, such as government borrowing, corruption, bureaucratic quality, and the provision of education and other public goods, affect the economic arena. These influence macroeconomic context, the probability of an enterprise's success, and the likelihood and willingness of borrowers to meet their obligations and adhere to their commitments. Inflation, foreign exchange fluctuations, property rights, and price volatility may appear as economic variables, but they incorporate political components. National political capacity, political institutions, public policies, and the stability of those arrangements influence the likelihood of lenders recouping their loans and reaping profits on their investments. Looking at the other side of the exchange, such arrangements affect the likelihood of a borrower successfully approaching the global capital markets. Increasing globalization of financial relations rests upon a local (or national) political-economic foundation.

> Any uncertainty about economic policy, and especially political or military instability so great that it creates skepticism about whether any investment in durable capital goods will be protected, will tend to reduce productive investment. (Olson 1982, 4)

The appeal of diversification across national boundaries compels investors to consider the implications of multiple political jurisdictions upon their investment portfolios. The rich diversity of political arrangements across nations generates threats and incentives to investments that vary by nation. Investors must now assess how foreign exchange movements, different national regulatory regimes, national variations in the informal pathways of "doing business," and other nation-specific factors affect their investments. They search for signals that provide information about the insulation of their investments from risks originating in political arenas.

Investors must rely upon political authorities in other nations to protect their interests and investments, as no binding or enforceable international mechanisms exist in the nation-state system (Carr 1946; Waltz 1959, 1979).

There is no international debtors' prison or international bankruptcy court to impose discipline upon borrowers, enforce contracts, and assign property rights and penalties. Investors' home governments may attempt to provide extraterritorial protections for their residents' interests across borders. This is a last resort, highly inefficient and available to only limited numbers of investors in a few large nations with sufficient power capabilities to project cross-border influence, and then only under highly unusual circumstances.

Many assessments of political risk and stability highlight the incidence of political violence such as coups, assassinations, revolutions, or labor unrest (Balkan 1992; Barro 1991). These behavioral measures contain, implicitly or explicitly, two assumptions: (1) these are valid and reliable measures of the political factors that affect investments and (2) borrowers in states defined as more or less risky by such indicators are more or less likely to slip on their financial obligations. Certainly such activities concern lenders, but they fail to specify the political risks central to investors' calculations and obscure the fact that states engage in many functions, some unrelated to international investment.[25] At best, such indicators offer an incomplete picture of the political factors that concern investors. They fail to capture the processes by which the state affects default, inflation, and price volatility risks central to investors' interests. They ignore economic policy stability in nations independent of regime change, labor strife, or political demonstrations. State policies and institutions in the economic arena can remain stable amid demonstrations, violence, and regime change in the political sphere. Conversely, a dictator or regime with no outward opposition could arbitrarily change the rules in the economic arena to the detriment of international investors. The political behavioral measures do not delineate a casual mechanism by which the behavior they measure affects the economic arena—especially those components that concern investors.

A nation's political capacity, policies, and institutions concern investors at least as much as the behavioral considerations that dominate political risk analyses. Political capacity involves resources and willingness. *Capacity* refers to the ability of the political system "to carry out the tasks imposed upon it by its own political elite, by other national actors, or by the international environment" (Organski and Kugler 1980; Jackman 1993). States with such resources are potentially more effective than low-capacity states in containing the risks and uncertainty that threaten investors' interests. A capable government can use its capacities to protect international investors' property rights, resist political manipulation of the economy to the detriment of international investors, and reduce uncertainties that hinder international investors.

Yet state capacity is insufficient to guarantee an attractive investment environment. Capable governments can better protect the interests of overseas investors than less capable governments can, but capable governments should also prove more effective at threatening investors' interests, extracting excessive rents, and implementing policies that depreciate investments. Capable governments generally prove better at policy implementation than less capable governments, independent of policy. Capacity constitutes a description of the ability to implement policies. It assesses the process and instrumentality of implementing policies, not their content. State capabilities may be highly correlated with policies that protect investors, but ex ante there is no reason to believe this must be so. Capacity is a necessary but not sufficient condition.

A government's willingness to employ its resources to promote stability in local conditions and protect overseas property rights is a second critical component. Claiming a willingness to promote a stable investment environment and protect overseas capital and actually doing so are separate activities. Talk is "cheap." Governments can be strategic or sincere in their assertions. Governments operate in political domains that are vulnerable to manipulation by strategic actors—private and public—depending upon a variety of nation-specific factors. At worst, borrowers employ differences in political and legal jurisdictions to deceive investors or manipulate the value of an investment. Alone, government statements contain minimal information about a state's commitment to an attractive climate for international investors.

How do governments credibly signal their commitments to a stable and safe investment environment for overseas capital? Governments convey valuable information about their "willingness" and commitments to overseas investors through their implementation of institutions and policies. Political institutions are the "rules of the game" (Knight 1992; North 1990).[26] If institutions are "the rules of the game," then policy choices are the outcomes within those rules. Institutions form the constraints within which policies are produced, limiting the range of policies.[27]

Government institutions and policies are signals (Banks 1990; Spence 1974) that provide investors with information about the risks and uncertainty investors face from the political arena. Institutional arrangements may look different across states but perform similar functions for borrowers and investors.[28] Regardless of intention, government policies and institutions signal investors about the safety of their investments from political manipulation, the political risks to their investments over time and space, and the willingness of governments to protect the property rights of investors from others and from government intrusion.

These establish property rights, access to information, standing to adjudicate claims, adjudication procedures, enforcement mechanisms, mechanisms to manipulate macroeconomic conditions, and the susceptibility of local economic conditions to political manipulation. Many institutions address informational concerns explicitly by promoting market transparency and access to key information (i.e., accounting standards, disclosure requirements, and reporting techniques). Other institutions indirectly supply information about price volatility, default, and inflation risks to investments that might arise from political arenas.

Monetary institutions and policies specify when and how governments intervene in the monetary sector to manipulate the money supply and the value of a currency. These policies and institutions supply policymakers with instruments that can affect a nation's balance of payments, realign exchange rates to produce relative price shifts in the international political economy, spark economic expansion, address employment concerns, deflate or inflate an economy, or export economic dislocations and transfer the costs of economic adjustment overseas upon other nations' constituents.[29] Differences among national central banks testify to wide variations in monetary institutions and policies across nations. Such differences help investors evaluate price volatility and inflation risks.

Property rights institutions and policies furnish investors with information about their default risks. States define property rights, which can vary quite dramatically across states. In the most extreme cases of political intrusion upon property, the state revokes private property rights and assumes ownership.[30] States also affect investors' property rights by means other than full expropriation. Taxes, licensing fees, bribes and extortion, political contributions, public utility costs, legal fees and court costs, laws mandating partial domestic ownership, bankruptcy laws, and other public policies supply information about the claims of investors upon the gains from their investments. Essentially they determine the distribution of the proceeds of the endeavor and delineate channels of redress available to investors. Borrowers may default on their obligations for purely economic reasons, but the channels of redress for an investor are defined by national political institutions, which stipulate the procedures for bankruptcy and the protection of lenders' rights. These institutions help define who has standing in the national adjudication mechanisms and how the state will treat investors' entreaties. National law and adjudication mechanisms (courts) may distinguish between domestic and overseas investors. Such national institutions and policies supply signals about how the state treats investors' entreaties and their exposure to default or property rights risks.

Policies and institutions contain inherent tensions. Stable policies and institutions reduce the flexibility of state actors and help shield policymakers from short-term constituent pressures and provide order to Hobbes's anarchic "state of nature."[31] They constrain behavior, bound expectations, and limit uncertainty (good or bad). This helps individuals plan over time. Yet at the same time they draw distributional boundaries in political economies, assign advantages and disadvantages, and organize and disorganize interests. A tapestry of competing interests with different time horizons poses obstacles to maintaining stable institutions and policies as political actors face conflicting pressures to maintain the status quo or redraw policies and institutions to alter distributional outcomes.

As such, stable institutions and policies are costly signals. They impose real costs upon national governments and politicians by members of society that prefer alternative arrangements. Such costs contribute to the credibility of these institutions and a government's commitment to maintaining them (Clark and Maxfield 1996; Keefer 1994; North 1990; Rodrik 1989; Sobel 1998). Credible signals act as incentive or insurance schemes (Kreps 1990, 629). They provide information that helps define risk and reduce uncertainty in the environment, allowing investors to price their risks with greater confidence. Consistency and stability are as important as fairness. Variability contributes to uncertainty and affects the ability of investors and lenders to form stable expectations about how to play the game. Political capabilities, strategies, or institutions that provide stability allow investors to price their political risk and concentrate upon economic risk, even if such mechanisms appear unfair to investors. Unpredictability, a lack of credibility, in such institutions undermines investors' abilities even to price their risks.

From lenders' perspectives, successful institutions stabilize expectations and reduce the political component of risk if they enhance the transparency of the investment environment, promote stability in local economic conditions despite potential short-term political pressures to the contrary, protect lenders' property rights, provide access to the adjudication and enforcement mechanisms of the borrower's state, protect their ability to obtain binding and enforceable decisions against borrowers that renege on their contractual obligations, and influence borrowers to abide by those institutions.

Figure 3 divided the world into more or less complete information environments before the addition of state institutions and national-level consideration (left and right columns, respectively). The incomplete information environment in the right column can generate a pooling equilibrium dilemma for investors, confounding their ability to distinguish types, raising the likelihood of adverse selection, and increasing the probability of suboptimal market

Political Context of Borrower

	Good	Poor
High	Low political risk Low uncertainty Loans without penalty	Market for lemons High uncertainty Adverse selection
Low	Political risk premium High uncertainty Adverse selection	Low uncertainty No/little lending

Lenders Expectations

Fig. 4. Lending under incomplete information with addition of political information

outcomes or market failures. Figure 4 takes the incomplete information environment in figure 3 and introduces information about national political arenas.[32] The result suggests how political capacity, policies, and institutions can help dismantle the pooling equilibrium and help investors distinguish among types—a separating equilibrium—and affect global capital access. The problem of adverse selection remains on one diagonal, but on the other the added information about the state helps destroy part of the pooling equilibrium and constrain part of the problem arising from asymmetric and incomplete information.

Convergence of lenders' expectations and borrowers' political context in the upper left cell reflects low uncertainty about the risks to investors from the political environment and indicates that the environment is favorable to international capital. Low uncertainty increases the likelihood of lenders accurately assessing lending risk associated with political context, and in this category those risks are low. This is an example of a highly conducive investment environment for international capital. Borrowers should find relatively good access to the international markets if their enterprises are deemed worthy. They should enjoy the greatest flexibility in their choice of borrowing strategies. Explicit consideration of political factors recedes relative to that of the other cells.

Moving along the diagonal to the lower right cell, political context and lender expectations converge negatively (low capacity and low expectations).

There is low uncertainty in this environment. Lenders and investors recognize the high permeability of a borrower's political arena and the lack of protections for their investments. The economic arena is highly susceptible to political manipulation. The state has low capacity to resist short-term pressures to the detriment of long-term interests. Investors may not recognize the political arena explicitly, but poor performance on the proxy economic indicators reflects the threats to international capital from a political arena that fails to create a political environment conducive to long-term economic growth. Borrowers in this category will encounter great barriers in their attempts to access international capital markets in general and disintermediated markets specifically. Political concerns will overwhelm economic considerations. Private overseas lenders will only provide capital to such borrowers at extremely high prices, if at all. Borrowers should be unwilling to pay such costs, nor will they be credible if they offer to pay. They will be forced to search for alternative financing mechanisms.

The other diagonal presents a much more interesting and challenging social dilemma for borrowers, lenders, and governments. This diagonal depicts a discontinuity between lender expectations and the underlying political context of the borrower (a false consciousness or confusion). This constitutes increased uncertainty about the investment environment and protections for global capital in the domestic political arena. This makes investors circumspect about their calculations of economic risk. The divergence between a borrower's political context and lenders' expectations increases the likelihood of lenders inaccurately assessing the risks that stem from political context. Increased uncertainty makes expectations unstable and can lead to perverse lending outcomes—penalizing good risks that are hard to differentiate from the bad and rewarding bad risks that are confounded with the good.

The lower left cell represents a perverse outcome of penalizing good borrowers from a good investment environment. Lenders systematically penalize borrowers from a political context that resists short-term constituent pressures and provides a stable and fair economic environment for international investors. The problem is that international investors are unsure of the political climate of that state. The state has failed to convincingly signal investors about its "type." Good borrowers in this state will find capital access more constrained and expensive than they would under conditions of more complete information or less uncertainty about that information. These borrowers will find less flexibility in their borrowing options than borrowers that are more easily identified as "good." This situation imposes a political risk premium upon a good borrower.

The upper right cell is similarly perverse in this context of heightened uncertainty. Lenders estimate, or implicitly assume, that the political risks of investment are lower than the underlying political situation warrants. This, too, is a problem of incomplete information or uncertainty about the information that is available. Some poor-risk borrowers may find capital more available and at lower costs than if lenders had more complete information. This is a political risk premium paid by the lender or a penalty imposed upon investors due to political context. This is a market in which "lemons" find better financing opportunities and flexibility than they deserve (Akerlof 1970). In times of financial distress and heightened systemic uncertainty, lenders may discover their weaknesses in identifying good borrowers and contexts. I expect lenders to retreat from this diagonal as they discover their shortcomings during financial crises, or at least retreat from the upper right cell and reevaluate the borrowers in the lower left cell.

If governments can commit to credible institutions and policies that constrain uncertainty and clearly signal investors about the safety of their investments, then, all else being equal, borrowers in those states should find capital more accessible than borrowers from states without such protections or borrowers from states with uncertain protections. These produce an expected ranking of access to capital and cost of capital.[33]

This book attempts to isolate the political components from other factors that affect borrowing and lending in global capital markets. This focuses upon just one aspect of the macroarena that affects microchoices. Obviously other factors, macro and micro, create incentives and disincentives in global capital markets, contributing to globalization and differences in access. The abilities and plans of individual borrowers are beyond the scope of this book, but they clearly dominate any investment decision independent of political context. Incomplete information, assessments of risk, and uncertainty about economic variables independent of the political arena strongly influence market outcomes.

CHAPTER 3

Domestic Policy, State Institutions, and Financial Globalization

The development of worldwide capital markets brought about by advances in computer and satellite technology and instantaneous global communications underlines the need to keep America's banking industry competitive with that of the rest of the world.

—Sen. James Sasser (S. Hrg. 100–481 1987, 5)

Technological developments have not only created the opportunities to invest across borders, but in a real sense they have driven the movement toward the liberalization of exchanges as markets have needed to stay competitive with each other and with competition outside the exchanges.

—Sir Nicholas Goodison, Chairman of the London Stock Exchange
(in *International Affairs*, May 1988)

Once-active global capital markets experienced a long period of stagnation and decay beginning with the Great Depression. This began to change in the 1960–70s. What awoke global financial markets from their long dormancy and stimulated the transformation of global financial relations? Popular explanations, as reflected in the comments of Sen. James Sasser and Sir Nicholas Goodison, emphasize systemic pressures such as technology and economic competition. These factors operate outside the domain of the nation-state and domestic politics and beyond the direct control of national policymakers, and they affect all states. From this perspective, state policymakers and policies reacted to exogenous pressures but did not create them in any fundamental sense. States responded to such pressures by lowering national barriers to exchange and re-

47

forming market regulations that created inefficiencies and hampered their industries and markets in the global arena.[1]

These "outside-in" explanations are consistent with the trend toward "open-polity" frameworks to understand the impact of international change upon politics within nations (Alt et al. 1996; Frieden 1991; Garrett and Lange 1995; Goodman and Pauly 1993; Keohane and Milner 1996; Maxfield 1990; Milner 1988; Rogowski 1989).[2] From such perspectives, the primary stimuli motivating political change resides in the global arena beyond the direct control of governments. At most, state policymakers, state policies, domestic socioeconomic divisions, or domestic political institutions intervene to mediate and translate the effects of such pressures. This intermediation produces variations or different "faces" of globalization across nations.

"Open-polity" analyses have evolved over several intellectual generations. Rogowski (1989) argues that pressures, or shocks, in the global political economy reward some factors of production and penalize others. He appeals to economic pluralism and ignores the collective action dilemmas of political mobilization and the problems of converting economic gains into political action. Rogowski translates economic gains and losses into domestic political cleavages along one of several dimensions depending upon the distribution (endowments) of the different factors of production in society: class (labor against land and capital) or urban-rural (land against capital and labor).

Frieden (1991) finds factors of production too broad a scheme but maintains an "outside-in" perspective. Crosscutting cleavages and conflicts exist within factors that undermine the political coherency of factors of production. Many interests, often fragmented and conflicting, comprise a factor of production. Frieden reduces the level of aggregation and suggests examining economic and industry sectors as an alternative. Milner (1988) follows a similar path but focuses upon the changing competitive stances of firms in the domestic polity. Alt et al. (1996) and Gilligan (1996) shift the focus to specific assets. Differences in the mobility of assets affect their bargaining power in "open economies" where mobile assets can exit. Alt, Frieden, Gilligan, and Milner construct the domestic polity differently than Rogowski, but they all share the causal structure of the international economy impacting upon the national political economy to favor some over others, which in turn affects domestic politics (Frieden and Rogowski, 1996) (see fig. 5a).

Garrett and Lange (1995) adopt a primarily outside-in and economic pluralist approach, but they add several important considerations involving domestic politics, its mechanisms, and its potential affect upon global economic relations. First, they recognize the role of domestic socioeconomic organiza-

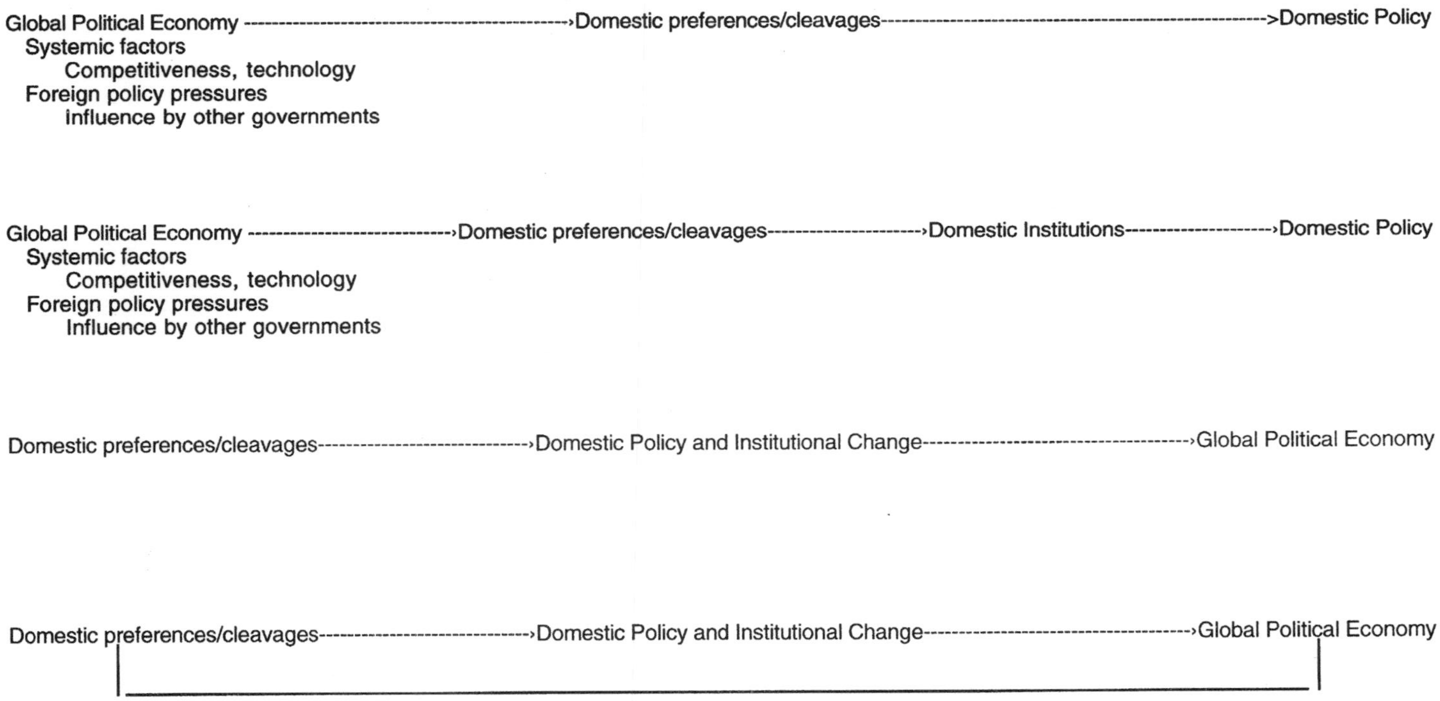

Global Political Economy --------->Domestic preferences/cleavages--------->Domestic Policy
Systemic factors
Competitiveness, technology
Foreign policy pressures
Influence by other governments

Global Political Economy --------->Domestic preferences/cleavages--------->Domestic Institutions--------->Domestic Policy
Systemic factors
Competitiveness, technology
Foreign policy pressures
Influence by other governments

Domestic preferences/cleavages--------->Domestic Policy and Institutional Change--------->Global Political Economy

Domestic preferences/cleavages--------->Domestic Policy and Institutional Change--------->Global Political Economy

Fig. 5 a–d. Stylized open-polity approaches

tions such as trade unions in overcoming barriers to collective action as preferences shift. Economic pressures do not immediately translate into political pressures. By focusing upon organized labor, Garrett and Lange implicitly include a
mechanism to overcome the barriers to political mobilization. Second, they in-
terject formal domestic political institutions between shifts in organized domestic preferences resulting from exogenous changes and policy outcomes (see
fig. 5b). Formal political institutions alter the effects of outside-in pressures
upon politics and policies within nations. They intermediate the outside-in
pressures and the translation of domestic preferences into policies. This helps
account for variations across nations. Milner also highlights the importance of
domestic political institutions in mediating international effects and responses
to those effects (1997).

Finally, Garrett and Lange alter the unidirectional causal framework. They
include feedback channels by which policy changes in domestic arenas that arise
in response to the global political economy feed back to alter domestic socioeconomic and formal political institutions. In turn, these changes alter future
mediation and translation of global effects. Garrett and Lange underplay this
feedback mechanism, choosing to focus primarily upon the translation of exogenous pressures into internal shifts and the role of domestic political institutional arrangements in producing variations across nations. But this feedback
loop constitutes an important refinement. It explicitly recognizes the possibility that causality can run in both directions and foresees the possibility for activities and events in domestic arenas to rearrange the global arena.

I find outside-in economic or technological explanations of financial globalization and liberalization problematic despite their appeal (Kurtzman 1993;
McKenzie and Lee 1991; Strange 1986; Wriston 1988). First, competition across
national financial markets results from financial globalization. International
competition requires mobility across markets, which occurs only after barriers
to such movements decline and market actors discover they can exit one market and move to another. At this point, globalization is well under way.[3] At some
point, competition may indeed spur national policy change, but it cannot be
causal until extensive global financial interactions create such pressures, and
such global financial interactions require the demise of national controls limiting international capital movements. Until the removal of national barriers to
capital mobility, competitive pressures across national markets remained constrained and could not be unleashed. Furthermore, an argument based upon
economic competitive pressures logically leads to expectations of multiple
rounds of competitive deregulations—a tit for tat competitive posturing. The
evidence (Sobel 1994, chap. 3) fails to conform to this expectation. At most, one

round of regulatory reforms took place, and those reforms were highly discontinuous in time and content.

Technological progress also proves problematic. Active global capital markets existed before the Depression (Zevin 1992). At the turn of the century, dealings in financial markets stretched beyond national boundaries. Financiers in London made great advances toward globalization (Polanyi 1957). Net capital flows across borders were quite large relative to the size of national economies prior to World War I. Foreign bond issues in New York accounted for 15 to 18 percent of all new issues yearly from 1921 to 1928 (Smith 1989, 23). Globalization reversed directions as the global market all but disappeared following the Depression. But technology did not regress to make global capital movements more difficult. On the contrary, information technologies advanced continuously. Many such advances appeared in national financial markets, yet those advances had little impact upon global dealings. If technology drives globalization, then the thirty- to forty-year reversal of globalization is difficult to understand in light of the technological advancements during that period. Furthermore, such explanations fail to account for significant, remaining, and persistent discontinuities across national markets.

Such exogenous pressures affect most nations all of the time, all nations some of the time, but never all nations all of the time. Outside-in economic and technological explanations neglect or discount domestic politics and the activities of states. They ignore the fact that state policymakers redefined global finance in an earlier era by erecting high barriers to international capital movements following the Depression. Financial sectors became the most regulated, protected, and domestically oriented sectors of national economies. Governments cushioned the impact of technology upon international financial dealings. At best, such exogenous explanations suggest that times and context have sufficiently changed to make governments and polities reactive to outside-in pressures (Frieden 1991; Frieden and Rogowski 1996; Kapstein 1989, 1994; Maxfield 1990; Rogowski 1989). From these perspectives, states and national political economies behave as price takers that respond to shifts in the global political economy.

Outside-in approaches offer accurate depictions of many states. Most are too small to unilaterally shape the global political economy, and they are extremely sensitive to events outside their borders. But external pressures originate somewhere. An outside-in focus neglects the possibility that such pressures may arise from policy and political institutional choices endogenous to a few specific states and spill over from these national political economies into the international arena. Policymakers within such states act as price makers in the international system by opening up their national doorways, liberalizing their domestic markets, restructuring the incentives of market actors, and unleashing the economic and technological forces that are confounded with financial globalization (Helleiner 1994; Moran 1991; Pauly 1988; Sobel 1994). Policy choices and institutional changes endemic to such states rearrange relations within the global political economy, alter the choices and incentives for private actors and other states' public actors, and change the nature of doing business (see fig. 5c). Other states cannot unleash such forces upon the international arena by their actions independent of the choices made by the key states.

This refinement recognizes that states are not equal in their abilities to affect or resist the international political economy. From this perspective, financial globalization and liberalization trace partly back to shifts in domestic policies and political institutions in such nations. These shifts altered the incentives of market actors, whose responses to such shifts aggregated to unleash the economic and technological pressures often awarded primacy by other explanations. This interaction of public and private spheres leads to a "bottom-up" construction of globalization. Financial globalization and liberalization emerge from local roots.

At first glance, this approach simply reverses the outside-in causal path by substituting an inside-out perspective. But this poses too sterile an alternative to the outside-in approach and falls into the same trap. A stark inside-out approach is just as overly rigid as a stark outside-in approach. Both may miss very important nuances.[4] Once unleashed by shifts in the domestic policies and political institutions of key nations and the reaction of private market actors to those shifts, financial liberalization and globalization become more than outcomes of endogenous processes. These outcomes are transformed into exogenous factors in a new decision cycle, which affects later policy and institutional choices—the genie has been let out of the bottle. The effects produced by the endogenous choices of a few become exogenous for all (see fig. 5d). Even large, relatively insulated states become sensitive to the effects of financial globalization. Policy choices rearrange the set of options in future decision environments (Pierson 1996). These outcomes can be intended or unintended (Boudon 1982; Pierson 1996; Sobel 1994). This introduces a feedback mechanism that allows such endogenous changes to restructure the exogenous world and feed back to alter future choices. This looks similar to the Garrett and Lange feedback channel (1995) but with several key distinctions.[5] I initiate the policy cycle endogenously, and they do so exogenously. My feedback cycle returns to the global political economy, but theirs goes to domestic socioeconomic and formal political institutions.

What one wants to explain affects the appropriateness of these alternative approaches. In this chapter, I explore the local origins of global phenomena such as financial globalization and liberalization. Choices and actions in key domestic political arenas promote four shifts that alter decision environments, affect the alternatives and incentives of investors and borrowers, and fundamentally transform the international borrowing environment: (1) capital's increasing international mobility, (2) growing securitization and disintermediation,[6] (3) emergence of intangibles as commodities, and (4) participation by Russia, Eastern Europe, and China in global financial markets. These changes involve interactions between public and private, domestic and international, and social context and individual choice. Parts of the following analysis are broached elsewhere in the literature (Aronson 1977; Grabbe 1996; Helleiner 1994). Here, I marshal systematic empirical evidence for the central role of policy and political institutional shifts in key states in explaining the reemergence of global finance and financial liberalization.

Increasing International Capital Mobility

For much of the time since 1929, most governments have employed regulatory constraints—institutions—that limited capital flows across their borders. National capital controls restricted the outflow of a nation's currency and less frequently the inflow of other nations' currencies. These politically constructed limits upon capital's international mobility made accumulation within national boundaries central to the availability and cost of capital. Three major institutional changes by key nations in the global political economy affected the overall opportunities for international lending and borrowing: (1) U.S. adoption of capital controls in 1963, (2) the demise of U.S. controls a decade later, and (3) the demise of capital controls in other major financial centers by the late 1970s and early 1980s.

Political institutional reforms lowered national barriers to capital movements and freed capital from its national cage. Such changes in national regulatory institutions reduced disincentives for moving or raising capital abroad, enlarged financing options for borrowers, allowed investors to balance risk and rate of return internationally, and generated international pressures on the pricing of capital. These three shifts, intentionally or not, fundamentally influenced the choices of private and public market actors, which accumulated to unleash international capital mobility and transform the global financial arena. These institutional shifts delineate four distinct periods in the reemergence of global finance: pre-1964, 1964–73, 1974–80, and 1981 to the present (see fig. 6).

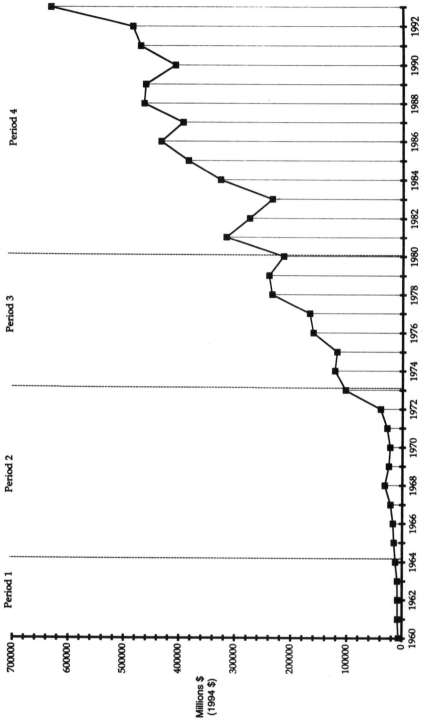

Fig. 6. International borrowing by period

The United States was noteworthy for its lack of capital controls following World War II. New York offered the deepest and most efficient capital market in the world—appealing qualities to borrowers. Borrowers found other nations' markets undercapitalized, inefficient, and protected by capital controls. As the primary source of overseas capital for borrowers and international liquidity since the end of the war, U.S. capital supplied a key fuel for the reconstruction of war-torn economies and the resurrection of the global economy. But the continual outflow of capital from the United States began to worry American officials. American policymakers became increasingly concerned over the growing deficit in the U.S. capital account. Dollars held overseas exceeded U.S. official gold reserves by 1960. An increasing outflow of dollars to fund U.S. multinational corporations' (MNC) overseas projects and a massive dollar overhang (dollar holdings outside the country) eventually threatened dollar convertibility and consequently the Bretton Woods monetary arrangements (Triffin 1961).

The Kennedy and Johnson administrations adopted policies intended to restrict this dollar outflow and preempt the potential threats to dollar convertibility which was the heart of the Bretton Woods system. The Interest Equalization Tax (IET) of 1963 taxed borrowings in U.S. bond markets for foreign purposes. As of February 1965, the IET was expanded to cover loans of one to three years' maturity borrowed in U.S. commercial lending markets for overseas purposes. The Voluntary Foreign Credit Restraint Act (VFCR) of 1965 limited the ability of U.S. banks to make overseas loans from their domestic offices. The VFCR established "voluntary" quotas on lending by American banks to U.S. MNCs for their foreign direct investments. These "voluntary" quotas became mandatory in 1968.

At first glance, these institutional changes look like obstacles to global finance, but U.S. MNCs were not going to cease their foreign operations. They continued to expand their overseas operations and production facilities, and they still needed capital for such operations. The IET and VFCR imposed costs upon borrowing in U.S. markets for overseas purposes, which reduced the differential in costs between borrowing in the United States and abroad. These government-generated costs were intended to make U.S. MNCs or other borrowers indifferent between domestic and overseas capital markets when borrowing for overseas operations at the very least. They might even prefer overseas markets. At best, policymakers hoped that borrowers for domestic operations might access foreign capital markets and reverse some of the capital outflows from the United States.

The IET and VFCR pushed U.S. MNCs toward offshore markets to fund their overseas activities, creating opportunities for the small international markets. As noted, the amount of dollars held outside the United States was huge. The changes in statutes and tax policies created incentives for U.S. MNCs to access that pool despite the inefficiencies of the overseas market mechanisms. As U.S. MNCs began to access dollars held overseas, American banks reacted to preserve their privileged relations with them. U.S. banks expanded overseas branches and began raising capital in foreign markets to service their domestic industrial clients' non-American operations. Private American financial institutions brought their more efficient market-making skills and operating procedures to the overseas markets. This introduced more efficient practices into those markets and helped reduce the costs of raising capital in the overseas markets. U.S. capital controls spurred expansion of the euro markets, and dollar borrowings by U.S. MNCs initially drove the expansion.

The demise of the IET and VFCR during the Nixon administration marks the second period. Intended as only temporary measures (Volcker and Gyohten 1992), the IET and VFCR remained in place for a decade. Their repeals in 1973 and 1974 removed institutional hindrances to capital leaving the United States. American MNCs and foreign borrowers could again easily access U.S. markets to raise capital for overseas investments. But the change proved to be more than simply a reversion to pre-IET and VFCR times. The private financial world had undergone significant changes since their introduction. American financiers responded to the earlier policy shifts embodied in the IET and VFCR by expanding their geographic scope and developing an appreciation for overseas markets. They became international firms. Overseas offices enabled U.S. banks to circumvent domestic reserve requirements and interest rate ceilings. They established relations with foreign industries and financial firms. Their operations stimulated the nascent global market. Private responses to the IET and VFCR fundamentally altered global financial dealings.

Two other significant events during this period reinforced the movement toward enhanced international capital mobility. First, petrodollars from the Organization of Petroleum Exporting Countries (OPEC) flooded Western banks. The increase in oil revenues (petrodollars) arose out of political events that led to the manipulation of oil prices by OPEC. Banks faced the ironic dilemma of receiving too many deposits too fast. This stimulated all lending as banks sought ways to make these deposits perform. Second, the fixed rate exchange mechanism designed as part of the Bretton Woods system and incorporated in its successor, the Smithsonian, collapsed. The United States and many of the advanced industrialized nations allowed their exchange rates to float at this time. Global money markets became key to the pricing of national currencies. Private market participants now found these markets important, as they affected the currency risk of international trade. Price movements in such markets affected currency risks, created opportunities for speculation, and supplied a means for hedging against currency risks. These promoted international mobility in money markets—as distinct from capital markets.

As the deepest and most liquid capital markets in the world became more accessible due to institutional reforms, the financial firms most capable of incorporating those markets into the emerging global market enjoyed an advantage of nationality. American financial firms were especially well poised to take advantage of the new U.S. openness. The global markets grew following the 1963–65 controls, but their expansion paled in comparison to that following the demise of those controls. Growth in international and foreign loans and bonds literally exploded.

The removal of controls in the United Kingdom and Japan, the two largest financial centers after New York, introduced the third major institutional shift. The British and Japanese ended their controls and lowered national barriers in 1979 and 1980, respectively. This enabled British and Japanese capital to more easily enter the emerging global market. Other policy and institutional reforms reinforced the effects of changing capital controls. May Day 1975 in the United States, Big Bang and the Financial Services Act in the United Kingdom, and regulatory reforms in Japan during the 1980s liberalized domestic markets. Appendix A describes many of these reforms and the events leading to them. Improvements in foreign access to capital markets accompanied domestic reforms during this period (Sobel 1994). Domestic liberalization of market institutions spurred the innovation of financial instruments and investment strategies, which helped unleash market pressures. Sophisticated bankers and institutional investors could take advantage of new instruments and other nations' markets to spread risk and seek higher rates of return. The domestic and international reforms interacted—creating new synergisms—and fed the deepening of national and global financial infrastructures.

Figure 6 shows the growth of international and foreign borrowing in primary bond and loan markets from 1960 to 1993. Changes in borrowing correspond to the major institutional shifts discussed previously. International borrowing takes a leap following 1964, again following 1973, and again after 1981. Table 2 compares and tests for differences in the mean levels of borrowing for adjacent periods. The mean levels of borrowing in adjacent periods differ statistically, the differences are statistically significant, and they are in the right direction. Testing differences in the average rates of change across adjacent periods produces more ambiguous results. Average rates of change across periods 1 and 2 are not statistically different. Average rates of change across periods

TABLE 2.   Comparison of Means

Comparison Periods	t-test	df	Prob > |t|
Period 1 (1960–63)			
and period 2 (1964–72)	3.535	11	.005
Period 2 (1964–72)			
and period 3 (1973–80)	8.043	15	.000
Period 3 (1973–80)			
and period 4 (1981–93)	5.900	19	.000

2 and 3 and periods 3 and 4 are statistically different but not significantly. It appears that with the advance of time the differences in average rates of change are closing in on statistical significance. This could be interpreted as financial globalization picking up speed and impetus as private actors adapt to the liberalizing shifts in national regulatory structures. Clearly, options for investors and borrowers increased with the growth of the global market after 1960, but removal of political institutional constraints upon capital mobility in the major financial centers created the preconditions for global markets. This did not guarantee global markets, nor were they necessarily the intention of the institutional shifts. Private actors still had to cross national boundaries.

Securitization and Disintermediation: Policy and Institutional Change

Increasing securitization and disintermediation constitutes a second major shift in finance. This shift hit domestic and global markets. During the 1980 and 1990s, capital increasingly found its way to disintermediated markets. Disintermediated markets are the fastest growing markets in finance. Macroeconomic conditions, policy changes in response to those conditions, regulatory changes, increasing government deficits, and privatization of state enterprises combined to enhance the appeal of securitization and disintermediation. These changes affected borrowing costs across types of markets, contributed to depth and liquidity in disintermediated markets, and enhanced the appeal of securitized instruments for resolving what initially appear to be conflicting preferences among borrowers—to stretch obligations over longer periods and ensure the liquidity of investments.

Double-digit inflation swept the industrialized economies in the late 1970s. Central bankers and finance ministers tightened money supplies in an attempt to control inflation. They raised the interest rates they charged to banks, bought currencies on the open market, and tightened reserve requirements to reduce the amount of money in the system and constrain monetary expansion. Commercial bank lending rates increased as a result of these public policies. Prime rates, those a bank charges its best customers, steadily increased at the end of the 1970s. Figure 7 details such interest rates in three key markets. These reflect the best cost of capital for borrowers in commercial loan markets. Borrowers considered ineligible for the prime rate discovered even higher costs of capital.

Prime rates display significant variation over time, particularly after 1980. Such fluctuations hinder lenders' and borrowers' abilities to form stable expectations about capital's pricing over time. Nonprime rates fluctuate even more. Adding currency movements to interest rate shifts compounds the difficulty in forming long-term stable expectations for the cost of capital across national boundaries. Commercial lenders, worried about inflation, changing interest rates, and fluctuations in monetary valuation, hesitate to commit capital to fixed rate loans for extended periods. They reduce risk by constraining the length of such loans. Adjustable rate instruments can reduce lenders' fears if rate changes do not create substantial incentives for borrowers to default on their obligations, as in the Third World debt crisis. The Third World debt crisis gave such adjustable rate instruments a bad reputation. Borrowers also face risks from rate fluctuations but generally prefer to stretch their obligations over longer periods—to extend the time horizon of a borrowing.

Prices and volatility in commercial loan markets—partly a function of government policies—created incentives for borrowers to consider alternative capital sources and for lenders to limit their time exposure. If prices and volatility in the commercial loan markets motivated borrowers and lenders to seek alternatives, how did disintermediated alternatives compare with commercial markets? Figure 8a–c compares the cost of loans and bonds in three major domestic markets.[7] Differences between pre- and post-1980 are apparent. Interest rates in the three intermediated markets show a widening disparity with bond yields. Borrowers able to issue securitized instruments found more stable long-term capital at a lower cost. At the same time, investors could increase their returns by accepting lending risks directly instead of paying banking institutions to intermediate that risk.

Borrowers that could securitize their borrowings via public offerings in the disintermediated markets found longer-term instruments to accompany reduced capital costs and less volatility. Extended terms are more typical in disintermediated than intermediated markets.[8] Expansion of active secondary markets in disintermediated instruments furnished investors with greater control over the duration of their investments. Active secondary markets allow investors

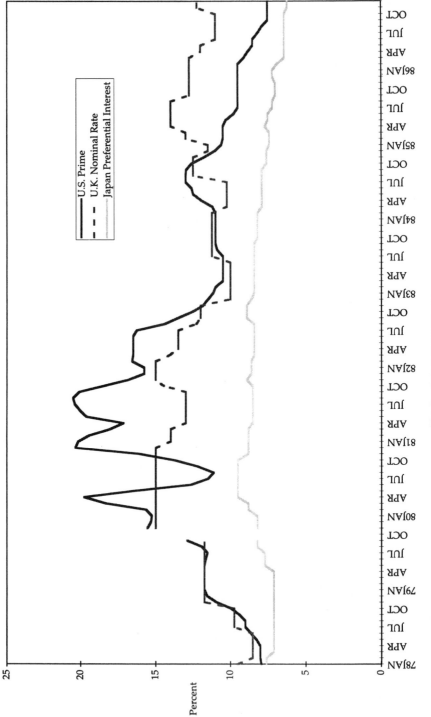

Fig. 7. Prime interest rates

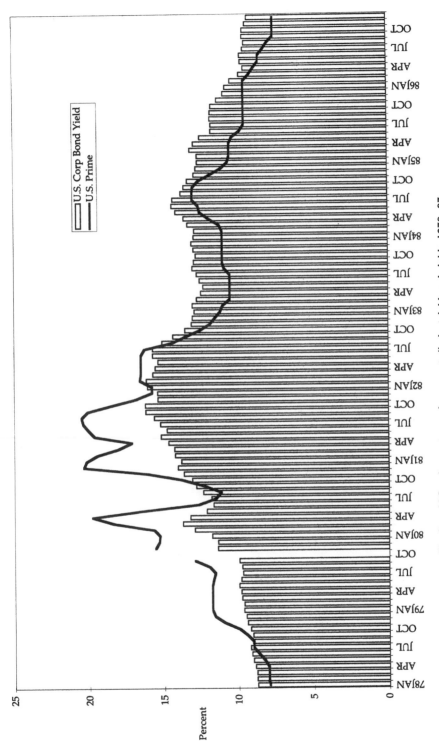

Fig. 8a.   U.S. prime rates and corporate/industrial bond yields, 1978–87

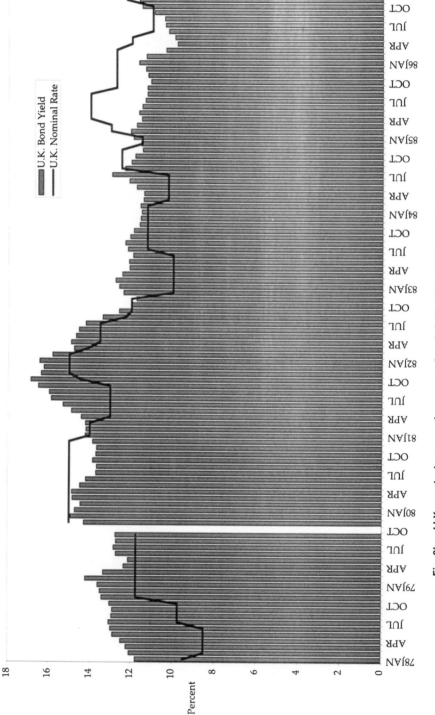

Fig. 8b. U.K. nominal rates and corporate bond yields, 1978–87 (twenty-five-year bonds)

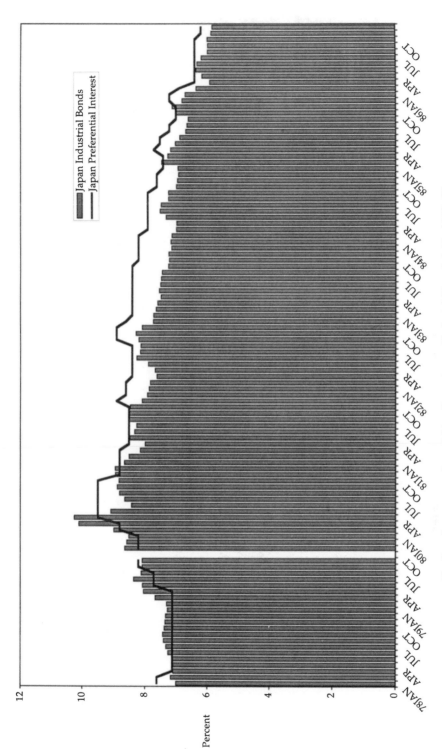

Fig. 8c. Japanese preferential lending rates and industrial bond yields, 1978–87

to buy and sell debt obligations before they reach maturity. Active secondary markets enable exchange between borrowers desiring long-term obligations and investors wanting mobility in their investments. Investors can buy an IPO with a long time horizon and shorten that horizon by selling the security in a secondary market.

Government policies in the major capital markets created incentives to switch borrowing and investment strategies. Borrowers and lenders apparently reacted to such shifts in incentives. Figure 9 separates primary international borrowing into loans and bonds. Prior to the 1980s, the growth in international borrowings did not really discriminate among bond and loan instruments, although loans appear to have been slightly more appealing during the 1970s.[9] But preferences over instruments shifted in the post-1980 period as borrowers increasingly employed bond instruments. Borrowing by loan instruments peaked in 1981. Bond issues increased, and by 1993 they exceeded loans threefold. Figure 10 disaggregates international borrowing further and reveals a hierarchy of preferences among types of bonds and loans. Government policy choices affected the costs and stability of instruments, which in turn affected how borrowers borrowed and investors invested.

Three other governmental shifts contributed significantly to securitization. First, policy conflicts among segments of domestic financial services industries led to regulatory liberalization in the major markets (Moran 1991; Sobel 1994), affecting international and domestic financial services. Major regulatory reforms such as May Day 1975 in the United States, Big Bang and the Financial Services Act of 1986 in the United Kingdom, and changes in Japan unleashed tremendous pressures upon investment banks (see appendix A). Liberalization encouraged competitive pricing of capital. Deregulation of fixed commissions and changes in regulatory boundaries led to a decline in brokerage earnings but also removed many restraints upon invention of securitized instruments and investment strategies. Policy reforms pushed investment banks to shift more emphasis to underwriting, inventing instruments and markets, and putting together deals such as mergers and acquisitions. These reinforced the trend toward greater disintermediation and securitization.

Second, deficit spending by governments of the industrialized nations expanded during this period. Policymakers could have cut programs, increased taxes, or resorted to seignorage to finance their deficits. Governments avoided such politically unpopular avenues by borrowing in securitized markets. Government liberalization of financial markets reduced transaction costs, lowered barriers, and enlarged the pool of those able to operate in these markets. These fed increased market size and liquidity, which enhanced governments' abilities

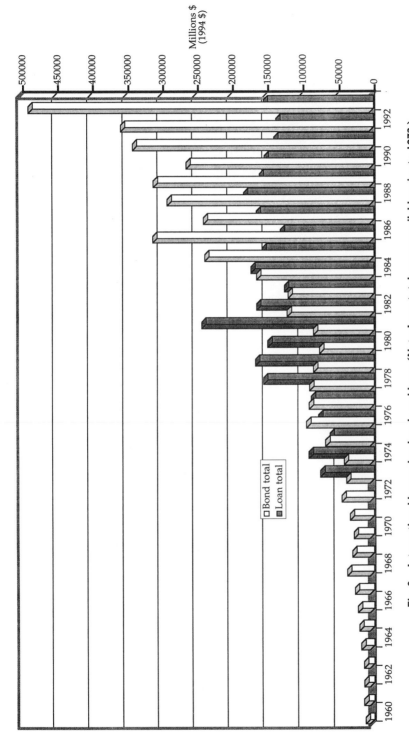

Fig. 9. International borrowing: bonds and loans (**Note:** Loan totals are unavailable prior to 1972.)

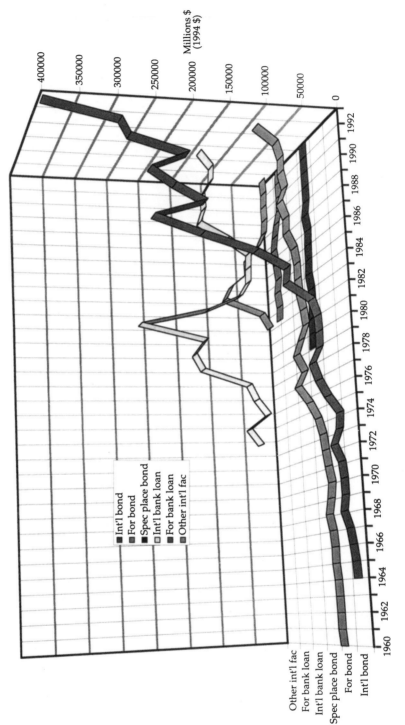

Fig. 10. International borrowing by instrument

to borrow to fund their shortfalls. The expansion of disintermediated markets allowed government policymakers to avoid increasing taxes, cutting spending, or using seignorage.

Third, many states embarked upon a privatization spree. In many nations, the government owned railroads, airlines, national banks, telecommunications enterprises, defense firms, and other companies. Governments used equity issues in disintermediated financial markets to transfer ownership of such state-owned enterprises to private shareholders. In Europe, these issues led to large increases in market capitalization. Deep and efficient disintermediated markets were in many governments' immediate interests as they sought to market the equity issues of their state-owned enterprises. In light of this newfound interest by governments in efficient and deep markets, it is not surprising that they altered the regulatory frameworks of disintermediated markets.

Borrowers did not rush back to the intermediated markets even with declines in commercial interest rates. Return to the nominal prices preceding 1979 did not mean a return to pre-1979 practices. The political-institutional and policy shifts created a new financial environment to which many actors had adapted. Many borrowers and lenders had shifted to the disintermediated markets, which offered more flexible financing and investment options. Regulatory liberalization spurred the invention of financial instruments, transformed the financial services industry, and stimulated securitization and disintermediation. Privatization and increased government borrowing produced greater depth and liquidity in disintermediated markets. The influx of capital resulted in deeper and more liquid secondary markets. Borrowers and lenders now enjoyed a greater menu of possibilities. Government policies and institutional reforms, which prompted private and public market participants to switch borrowing and lending strategies, spurred the expansion of the more decentralized disintermediated markets and transformed the decision environment of future public policy deliberations. As a consequence of government actions and private reactions to them, capital became increasingly heterogeneous and mobile across types of markets to accompany its new international mobility.

Intangibles as Commodities

Domestic regulatory reforms enabled and stimulated the invention of a new form of financial instrument, which fundamentally altered financial markets: financial derivatives and futures. Commodities markets already traded futures and options in tangible goods (e.g., pork bellies, rice, cattle, oil, corn, and coffee). In some cases, futures markets for such tangible commodities have existed for centuries. Intangibles began trading as commodities only in the early 1970s. Such markets grew vigorously. In 1993, derivative markets surpassed $5 trillion in capitalization, and by 1995 they had grown to approximately $8.5 trillion.

Two political institutional reforms opened the door to such markets and stimulated their expansion. First, in the early 1970s the U.S. Congress reformed statutes pertaining to commodity trading and redefined what constituted a commodity. This opened the door to trading intangibles as commodities and allowed the construction of financial futures and derivatives tied to financial instruments in other markets. Active financial derivatives markets emerged and grew faster than anyone could have forecast. Invention of financial instruments exploded. A succession of innovative financial instruments quickly began trading on the Chicago commodities and financial markets.

Warrants began trading in 1970. The Chicago International Monetary Market introduced options linked to U.S. Treasury securities in 1972; the Chicago Mercantile Exchange began trading financial futures and options the same year; the Chicago Board Options Exchange initiated options linked to U.S. Treasury securities and the Standard and Poors Composite Indices in 1973; and the Chicago Board of Trade introduced Treasury bond futures in 1977.[10] The New York Futures Exchange opened in 1980. Index options, the New York Stock Exchange (NYSE) Composite Index Futures, and the NYSE Composite Index began trading in 1983. In 1985, the NYSE began trading financial instruments pegged to equities listed elsewhere, options on over-the-counter stocks. These innovations spread overseas. Financial options began trading in London in 1978, and the London International Financial Futures Exchange opened its doors in 1982. The Japanese Diet amended the Japanese Securities and Exchange Law in June 1985 to permit financial futures. Index funds were soon introduced. The Tokyo Stock Exchange (TSE) began trading bond futures in October 1985. A stock futures portfolio based on a basket of fifty Japanese stocks, the "Stock Futures 50," began trading on the Osaka market in 1987. These markets expanded the range of investment opportunities, provided mechanisms for hedging risks in other markets, and competed with other markets for investors' capital.

Second, as mentioned earlier, the Nixon administration abandoned the Bretton Woods–Smithsonian fixed exchange rate system and moved to floating rates in 1973. Exchange rates affect the value of transactions that take place across borders. Floating rates increase uncertainty about the future value of such transactions. They create an inherently more uncertain environment for global trade and investment. International monetary relations based upon floating rates created a functional demand for mechanisms to limit the newly expanded exchange rate risk.

These political-institutional shifts, defining intangibles as commodities and the movement to floating exchange rates, were mutually reinforcing. The second change increased the uncertainty surrounding economic exchanges across borders, and the first allowed the development of financial mechanisms that constrained that uncertainty. Government actions, particularly those of the United States, created a demand for and the possibility (supply) of some device to manage such risks. Futures and options in foreign exchange markets permitted hedging against exchange rate risks. Legislative reforms permitted the growth of financial derivatives markets, and the movement to floating rates stimulated their expansion. These markets have exploded since the early 1970s.

The position of derivatives markets in the financial infrastructure is as important as their appearance and growth. Previously, most linkages across financial markets were more implicit and psychological. Yet the very nature of the financial instruments in derivatives markets links these markets to other financial markets. These markets trade instruments whose values are tied to financial instruments in other markets. This creates explicit connections across types of financial markets. These explicit linkages allow the use of a derivative to lower overall risk if it is used to hedge an investment in another market. But these explicit linkages between derivatives and instruments in other financial markets could also transmit shocks during a crisis.[11] Political-institutional reforms enabled financial derivatives and stimulated their growth and consequently led to a more tightly interconnected financial infrastructure across markets and boundaries. Markets in financial derivatives grew out of domestic policy reforms, but their extraordinary growth and their connections to other financial markets transformed the international financial environment, creating uncharted territory for private and public decision makers.

The Former Command Economies and Global Capital Markets

Political change in the form of détente in the early 1970s, economic liberalization in the People's Republic of China, the dismantling of the Soviet Union and its sphere in the 1980s, and the ongoing transformation of those political economies altered the way they interact with the global political economy. Domestic political shifts since détente, democratization of political enterprise, and privatization of economic enterprise constitute stunning transformations in their state-society relations. As the changes in the former Eastern bloc economies were such unusual and dramatic events, with potentially huge ramifications for global financial relations, I use the next chapter to take a more detailed look at the shifts that led to these economies' increased interest in global capital markets.

During the Cold War, the Eastern bloc states accumulated capital almost independent of Western capital markets and international financial mechanisms. With détente, these nations expanded their interests in the global economy in general and in global financial mechanisms specifically. Borrowers in these states began to approach Western capital markets for long-term financing. In 1971, the National Bank of Hungary issued the first eurobond by a Council for Mutual Economic Assistance (Comecon) nation. Borrowers from these states now approach global markets with potentially ravenous appetites. These nations enjoy educated and semi- to highly skilled labor forces, but they need capital to transform their economic infrastructures. They offer potentially attractive investment opportunities. Since it is too soon to forecast the long-term capital demands of borrowers in these states, many in the developing world fear that the economic appeal and capital appetites of these borrowers will crowd out others.

Figure 11 shows the international borrowing behavior of Russian and Eastern European borrowers. Although relatively small in absolute size compared to Western borrowing, appreciable absolute growth has occurred since détente. Comecon medium-term bank loans made up one of the most rapidly expanding components of the euro markets by the mid-1970s. A second surge in borrowing by the Eastern European economies appears following the disintegration of the Eastern bloc and the demise of the Soviet Union, despite the accompanying political uncertainty and instability.

These participants' interests in global capital markets, unleashed by domestic political shifts, have interacted with the increasing heterogeneity of those markets. The aggregate trends in figure 12 suggest that at least some borrowers from the former command economies are adopting strategies similar to Western borrowers by shifting to less costly and more flexible disintermediated instruments. The data demonstrate a shift in preferences over financing strategies and an ability to act on those shifting preferences. Economic liberalization and the increasing interest of these political economies in global financial markets followed from fundamental shifts in their domestic political arenas—endogenous changes that restructured relations between these states and global financial markets. But the potential scope and size of their involvement in global cap-

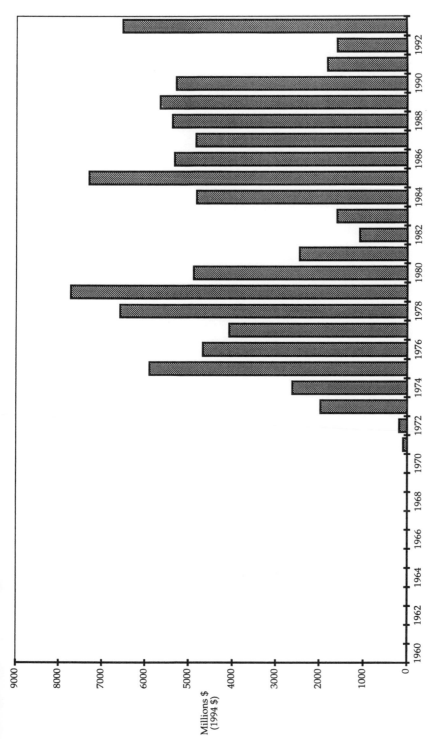

Fig. 11. Eastern European and Soviet/Russian borrowing

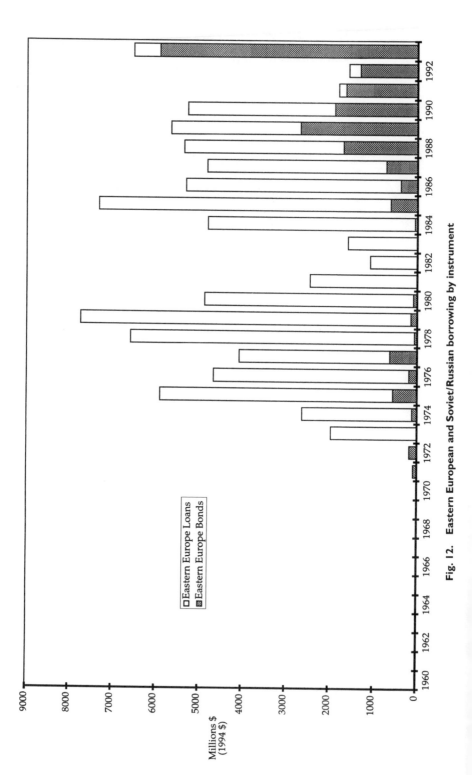

Fig. 12. Eastern European and Soviet/Russian borrowing by instrument

ital markets could eventually affect future decision environments and become exogenous factors for all.

Conclusion

In this chapter, I have described four fundamental changes in global finance from the 1960s to the 1990s. These changes go far deeper than the simple expansion of cross-border capital flows. First, increases in international capital mobility have made national markets potentially international and created greater linkages across national economies. Second, capital's heterogeneity has exploded with the invention of instruments and increasing disintermediation. Third, financial derivatives have increased linkages across financial markets. Capital mobility and linkages have increased across markets—within and across borders. Fourth, new participants have entered the global capital markets. I focused upon those from the former command economies of Russia and Eastern Europe, but new participants from around the globe continue to seek access. Financial markets have become more global, heterogeneous, interconnected, and encompassing. These changes—produced by the interaction of public and private behavior, domestic and international arenas, and social context and individual choice—have transformed the environment in which private and public decision makers now operate.

Unlike outside-in stories, political institutional shifts and policies endogenous to a few nations underpinned these fundamental changes in global financial relations, which led to the vibrant reemergence of global finance. Decisions in domestic political arenas restructured market rules, created incentives for financial actors, and proved pivotal to globalization. Faced with shifts in their incentive structures, market actors altered their behavior—in some cases negating the intentions of the public policy shifts. When aggregated by a market mechanism, these choices transformed the international political economy. Intentional or not, the revitalization of global finance can be traced back to state choices.

After decades of unfettered capital flows, American political leaders created institutions that hindered U.S. capital outflows. U.S. industries and MNCs shifted their borrowing for foreign operations to overseas markets, stimulating the development of the euro markets and neutralizing the objectives of the policymakers. American financial firms followed their industry clients. Ten years later, U.S. policymakers repealed the capital controls—which had proved fruitless in the long term, as private actors devised routes around the restrictions—and began liberalizing American capital markets. Later, central bank policies led to higher interest rates in commercial lending markets, which proved instrumental in shifting preferences toward disintermediated instruments. Government decisions to increase borrowing and privatize state enterprises also contributed to this shift in preferences. These moves increased the capitalization and liquidity of disintermediated markets, further enhancing their appeal to investors. Within the American political arena, the decisions to reject fixed exchange rates and recognize intangibles as commodities fed the development of financial derivatives markets. Political-institutional changes such as liberalization and market-oriented reforms brought new participants to the global markets.

In all states, policy choices and political institutions temper the external pressures that come with global integration. But such pressures originate somewhere. Technology and economic competition did not simply appear in the mid-1970s after a forty-year absence and steamroll policymakers. Discontinuities across national markets and temporal inconsistencies highlight the weaknesses of explanations of financial globalization that focus primarily upon technological change and international economic competition. Choices endogenous to key governments unleashed such forces. This amounts to a "size principle" that discriminates among states and their capacities to play causal roles in transforming the international political economy. Yet relying solely upon an inside-out explanation neglects the fact that changes endogenous to several states, which transform the global political economy by affecting the choices of market actors, can then produce exogenous pressures on all states. Politics and markets are intricately connected, and the relationship between the two is constantly evolving. Capital markets rely upon political systems, humanly devised scaffolding that affects the likelihood of exchange beyond small-scale local interactions.[12] As the scaffolding changes, so does exchange.

CHAPTER 4

Global Capital Markets and the Command Economies

The increasing participation of the Soviet, Eastern European, and Chinese economies in global capital markets constitutes a sharp departure from the past, a notable shift since the 1960s that for three primary reasons deserves special attention despite the relatively limited role these nations play in the global economy. First, the shift in outlook by these nations reflects huge changes in their domestic political-economic arrangements. Massive transformations have reoriented their domestic dealings and their relationships with the international political economy. As a rough gauge of importance, Western academics, development experts from international organizations, private consultants, and firms have poured advice, recommendations, assistance, and investments into these economies. Second, the shifts in domestic political-economic relations amount to shifts in key independent variables. These political economies provide quasi-experimental arenas in which we can observe the effects of changes in domestic political-economic society upon the integration of such nations into the global political economy. It is the variation that makes these cases so appealing as social science laboratories in which to observe the effects of domestic political institutions and policies upon behavioral outcomes in global markets. Third, despite the relatively limited role these nations enjoy in the global economy today, long-term counterfactual reasoning suggests that they have the potential to become significant contributors to the global economy and vastly more integrated. Large educated populations, potentially large domestic markets, ample supplies of raw materials, and growing foreign direct investment suggest that these economies will become increasingly important to the global economy.

The nations comprising Comecon participated in global finance to only a small extent prior to the late 1960s. Two banks with Eastern bloc ties, the

Moscow Narodny in London and the Banque Commerciale por l'Europe du Nord (Eurobank) in Paris, helped create the euro dollar market and handled most Comecon activity in global markets. In part, a fear of being stuck with dollar holdings in the event of an East-West crisis pushed the Soviets to recycle dollars through these eurobank connections. Nevertheless, Eastern bloc participation in global finance remained relatively small for many years, as Cold War tensions hampered East-West economic interactions. Eastern bloc political leaders limited their nations' interactions in global financial markets. Western governments limited Eastern bloc access to Western capital as one strategy of containment, and Western financiers appeared reticent to operate in these economies. What, then, fed the shifts that began in the late 1960s and early 1970s? What are their magnitudes? What are the implications for these political economies? And, finally, what are the implications for other political economies that may compete for the same capital?

The changing participation in global capital markets by Eastern bloc countries occurred within a context of significant political and economic shifts, which highlight the linkages between the political-security and political-economic arenas. First, I examine why these nations turned to global capital markets during the 1970s, why international investors and lenders responded to their entreaties, and which changes in the domestic and international political-economic arenas helped initiate the integration of these economies into global capital dealings. The changes fall into two periods. First, a thaw in political-economic relations, highlighted by détente in the late 1960s and early 1970s, promoted the integration of these economies into the global political economy generally and global financial markets specifically. Second, economic and political liberalization in the late 1980s and early 1990s appears to have fueled further integration.

Next, I describe the activities of these nations in global capital markets. I look at overall changes in their borrowing. Global activity by borrowers from these nations constitutes a relatively small segment of the global markets, but their absolute borrowing has grown since détente. Borrowers from these states reveal an increased interest in global capital *and* changing preferences over how they borrow. Some Eastern bloc borrowers began shifting their strategies in global capital markets in the mid-1970s to mimic strategies employed by Western industrialized borrowers. Nevertheless, popular versions of the integration of these nations into global capital markets hugely overstate such shifts.

Third, I consider the implications of these changes. The potential demand for global capital from these states is enormous. This concerns other borrowers, particularly those from developing nations that seek scarce global capital. Is there a potential that borrowers from the former command economies could "crowd out" other borrowers in the international markets? The integration of these economies into global capital markets may portend hardships for others as international investors select among investment options. To date, the evidence fails to provide a clear answer. Borrowers from some of the former command economies gained improved access to global capital following the reforms of the late 1980s and early 1990s, but borrowers from others appear to have enjoyed better access prior to liberalization and democratization. The evidence casts shadows upon the sunny expectations that first accompanied such reforms.

Explaining Changing Participation

Pinpointing a single cause for the growing integration of the centrally planned economies—later the former centrally planned economies—into global financial markets is difficult and can be misleading. Shifts in their domestic political economies and the global political arena contributed to their increased involvement. Externally imposed barriers to their participation gradually fell away. Concurrently, shifts in the internal dynamics of these nations spurred their interest in global capital. International investors became more curious about economic opportunities in these nations *and* the nations became more interested in accessing global capital. The shifts fall into two distinct periods: détente, beginning in the late 1960s, and the era of political and economic reform that began in the mid to late 1980s.

Détente and Shifts in the International Political-Military Context

The Cold War was in full swing in 1960, but within the decade tensions thawed and opened the door to political-military détente between East and West. This restructuring of political-military relations spilled over into the economic sphere. Several key shifts in the political-military arena reduced Cold War tensions and engendered more constructive East-West engagements. First, the narrowing of the U.S.-Soviet strategic gap and the Cuban missile crisis led to greater East-West cooperation, which aimed at reducing the likelihood of catastrophic military conflict. Second, the ascension of Willy Brandt and his political agenda in West Germany promoted the resolution of issues that had persisted since the end of World War II, obstructing a political settlement in Europe. Third, the American experience and subsequent disengagement in Vietnam opened the door to more amicable relations between East and West. Fourth, the rise of Sino-Soviet tensions and discontent within the communist bloc created opportunities for the West to play the "China card" and seek rapprochement with both the Chinese and the Soviets.

Strategic and Nuclear Parity

The Cuban missile crisis in 1962 unleashed forces that helped alter East-West political, military, and economic relations. Khrushchev's attempt to base Soviet intermediate-range missiles in Cuba to effect a balance of nuclear capabilities punctuated the inferiority of the Soviets' long-range strategic weapons programs and their inability to challenge U.S. supremacy as a global power beyond the Eurasian landmass. The Soviet retreat during the Cuban crisis embarrassed Khrushchev and the Soviet Union. The crisis undermined Khrushchev's leadership and fueled the internal political maneuvering that led to his downfall and the eventual ascendancy of Brezhnev—a key shift in the Soviet domestic hierarchy.

Soviet embarrassment over the Cuban crisis strained the already tense Sino-Soviet relationship. The Chinese had earlier begun to distance themselves from the Soviet-dominated bloc. Soviet backpedaling in the face of American military and diplomatic pressures exacerbated the underlying tensions between the Soviets and Chinese. This accelerated the pace of the Chinese defection. The monolithic communist bloc began to show more cracks as Sino-Soviet tensions fed dissension in the satellite nations.

The Cuban fiasco led to shifts in American and Soviet diplomatic and military strategies that helped improve East-West relations within a decade. Soviet strategy shifted away from the confrontational policies that had led to the Berlin and Cuban crises, giving way to more constructive engagement. After going to the brink of nuclear confrontation, Soviet and American interactions focused upon reducing the likelihood of similar crises. Arms control negotiations and agreements became the cornerstone of this policy shift. The Test Ban Treaty, Hot-Line Agreement, Outer Space Treaty, Non-Proliferation Treaty, SALT I, SALT II, and the Mutual Balance Force Reduction talks arose from the diplomatic engagement precipitated by the Cuban crisis. These negotiations and agreements restructured the international political-military landscape, eased East-West tensions, and created precedents for interbloc cooperation. This generated opportunities for greater East-West political and economic détente.

Concurrent with political initiatives to reduce potentially devastating mishaps in the nuclear relationship, the Soviets moved to achieve strategic parity with the United States. They increased the pace of their long-range weapons programs, built up their strategic intercontinental missile forces, improved their intermediate-range nuclear weapons for the European theater, enlarged their submarine-based nuclear missile capabilities, and created an oceangoing surface fleet capable of projecting Soviet power beyond the Eurasian landmass. The Soviets had gained strategic parity with the United States by the time the Nixon administration took office.

At first glance, the improvements in Soviet military capabilities seem paradoxical to better interbloc relations and the integration of the Eastern bloc economies into the global economy. But narrowing the military gap between the United States and the Soviet Union actually provided a basis for improved relations—perhaps a necessary precondition for negotiations between equals. The shifts in military strategy and weapons development empowered the Soviet diplomatic move toward engagement. Strategic parity and a threat of mutual destruction illuminated the dysfunctional nature of an uncontrolled and unwinnable arms race. Both sides found a common interest in limiting the nuclear race and the destabilizing competition between the superpowers. A reduction in political-military tensions created opportunities for improved relations between the two spheres along other dimensions. The Cuban crisis pushed the Soviet Union down a path that led to strategic parity and U.S.-Soviet constructive engagement. Arms control negotiations eased diplomatic tensions and created channels for future interactions. The thawing of political-military tensions was a precursor to increased trade and investment.

Political Settlement in Europe

The Berlin crisis, the division of Germany into two states in 1949, and the Cold War reinforced the post–World War II partition that left Europe divided into two blocs. Prospects for normalization of relations between the Eastern and Western blocs depended upon a reduction in bipolar tensions. This ultimately rested upon the fate of the two German states, Berlin, and West German territorial disputes with Poland and Czechoslovakia from the redrawing of their national boundaries in 1945. Konrad Adenauer, the West German chancellor, rejected East German sovereignty and held out for a united Germany. The Hallstein Doctrine enshrined this position in 1955 by claiming for the West German government the sole right to represent all Germans. The Hallstein Doctrine rejected the authority of the East German state and declared that the West German government would regard diplomatic recognition of East Germany as an unfriendly act. West Germany severed diplomatic relations with Eastern European governments that recognized East Germany.[1] West German hopes for uni-fication and the redrawing of postwar boundaries concerned the Soviet and other Eastern European governments. This posed a major obstacle to thawing the Cold War and normalizing economic relations.

The Cuban missile crisis revealed cracks in the communist bloc, but the Western bloc also began to exhibit some stresses. With postwar recovery, West-ern Europe began to emerge as a political and economic force in world affairs distinct from the United States. The European Economic Community devel-oped into an economic bloc with its own agenda. In France, Charles De Gaulle's government employed a variety of strategies to drive wedges into the Atlantic alliance and distance Europe from the United States. An increasingly indepen-dent Western Europe became more amenable to relaxing East-West tensions. Yet West Germany's refusal to accept the political and territorial status quo re-strained its allies from seeking normalization of relations and continued to fuel Soviet and Eastern European fears.

West German intransigence began to soften in 1966. When a new govern-ing coalition took power, it elevated Willy Brandt (a Social Democrat) to for-eign minister. Brandt introduced his "Ostpolitik," or eastern policy, which sig-naled a significant shift in the West German policy position. Ostpolitik targeted the normalization of West German relations with Eastern European states and a relaxation of East-West tensions, even if this meant foregoing German unifi-cation and the country's claim to the territories ceded to Poland and Czecho-slovakia at the end of World War II. Brandt did not reject unification as a goal, but Ostpolitik dropped unification as a precondition for the normalization of relations. Essentially, he altered expectations about the sequence, time horizon, and context of unification.

Under Brandt's leadership, and contrary to the Hallstein Doctrine, the West German Foreign Ministry began to normalize relations with Eastern European governments. West Germany established formal diplomatic ties with Hungary in 1967 and continued to work toward normal relations with other states. East-ern European governments demanded recognition of East German sovereignty and the territorial status quo in Europe as the price of normalization. West Ger-many took a major step toward this goal in the 1969 West German elections. Brandt's Social Democrats dominated the coalition government that emerged from the elections, and he ascended to the West German chancellorship.

As chancellor, Brandt increased his efforts to normalize West German rela-tions with Eastern Europe. He reduced Soviet fears of a reawakened, aggressive Germany by signing the Nuclear Non-Proliferation Treaty. He then negotiated a nonaggression agreement with the Soviets, which recognized the territorial status quo in Europe. Next Brandt entered into a nonaggression treaty with

Poland that accepted the German-Polish boundaries imposed at the end of World War II. In 1973, West Germany formally recognized the existing German and Czechoslovakian borders and renounced the Munich Pact of 1938, giving up any claim on the Sudetenland. West German territorial claims that obstructed a political settlement in Europe, and consequently served as obstacles to the normalization of East-West relations, no longer existed.

These shifts in West German policies left the question of East German sovereignty as the major remaining barrier to normalization of European political relations. The demise of Walter Ulbricht as the East German leader and the rise of Erich Honecker opened the door to a resolution. The four occupying powers in Berlin (the United States, the United Kingdom, France, and the Soviet Union) formally recognized the special relationship between West Berlin and West Germany. This recognition rejected East Germany's demand that it be allowed to control access to Berlin. The Soviets pressured their East German patron to sign the Basic Treaty with West Germany in December 1972. The treaty called for greater commercial ties between the two Germanies and the exchange of diplomatic missions. In 1973, East and West Germany gained membership in the United Nations as individual sovereign states. The resolution of German territorial demands and sovereignty issues underpinned the political settlement in Europe, transformed the global context, and substantially lowered barriers to improved East-West commercial relations.

Vietnam

Ironically, the bitter American experience in Vietnam contributed to the relaxation of East-West political and economic relations. Vietnam led to U.S. political-military retrenchment in the global arena. American policymakers took away from Vietnam lessons about the limitations of American power. After Vietnam, they became more cautious and skeptical about projecting American influence overseas. They became more amenable to East-West cooperation, which could reduce tensions and limit American military exposure overseas.

The United States became engaged in Vietnam in the early 1950s when it recognized the French puppet government of Emperor Bao Dai and subsidized a significant portion of the costs of the French-Vietminh military confrontation. Though the French subsequently withdrew, the United States remained involved. American involvement unraveled twenty years later. Domestic disagreements over the country's involvement tore apart the polity, revived isolationist tendencies, and increased American wariness of foreign entanglements. Calls for retrenchment bubbled up in the American polity.

A Senate resolution, sponsored by Mike Mansfield, reflected such pressures by calling for reduced U.S. troop levels in Europe. The resolution failed, but it garnered substantial support and attention. This raised questions about the American commitment to its Western European partners. The European allies faced the possibility of a reduced American military commitment to Europe, which could lead to politically unpopular increases in their own defense expenditures. An alternative was a reduction of East-West political-military tensions in Europe. Vietnam helped create conditions conducive to détente in Europe.

American withdrawal from Vietnam removed a major obstacle to Soviet-American and Sino-American rapprochement. Despite the appeal of rapprochement and the pressures of increasing Sino-Soviet tensions, the Soviets and Chinese could not normalize relations with the United States as long as the Americans continued to wage war against their client North Vietnam. Opportunities for rapprochement grew as the United States embarked on a diplomatic course to end active American military involvement.

The end of America's involvement in Vietnam transformed the international political-military arena and created opportunities. The American public grew disillusioned with the Cold War. U.S. foreign policy became more conservative. European governments feared a U.S. retrenchment in Europe and the implications for their own military expenditures. With the U.S. withdrawal from Vietnam, the Soviets and Chinese lost an important motivation for presenting a common front. Repressed Sino-Soviet tensions emerged full-blown in a bitter dispute. The Soviets sought to stabilize their European flank as prospects for a military confrontation with the People's Republic of China increased. In Europe, all the major parties recognized the advantages of normalizing East-West relations, pursuing détente, and stabilizing military relations. The Mutual and Balanced Force Reduction negotiations in Vienna and the European Security Conference in Helsinki in 1973 grew out of this recognition.

Sino-Soviet Tension, the China Card, and East-West Rapprochement

During World War II, a common enemy, the Japanese, prompted an uneasy truce in the Chinese civil war between Mao Zedong's Communists and Chiang Kai-shek's Nationalists. That truce ended with the conclusion of the war. The Communists triumphed in 1949, and the remnants of the Nationalist forces retreated to Taiwan. Distressed by excessive corruption, the United States had withdrawn its support from the Nationalists during the civil war. The United States may have been willing to recognize the triumphant Communist regime in China, but the Korean War broke out before American policymakers could decide. With the hostilities in Korea, American foreign policy lumped China and the Soviet Union into a monolithic communist bloc. The United States resumed providing economic and military aid to the Nationalists and negotiated a U.S.-Taiwan mutual defense agreement. The Korean conflict destroyed the prospects for Sino-American rapprochement during the 1950s and pushed the Soviets and Chinese closer together.

From its onset, the Sino-Soviet alliance proved to be an uneasy coalition. Prior to the Communist victory, the Soviets recognized the Nationalists as the government of China and pressured the Communists to compromise with them. After the defeat of the Nationalists, and despite earlier Soviet equivocation, the Chinese Communists looked to the Soviets for economic and technical assistance. The Soviets responded with military assistance during the Korean War. After the war, in the 1950s, the Soviets committed to long-term development loans and became China's primary trading partner. But Soviet assistance was costly. The Soviets required repayment for military assistance extended during the Korean War, and economic aid fell far below Beijing's expectations. The disappointing levels of assistance became glaringly obvious when Soviet economic development aid to India and other noncommunist states exceeded their aid to China. Much of the aid came tied to Soviet access to Chinese resources (at the expense of Chinese interests and sovereignty).

Territorial disputes revealed significant tensions and disagreements in the Chinese-Soviet coalition. Moscow remained officially neutral during Sino-Indian border clashes in 1959 and 1962, but the Soviets provided aid and comfort to China's foe in the form of economic and military assistance. The Soviets remained officially noncommittal during the Quemoy and Matsu crisis. The Sino-Soviet border dispute provided more dramatic and prescient signs of tense relations. The Chinese disputed Soviet claims to a large amount of territory that Russia had obtained by treaty during the 1800s. The territorial dispute grew violent when Chinese and Soviet troops clashed along the disputed border.

Nuclear weapons were another major source of friction. In 1957, the Soviets promised technical assistance to China's nascent nuclear program but only if China agreed to Soviet control of Chinese nuclear weapons and greater coordination of their foreign policies. The Chinese rejected the stipulation as an infringement upon Chinese sovereignty. The Soviets responded by withdrawing their offer to assist China's nuclear program.

Sino-Soviet disagreements became increasingly public during the 1950s and early 1960s. The emerging split fueled other cracks in the communist bloc. Some Eastern European states followed China's lead and began asserting greater policy independence from the Soviets. By the mid-1960s, the West faced an opportunity to exploit the growing divisions in the communist bloc, but Vietnam intervened. Vietnam postponed the improvement of East-West relations even though Sino-Soviet relations continued to deteriorate.

By the end of the decade, Vietnam had begun to fade as an obstacle to improved East-West relations. The Nixon administration took office in 1969 and pursued peace negotiations with North Vietnam. Sino-Soviet military confrontations escalated over territorial disputes in Northwest China. The Soviets redeployed troops, aircraft, and nuclear weapons from Eastern Europe to the Chinese frontier. In this environment, the United States embarked on a diplomatic strategy to normalize relations with China and exploit the split in the communist bloc. Hoping to take advantage of Sino-Soviet tensions, the United States began playing the "China card."

The Americans offered the Chinese an opportunity to normalize economic and diplomatic relations. Relaxation of American trade and travel restrictions, ping-pong diplomacy, shuttle diplomacy by Henry Kissinger, American support of Pakistan against China's enemy India, and significant changes in the U.S. policy toward Taiwan paved the way for Nixon to visit the Peoples' Republic of China. Sino-American rapprochement allowed China to balance the Soviet military buildup by redeploying troops to the northwestern Chinese frontier. The Soviets, fearing escalation of tensions with China, sought to reduce East-West differences in Europe. The restructuring of Sino-American relations in the early 1970s transformed the international political-military context and afforded opportunities for normalization of East-West economic relations.

Domestic Shifts during Détente

At the same time that the global political-military context was becoming conducive to improved East-West relations, domestic conditions in the Eastern bloc led to a growing interest in greater integration into the global economy. Comecon's inability to keep pace with Western European economic growth, Polish food riots in 1970, and increasing tensions over Soviet economic exploitation of its Eastern European satellites revealed dissatisfaction with Eastern economic policies. Economic disparities between the East and West increased. Eastern bloc economies failed to meet domestic consumer demands. Growing frustration among the Eastern bloc polities produced domestic pressures for increased economic openings to the West.

After Khrushchev's downfall, Brezhnev outmaneuvered Kosygin to gain the Soviet premiership. Brezhnev reversed the policies of limited economic interaction with the West. He viewed stronger ties as a means of stimulating economic growth. The Soviet bloc turned to Western sources for capital, technology, and other assistance to develop their raw materials and modernize their industrial base. The Soviets aimed to develop industries and resources that would generate the hard currency income they needed to underwrite domestic development.[2] Yet the Soviet bloc continued to face a hard currency shortfall—a recipe for chronic balance of payment shortfalls. The natural resources that could earn hard currency in global markets were located mostly in the Soviet Union and Poland. Other Comecon states confronted rising imports and small export markets. The Eastern bloc shortfall in its balance of payments with the OECD more than doubled from 1974 to 1975 (*Euromoney* January 1976, 16).

The gap between imports and exports continued to grow as imports of Western grain increased in the mid-1970s. OPEC's actions led to large increases in the price of energy. Increasing energy costs reduced Western consumption of other foreign goods and squeezed nonenergy export markets. Eastern bloc exports to the West slumped. This hindered Eastern states from financing their domestic development with hard currency earnings. The effect upon the Eastern bloc nations' balance of payments deficits reflected a dependence upon Western markets and an expanding demand for Western capital and products. This developing East-West economic interdependence was more one-sided than mutual and had implications for Eastern bloc growth and development. Socialist policymakers faced limiting Western imports to reduce the balance of payments deficit and the hard currency earnings shortfall. This option ensured that they would fall short of the economic targets specified in their 1971–75 five-year plans. Slowing the flow of Western goods, technology, and expertise would mean delays in developing the East's resources and constructing and converting industrial plants to produce export goods. This would create shortages and increase the dissatisfaction of Eastern bloc consumers.

The high cost of restraining import growth pushed Socialist planners toward the global capital markets as an alternative. Eastern bloc states turned to global capital markets to cover their chronic balance of payment deficits and to finance continued economic expansion. Global borrowing by Comecon states between 1974 and 1975 more than doubled as these states accessed approximately $2.1 billion in eurocurrency credits and $140 million in international bond issues (*Euromoney* January 1976, 12).

An Interlude in East-West Rapprochement and Economic Integration

Comecon nations increased their trade with the West and borrowed heavily in the euro markets in pursuit of growth and development. They imported Western goods and services to transform an inefficient economic infrastructure and alleviate consumer shortages. They borrowed capital to finance those purchases and pay for capital improvement projects. Opening the doors to greater East-West economic exchange produced rapidly expanding trade deficits and debt levels in the Comecon states. Their trade deficits and global borrowing grew dramatically in 1974–75 as they strove to meet the targets of economic five-year plans that ended in 1975.

A new five-year planning cycle began in 1976. Central planners in the Comecon states lowered their targets and sought to improve the imbalance in East-West economic relations. This meant restraining the growing appetite for Western goods, services, and capital that had produced the trade deficit and debt burden; expanding the export of goods to the West to balance imports; or both. It was far easier said than done. An economic slump in the West slowed the import of Eastern bloc goods by Western economies, but the demand for Western goods and capital continued unabated in the East and exacerbated the imbalance.

Western bankers and governments began worrying about the Eastern bloc's debt in relation to its hard currency earnings from exports. The trade deficits and debt service ratios of most Comecon nations rose to disquieting levels by the mid to late 1970s. Questions and doubts appeared about the ability of Eastern bloc borrowers to service their growing debt obligations as the trade imbalances restricted hard currency export earnings of the Comecon states. Hard currency earnings were necessary to service the external debt acquired in global capital markets. Bankers and borrowers alike began to worry about these levels of debt. Senator Henry Jackson noted:

By all accounts Soviet and East European indebtedness to the West has reached major proportions. And yet, estimates of that debt vary widely— from about $27 billion to about $45 billion overall. By any measure, these sums are substantial—and they are growing. It is all the more disturbing that official and private estimates of that debt diverge so greatly. An apparent inability to gain consistent and reliable information about the extent of Soviet and East European borrowing is, itself, a significant part of the problem.

Large scale loans to the Soviet Union and the East European countries were once thought of as a way to gain "leverage" over these governments. What may be happening instead is that the debtors are on the verge of obtaining leverage over Western governments by the substantial interest in repayment that the Western banking system may be acquiring. . . .

Are we on sound ground if we assume that the Soviet Union and the states of Eastern Europe will be able to earn enough hard currency to repay their mounting obligations?[3]

Secretary of State Henry Kissinger addressed the same concerns when he asked his fellow OECD ministers at the June 1976 ministerial meeting:

> What are the implications of the growing external debt of the communist countries?[4]

Increasing uncertainty about Eastern bloc nations' ability to meet their obligations reached beyond the offices of Western governments. Richard Portes, an economist from the University of London, noted that:

> The East Europeans are paying close to $2 billion a year in interest to Western banks. Meanwhile they are running substantial deficits in their international trade. At the same time their indebtedness continues to climb.
>
> Bankers are "terribly genuine" about lending to Eastern Europe. Either they don't know what they're doing or the individual [exposure] limits are so low it doesn't matter. But in the aggregate, the amounts are absurdly large. There is no justification for it unless you can agree that there are political advantages for the West, which I don't see.[5]

By 1976, Poland was devoting 30 percent of its hard currency earnings from trade to refinance its external debt obligations.[6] Accounts estimate the Soviet and East German debt service ratios at 25 percent, 20 to 25 percent for Hungary, and less than 20 percent for Romania. This was before repayment of principle began—an optimistic view. In 1975, Bulgaria's external debt reached 3.1 times its hard currency earnings. East Germany, the Soviet Union, Hungary, Romania, and Poland had ratios of 1.9, 1.3, 1.2, 1.1, and 2, respectively. Only Czechoslovakia, which had followed conservative borrowing policies, had a debt-to-export earning ratio of less than 1.[7] These ratios did not dramatically differ from those of the developing nations, but the information disclosure by borrowers did. Eastern bloc borrowers provided far less information about their economic conditions. Decision makers at Western financial institutions partly assumed, mistakenly or nor, that the centralized management of the Comecon economies could exercise sufficient control over their economies to protect against failures to service external debt obligations and that the Soviet Union would stand behind the external obligations of the other Comecon states. No developing borrowers received such special consideration in terms of information disclosure.

The lack of information about Comecon indebtedness, creditworthiness, and economic projects began to feed uncertainty and affect the willingness of Western financial institutions to extend credit to Eastern bloc borrowers.

On the political front, East-West tensions appeared to have relaxed by the mid-1970s. Policymakers in the East and West looked forward to improving relations. The 1975 Helsinki conference marked the formal end of the Cold War in Europe, as it resolved the territorial and sovereignty issues that had plagued East-West relations since the end of World War II. Sino-American rapprochement proceeded as the United States accepted as a fait accompli the demise of Western-supported regimes in Southeast Asia. The Soviets, Chinese, and Eastern Europeans used political rapprochement to enhance economic interactions with the West. Increasing economic linkages via trade, technology, and capital flows glossed over East-West political divisions.

Despite the trend toward improving relations, political and economic détente stalled in the late 1970s. East-West rapprochement faltered, and Cold War tensions reemerged. U.S.-Soviet arms control negotiations stumbled over technological advances in Soviet strategic weaponry. Theater nuclear weapons in Europe became a central issue as the Soviets replaced its old intermediate-range missiles with new and more capable systems. The Carter administration responded to Soviet weapons development by accelerating development and deployment of American weapons. The U.S.-Soviet arms race was renewed after the lull of the early 1970s.

Another political obstacle interrupted rapprochement when Soviet troops entered Afghanistan to support the pro-Soviet government in Kabul against militant opposition. Soviet military involvement in Afghanistan marked the first time since World War II that Soviet troops formally intervened outside the boundaries of Eastern Europe. Earlier that year, the overthrow of the shah of Iran by Muslim fundamentalists severely damaged American strategic capabilities in the region. With this shift in the geopolitical landscape of the region, President Carter viewed Soviet military adventurism in Afghanistan as a potential threat to vital American interests in the region—specifically access to oil resources. He declared with the Carter Doctrine that the United States would intervene militarily in the region if necessary to protect such interests. In addition to the Carter Doctrine, U.S. policymakers sought other avenues to contain Soviet influence in the region. American policymakers repaired damaged relations with the military regime in Pakistan, sought military facilities in the region to replace those lost in the downfall of the shah, provided assistance to the Afghan rebels fighting the Soviet-supported Kabul government, created a rapid deployment force for the Persian Gulf, and increased U.S. military capabilities in the region. The Reagan administration continued and accelerated these initiatives.

The expansion in East-West trade, capital flows, and technological exchange that characterized the early 1970s slowed considerably by the late 1970s and early 1980s as political and economic pitfalls befell détente. Nontrivial disagreements in foreign policies highlighted the lack of Western political leverage over the choices of Eastern bloc policymakers. Expanded economic ties failed to constrain political activities and disagreements to the degree expected by many public and private decision makers. The reappearance of disagreements contributed to the wariness of Western lenders.

Renewal of East-West Economic Integration

The reappearance of Cold War tensions, uncertainty about the ability of Eastern bloc nations to service their debt burdens, the paucity of accurate data about Eastern bloc accounts, and the Third World debt crisis interrupted the expansion of Eastern bloc borrowing by the early 1980s. This interruption proved to be a temporary interlude on the path to greater participation by the Eastern bloc nations in the global economy. Evidence of continued interest on the part of Eastern bloc borrowers and renewed interest by Western lenders appeared even during the retrenchment.

China provided a hint of things to come. In 1978, it announced that it was seeking overseas development assistance and direct loans (Harding 1987, 152). Under the leadership of Deng Xiaoping, China openly rejected the self-reliant and centralized development strategies of the Mao era. The Chinese embraced export-oriented production, a limited free market, and an increasing amount of private ownership. They sought capital, skills, and technology from abroad. Exposure to global trading and financial markets provided external discipline to the economy.[8]

China joined the World Bank, the International Monetary Fund (IMF), and the Asian Development Bank. In 1978, it requested assistance from the United Nations Development Program (UNDP) and soon became the largest recipient of UNDP Funds (Keylor 1996, 442). This concerned others in the developing economies. In 1980, China began receiving IMF and World Bank funds. China's access to overseas capital grew dramatically. It moved cautiously in the early 1980s despite its growing access to global capital through international development assistance, credits from foreign governments, and borrowing in global markets. Chinese policymakers sought overseas capital but also tried to restrain China's level of external indebtedness (Harding 1987, 152). By the mid-1980s,

Chinese policymakers had abandoned their conservatism and restraint with regard to overseas indebtedness.

While overseas capital and investment flowed to China in the early 1980s, in other communist states such flows stagnated. Some of this reflects the appeal of China's potentially huge domestic market, but it also represents the success of Sino-American rapprochement and mutual American-Chinese apprehensions over Soviet political-military activities. Chinese and American policymakers deplored the Soviet military intervention in Afghanistan. The invasion of Cambodia by Vietnam, a Soviet client, reinforced such concerns. Events in the political-military arena, which exacerbated Soviet-American tensions, helped strengthen Sino-American relations. Spillover from the political-military arena that restrained the willingness of overseas investors to extend credit in the Soviet bloc worked to China's benefit.

The revived U.S.-Soviet tensions proved to be relatively short-lived. Mikhail Gorbachev ascended to the leadership of the Soviet Communist Party. He moved to reverse the deterioration of the Soviet economy, which had continued under his predecessor. He introduced significant policy changes, which ultimately contributed to the dismantling of the Soviet bloc in Eastern Europe and the breakup of the Soviet Union. These initiatives took place on both the international and domestic fronts.

Internationally, Gorbachev moved to improve U.S.-Soviet relations. He sought to curtail the arms race, which had sapped resources from productive enterprises. He planned to redirect the resources consumed by the arms race toward revitalizing the Soviet economy. After nearly a decade of stalled arms control negotiations and increased military expenditures, the United States and the Soviet Union reached several agreements. In 1987, they agreed to remove intermediate-range nuclear missiles from the European theater (the INF Treaty). The Strategic Arms Reduction Talks (START) led to a strategic arms control treaty in 1991. The Conventional Armed Forces in Europe talks (CFE) produced a treaty in 1990, which provided for a balance of conventional forces in Europe. The Soviets withdrew conventional forces to meet the CFE targets. Gorbachev's international appeals and successful arms control negotiations led to improvements in East-West relations, which helped renew investor and lender interest in the Eastern bloc.

Gorbachev's international initiatives pale in comparison with the political and economic changes he unleashed domestically. He moved to restructure the entire Soviet economic framework. His economic reforms, labeled perestroika, introduced market mechanisms and pressures into the Soviet economy. These encouraged consumer demand, decentralized decision making and industrial management, and supported private economic initiatives. The political reforms of glasnost accompanied the economic reforms of perestroika. Perestroika encouraged consumer choice and individual initiative in the economic arena. Glasnost promoted choice and participation in the political sphere.

Glasnost and perestroika generated unexpected results. Soviet economic and political reforms spilled over into Eastern Europe. Eastern European proponents of reform took strength from the Soviet initiatives and pressed hard for changes in their domestic arenas. The unleashed pressures for reform in Eastern Europe outpaced the demands for reform in the Soviet Union. The policies and leadership of the Eastern European communist parties came under severe pressure from their polities, which undermined their legitimacy. Unlike Hungary in 1956 or Czechoslovakia in 1968, the Soviets refrained from intervening to halt the sweeping changes unleashed in Eastern Europe.

In 1989, the populations of many Eastern European states rejected communist rule. The rest of the region soon followed. Privatization and democratization led to a stunning transformation, arguably the most dramatic of the European political-economic landscape in the twentieth century. By late 1990, the two Germanies had reunited, the Warsaw Pact had disappeared, and Comecon had been disbanded. Popular pressures and uprisings led to the demise—sometimes violent—of communist leaders throughout Eastern Europe and the transfer of political leadership to new hands.

Although stunning, the political transformations within the Soviet satellites pale in comparison with events in the Soviet Union. Glasnost and perestroika raised expectations that remained unfulfilled. Aggregate economic conditions barely improved. For many Soviets, they deteriorated or fell far below expectations. Agriculture and oil production declined. GNP fell. Economic stagnation and the resulting shortage of basic goods plagued the Soviet leadership. Pressures for greater political decentralization and fragmentation grew as nationalist and ethnic movements appeared in the Soviet republics. The Baltic republics pushed for autonomy and secession. Conflicts between Christians and Muslims arose in the Caucasus. Legislatures in other Soviet republics voiced preferences for greater autonomy if not political independence. The years 1990–91 proved to be a watershed in the Soviet Union, leading to its disintegration in the fall of 1991. Republic after republic announced its secession and independence. The transformed and newly independent states had potentially huge appetites for foreign resources, capital and investment, and technology. Borrowers from these states now approached overseas lenders under new political institutional arrangements.

Shifts in Borrowing: Empirical Evidence

An initial inspection of aggregate global borrowing by these economies appears to conform to expectations. As a category, global borrowing by these economies increased following the warming of political-military relations as described in the previous section. Figure 11 (chap. 3) shows that aggregate Eastern bloc borrowing in the global markets expanded following détente in the late 1960s and early 1970s. Borrowing activity increased until the resumption of East-West tensions at the end of the Carter administration and during the early Reagan years. Eastern bloc borrowing declined following the invasion of Afghanistan, and the renewed devotion of resources to the arms race resulted in increased East-West tension. The ascension of Gorbachev, increased Chinese integration into the global economy, and an easing of East-West tensions fueled the revival of Eastern bloc borrowing by the mid-1980s. Aggregate borrowing temporarily declined again amid the revolutionary changes of the late 1980s, but it appears to be on the rise again.

Figure 12 (chap. 3) suggests that some Eastern bloc borrowers changed strategies over the period of changing East-West economic relations. With few exceptions, Eastern bloc borrowing consisted almost entirely of intermediated commercial loans during the initial phase of greater East-West economic interaction. In the mid-1980s, some Eastern bloc borrowers began to shift strategies and access capital in the global disintermediated markets. These instruments generally offer greater flexibility and better terms than those in the intermediated markets. By the early 1990s, disintermediated financing began to rival intermediated approaches as a means of accessing global capital.

Aggregate numbers suggest increasing access to global capital, yet examining the individual nations of the Eastern bloc introduces questions. Table 3 shows the global borrowing of all debt instruments (bonds and loans) by nationality of borrower from 1972 to 1995. The results are not nearly as positive as the higher level of aggregation suggests. Almost all the command economies experienced some success in accessing global capital markets during the first stages of the East-West thaw, but only a handful of the former command economies have expanded their borrowing during the ongoing transition to market-based economies and the increasing democratization of their political arenas. Of all the Eastern European nations that initiated market and political reforms, only Hungary, the Czech Republic, and the Slovak Republic significantly expanded their global borrowing following the rejection of communist rule. The most successful borrower, China, avoided the political liberalization that marked the Eastern European transitions. China, Hungary, the Czech Republic, and the Slovak Republic drive the aggregate borrowing by the former command economies after 1989, as most of the former command economies borrowed less than they had before the reforms. Poland and perhaps several of the former Soviet republics appear to be gradually gaining access to the global markets, but the data limit speculation.

Comparing types of borrowing across the former command economies after 1989 uncovers even more dramatic differences and reinforces skepticism. Tables 4 and 5 separate borrowing by intermediated instruments (loans) and disintermediated instruments (bonds), respectively. Whereas the distribution of borrowing falls along a broader spectrum for loans, only a few nations access capital in the global bond markets. China, Hungary, the Czech Republic, and the Slovak Republic appear to be the only borrowers in the disintermediated markets despite the ambiguous presence of several other states that first appear in 1994–95 (Poland, Latvia, Croatia, and the Russian Federation).

Ironically, access to global capital seems to have diminished for many of the Eastern European nations and former Soviet republics since the tremendous transformations of the late 1980s and early 1990s. This does not reflect a reduction in the demand for global capital from these countries but a reluctance among international investors to lend their capital to borrowers in these nations. This reluctance is grounded in investor uncertainty concerning the investment environment and frustrations arising from recent interactions, as is revealed in a notice placed in the *Economist* by the Association Francaise des Porteurs d'Emprunts Russes (fig. 13). This may only constitute a temporary lull as international investors await the resolution of much of the uncertainty produced by such dramatic changes. Or it may represent a more persistent investor wariness. Regardless, at the very time that Western popular opinion enthusiastically welcomed the transformation of the socialist political economies, international investors acted cautiously toward borrowers in those states. If money talks, then the enthusiasm is more restrained and cautious than it first appears. This can be problematic for political economies in the midst of dramatic changes. International capital offers a tremendous resource in that transformation, as it can help fund economic expansion, cushion dislocations, and provide an important stimulus to struggling political economies.

Implications

The evolving interest and involvement in global capital dealings by citizens and governments of the former socialist economies constitutes a significant shift in the global political economy. Since the early 1970s, the global activities of bor-

TABLE 3. Borrowing: Loans and Bonds (1994 $ mil.)

Pre-Breakup	Post-Breakup	1972	1973	1974	1975	1976	1977	1978	1979	1980	1981	1982	1983
Bulgaria		40	115	160	125	240	245	239	182.2	0	0	0	0
China		0	0	0	0	0	0	0	3570	373.7	452.5	360	128.4
Comecon Bank		140	0	100	60	0	0	0	0	0	0	0	0
Cuba		49.8	30.1	119.7	237	140.5	10	16.8	126.3	0	59.4	0	0
CSFR	CSFR		0	0	60	200	150	230	450	475	30	0	50
	Czech Republic												
	Slovak Republic												
East Germany		35	15	12	280.3	260	692	782	600	397.1	516.1	68.9	386.4
Hungary		100	90	150	290.5	175	524.6	515	950	600	591.4	482.5	567.3
North Korea		0	65.4	65.4	0	0	0	0	0	0	0	0	0
Poland		20	370	508.7	475	545.9	99.9	435.1	931.8	735.8	0	0	0
Romania		0	0	0	105.7	0	125	725.3	420	458	337	0	0
Soviet Union	Soviet Union	0	0	0	750	282	0	400	320	50	25	152.6	67.5
	Russian Federation												
	Georgia												
	Kyrgyz												
	Latvia												
	Lithuania												
	Upper Volta												
Vietnam		0	0	0	38.1	0	74.1	60.9	0	0	0	0	0.8
Yugoslavia	Yugoslavia	270	303.1	612.9	91.5	155	465.7	871	1657.1	1869.3	1037.3	559	600
	Slovenia												
	Croatia												

Pre-Breakup	Post-Breakup	1984	1985	1986	1987	1988	1989	1990	1991	1992	1993	1994	1995
Bulgaria		0	475	45	260.2	193.9	580	0	0	0	0	0	0
China		307.9	1244.7	3335.9	4678.3	3846.4	1760.5	1513.6	2595.1	4043.2	6755.9	8157.2	6166.2
Comecon Bank		0	150	150	0	0	75	0	0	0	0	0	0
Cuba		0	0	0	0	0	0	0	0	0	0	0	0
CSFR	CSFR	0	100	100	242.2	329.5	334	437.5	278.3	39.5			
	Czech Republic									0	902.6	637.9	740
	Slovak Republic									0	240	330.6	427.3
East Germany		935.7	1172.8	81.3	209.2	0	0	0	0				
Hungary		1166.2	1642.1	1315.4	1950.6	1016.2	1708.1	986.9	1378.4	1446.1	5070.6	2541	3771.2
North Korea		0	0	0	0	0	0	0	0	0	0	0	0
Poland		180	0	0	30	0	163.1	0	4.7	8.7	0	2.8	298.5
Romania		0	150	0	0	0	0	0	0	0	0	0	158.2
Soviet Union	Soviet Union	866.8	1508.2	1821	1003.4	2679.3	1857.7	3250.1	0				
	Russian Federation									0	8	75	884.7
	Georgia									0	20	0	0
	Kyrgyz									0	0	0	140
	Latvia									0	0	0	40.8
	Lithuania									0	0	0	60
	Upper Volta									0	0	0	0
Vietnam		0	0	0	0	0	0	0	0	20	0	0	94
Yugoslavia	Yugoslavia	0	13.6	0	20	0	0	0	0	0			
	Slovenia									0	100	75	226.1
	Croatia									0	0	0	26

TABLE 4. Borrowing: Loans (1994 $ mil.)

Pre-Breakup	Post-Breakup	1972	1973	1974	1975	1976	1977	1978	1979	1980	1981	1982	1983
Bulgaria		40	115	160	125	240	245	239	182.2	0	0	0	0
China		0	0	0	0	0	0	0	3570	373.7	452.5	315.5	107.9
Comecon Bank		140	0	100	60	0	0	0	0	0	0	0	0
Cuba		49.8	30.1	119.7	237	140.5	10	16.8	126.3	0	59.4	0	0
CSFR	CSFR	0	0	0	60	200	150	230	450	475	0	0	50
	Czech Republic												
	Slovak Republic												
East Germany		35	15	12	280.3	260	692	782	600	397.1	516.1	68.9	386.4
Hungary		50	90	150	250	150	350	515	950	550	571.4	341	495.6
North Korea		0	65.4	65.4	0	0	0	0	0	0	0	0	0
Poland		20	370	508.7	475	498.9	19	405.1	859.1	735.8	0	0	0
Romania		0	0	0	5.7	0	125	725.3	420	458	337	0	0
Soviet Union	Soviet Union	0	0	0	750	282	0	400	320	50	25	152.6	67.5
	Russian Federation												
	Georgia												
	Kyrgyz												
	Latvia												
	Lithuania												
	Upper Volta												0.8
Vietnam		0	0	0	38.1	0	74.1	60.9	0	0	0	0	0
Yugoslavia	Yugoslavia	270	273.1	561.4	72.6	83.5	371.4	744.3	1560.8	1832.1	1037.3	549	600
	Slovenia												
	Croatia												

Pre-Breakup	Post-Breakup	1984	1985	1986	1987	1988	1989	1990	1991	1992	1993	1994	1995
Bulgaria		0	475	45	260.2	112.1	250	0	0	0	0	0	0
China		226.2	271.9	1854.1	3,263.0	2,734.8	1,610.1	1,513.6	2,332.1	2,736.9	3,604.2	4,046.1	4,226.1
Comecon Bank		0	150	150	0	0	75	0	0	0	0	0	0
Cuba		0	0	0	0	0	0	0	0				
CSFR	CSFR	0	100	100	242.2	150	260	0	0	24			
	Czech Republic									0	200	237.9	740
	Slovak Republic									0	0	81.1	363.3
East Germany		935.7	1172.8	81.3	209.2	0	0	0	0				
Hungary		830.7	945	814.9	1,356.0	200	765.5	40	140.5	211.3	262.1	820	451.3
North Korea		0	0	0	0	0	0	0	0	0	0	0	0
Poland		180	0	0	30	0	163.1	0	4.7	8.7	0	2.8	48.5
Romania		0	150	0	0	0	0	0	0	0	0	0	158.2
Soviet Union	Soviet Union	866.8	1508.2	1298.4	755.4	2,164.6	891	2,952.5	0				
	Russian Federation									0	8	0	884.7
	Georgia									0	20	0	0
	Kyrgyz									0	0	0	140
	Latvia									0	0	0	0
	Lithuania									0	0	0	0
	Upper Volta									0	0	0	0
Vietnam		0	0	0	0	0	0	0	0	20	0	0	94
Yugoslavia	Yugoslavia	0	13.6	0	20	0	0	0	0	0	0	0	0
	Slovenia										100	75	226.1
	Croatia										0	0	0

TABLE 5. Borrowing: Bonds (1994 $ mil.)

Pre-Breakup	Post-Breakup	1972	1973	1974	1975	1976	1977	1978	1979	1980	1981	1982	1983
Bulgaria		0	0	0	0	0	0	0	0	0	0	0	0
China		0	0	0	0	0	0	0	0	0	0	44.5	20.5
Comecon Bank		0	0	0	0	0	0	0	0	0	0	0	0
Cuba		0	0	0	0	0	0	0	0	0	0	0	0
CSFR	CSFR		0	0	0	0	0	0	0	0	30	0	0
	Czech Republic												
	Slovak Republic												
East Germany		0	0	0	0	0	0	0	0	0	0	0	0
Hungary		50	0	0	40.5	25	174.6	0	0	50	20	0	0
North Korea		0	0	0	0	0	0	0	0	0	0	0	0
Poland		0	0	0	0	47	80.9	30	72.7	0	0	0	0
Romania		0	0	0	100	0	0	0	0	0	0	0	0
Soviet Union	Soviet Union	0	0	0	0	0	0	0	0	0	0	0	0
	Russian Federation												
	Georgia												
	Kyrgyz												
	Latvia												
	Lithuania												
	Upper Volta												
Vietnam		0										0	0
Yugoslavia	Yugoslavia	30	51.5	18.9	71.5	94.3	126.7	96.3	37.2	0	0	0	0
	Croatia												
	Slovenia												

Pre-Breakup	Post-Breakup	1984	1985	1986	1987	1988	1989	1990	1991	1992	1993	1994	1995
Bulgaria		0	0	0	0	81.8	330	0	0	0	0	0	0
China		81.7	972.8	1362.1	1415.1	911.6	150.4	0	263	1,274	2,956.9	3,802.5	1,790.1
Comecon Bank													0
Cuba		0	0	0	0	0	0	0	0	0	0	0	0
CSFR	CSFR	0	0	0	0	129.5	74	437.5	278.3	15.5			
	Czech Republic									0	702.6	400	0
	Slovak Republic									0	240	249.5	64
East Germany		0	0	0	0	0	0	0	0				
Hungary		40.5	447.1	290.5	554.6	816.2	942.6	946.9	1237.9	1,234.8	4,808.5	1721	3,319.9
North Korea		0	0	0	0	0	0	0	0	0	0	0	0
Poland		0	0	0	0	0	0	0	0	0	0	0	250
Romania		0	0	0	0	0	0	0	0	0	0	0	0
Soviet Union	Soviet Union	0	0	0	0	333.2	891.5	297.6	0				
	Russian Federation												
	Georgia									0	0	75	0
	Kyrgyz									0	0	0	0
	Latvia									0	0	0	0
	Lithuania									0	0	0	40.8
	Upper Volta									0	0	0	60
Vietnam		0	0	0	0	0	0	0	0	0	0	0	0
Yugoslavia		0	0	0	0	0	0	0	0				
Yugoslavia	Yugoslavia									0	0	0	0
	Croatia									0	0	0	26
	Slovenia									0	0	0	0

RUSSIA
NOTE TO INVESTORS

Russia is about to issue bonds on the international market.

We wish to draw investors' attention to the fact that subscribing to such bonds entails ver considerable risks.

Russia has already issued bonds in France which are still quoted on the official list of the Par Bourse. However, contrary to all the rules of international law and of their issue contract, Russi has unilaterally stopped paying interest on and redeeming the bonds, thereby ruining hundreds thousands of subscribers who had put their trust in Russia.

Russia committed itself to redeeming the bonds when it signed the Franco-Russian treaty on February, 1992 in Rambouillet and when it sought membership of the Council of Europ However, so far it has not done so, which raises questions about its ability to fulfill its obligations.

We have therefore contacted the international rating agencies about the ratings recently attribute to Russia which do not take into account this major risk of default. Clearly, if Russia does n redeem the securities previously issued in France before the new bond issue, the rating agencie will be obliged to revise their ratings downwards.

International investors would therefore be well advised to ensure that Russia has met it obligations toward previous creditors before subscribing to the new bonds it is issuing, on pain running an unconsidered risk.

Association Française des Porteurs d'Emprunts Russes (AFPER)
9-11, avenue Franklin-Roosevelt, 75008 Paris.
Tél.: 0145-62-15-95. Fax: 0143-59-16-78

**Fig. 13. Advertisement signaling investors about potential risk in Russia.
(Recreated from the *Economist*, November 2, 1996, 100.)**

rowers from these nations have steadily increased. These nations competed ca-
pably in the political-military sphere with the Western bloc nations for more
than forty years. But they have lagged behind the West in addressing domestic
consumer demands despite having developed an educated and skilled work
force oriented toward producing formidable military capabilities. With the
demise of communist control and the liberalization of their political and economic arenas in the late 1980s and early 1990s, these nations face a challenge to
convert the heavy defense industry sector and address growing consumer demands. Global capital offers an important resource for the transformation of
economic activity and the constraint of divisive political pressures.

The demand for global capital and investment to help finance the transformation of these political economies is potentially staggering. Many in the de-

veloping states fear that Eastern bloc and Chinese borrowers could crowd out their own capital demands. This is not an unwarranted concern, but the evidence is mixed and open to interpretation. More than $7 billion of foreign direct investment flowed into China from 1979 to 1987. It became the largest recipient of UNDP funds within four years of approaching the UNDP for assistance in 1978. It obtained more than $5.5 billion dollars in World Bank assistance by the middle of the decade after gaining membership to the World Bank in 1980 (Keylor 1996, 441–43). These were funds that could have gone to other developing nations. This did not go unnoticed. During this same period foreign lending to borrowers in developing nations virtually ceased due to the Third World debt crisis.

In absolute terms, the growth in Eastern bloc and Chinese borrowing already seems stunning. Yet the expansion in Eastern bloc and Chinese borrowing parrots the growing expansion of global borrowing in general. This complicates the interpretation of increasing Eastern bloc demand for global capital. Does the increase in borrowing reflect a trend across all borrowers and lenders in global markets or do borrowers from the former command economies obtain capital at a faster rate of increase than other categories of borrowers in recent years? Given that the global capital pool grew significantly after the 1960s, did borrowing by the socialist economies, and later the former socialist economies, outpace other types of borrowers?

Figure 14 shows the year-to-year percentage change in borrowing in the global markets by category of borrower using real (1994) dollars. The results present less than a clear picture. Overall, total borrowing and borrowing by OECD borrowers expanded in all but a handful of years. A tight relationship exists between yearly changes in OECD borrowing behavior and the yearly changes in overall global borrowing. The expansion of global borrowing is only marginally related to the borrowing of either Eastern bloc or developing nations. This is consistent with the claim in chapter 3 that the actions of OECD borrowers and lenders generate the trends in global financial markets. The activities of Eastern bloc and developing borrowers prove to be difficult to describe as the year-to-year changes demonstrate far more volatility. This is partly a function of the smaller total amount of borrowing by these borrowers in the global markets. A sizable nominal change in borrowing produces a large percentage change for these categories, whereas for the OECD category a similar nominal change would produce only a small percentage change.

The volatile year-to-year swings suggest that developing and Eastern bloc borrowers may be competing for the same pool of capital—a higher risk and more adventurous capital that is more likely to move in and out of investments.

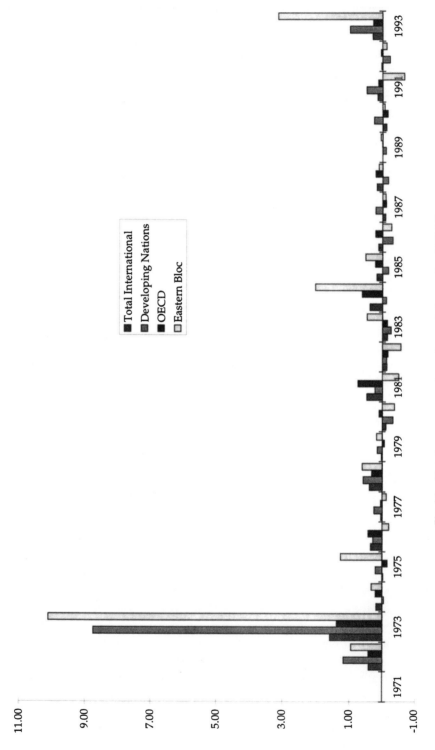

Fig. 14. Year-to-year percentage change in borrowing (1994 $)

In chapter 5, I compare shifts in access across categories of states. The results will furnish a more useful set of metrics and tools for examining the question of crowding out and differences in access across categories.

Conclusion

The empirical evidence provides mixed signals that sometimes support expectations and sometimes not. The command, and later former command, economies became increasingly integrated into global capital markets following key political changes in those nations and the international political-military arena. But their level of integration falls short of expectations. This is especially true in the climate of raised expectations that followed the momentous shift toward market liberalization and political reform at the end of the 1980s. This becomes especially evident when global borrowing by nationality of borrower is examined.

The rapid and dramatic changes in China, Eastern Europe, and the former Soviet Union may promote attractive environments for international investors. But borrowing, and changes in borrowing, vary greatly by nation. The monumental political changes in the Eastern bloc, which fundamentally transformed global political and economic relations, were unforeseen by most observers and analysts. Such dramatic changes may unsettle international investors in the near term. International investors may wait to see whether the transformations become ensconced, robust, and stable. Many aspects of the national political arenas shifted with the economic and political reforms beginning in the late 1980s. Reform varied by nation across the regulatory, judicial, and participatory states. Reforms along the political democratization dimension appear only loosely connected, if at all, with success in obtaining global capital. China, Hungary, the Czech Republic, and Slovak Republic succeeded in gaining the greatest access. These nations vary dramatically in their democratization but less so in their adoption of stable regulatory measures that affect the interests of international investors.

Liberalization and the consistency of the regulatory state appear to have greater impact upon global capital than democratization does. Governments and private borrowers in those nations recognize the importance of reassuring international investors about the stability of the investment environment. An advertisement by the Hungarian government in the *Financial Times* (fig. 15) reflects an awareness of the importance of at least claiming to have a stable, unified, and transparent legal framework for international investors.

The empirical results provoke several questions. Despite evidence of in-

REPUBLIC OF HUNGARY
PRIVATISATION MINISTER

To Investors
Worldwide

May 10, 1995.

Dear Sir,

I am pleased to inform you that the Hungarian Parliament yesterday passed the Privatisation Act, a comprehensive legislation which specifies the principles, priorities, techniques and competition rules of privatisation in a unified legal framework.

The Act reflects the clear intention of the Hungarian Government to successfully complete the privatisation of state owned assets.

The Act will come into force in a few weeks. At the same time a new single privatisation company, ÁPV Rt. will start operations, and will replace the two former organizations that have so far dealt with privatisation. More transparent tendering rules shall also become effective offering equal opportunity and a speedier conclusion of transactions.

I take this opportunity to thank you for your interest in Hungarian privatisation. May I assure you that on the basis of the commitment, the new operational and organizational structure offered by the Act we shall do our best to come to mutually beneficial transactions regarding your interests.

Yours sincerely

Tamás Suchman

P.S. For further information regarding the Privatisation Act and other related developments, kindly contact Privatisation Information Services:

H-1133 Budapest	POB: 1399 Budapest, Pf. 708
Pozsonyi út 56	Tel: (36 1) 269 8990
Hungary	Fax: (36 1) 269 8991

Fig. 15. Advertisement by the Hungarian government (Recreated from the *Financial Times*, May 11, 1995.)

creased integration and participation, what accounts for the ambiguous results, which suggest that borrowing by those economies fails to conform to popular expectations? Why does global capital fail to flood these nations as expected, especially during the initial euphoria of market and political reform? What explains the tremendous variations across these nations, particularly following the market and political reforms of the late 1980s and early 1990s? The results raise questions about the linkages between market liberalization and democratization, at least during the early stages of reform, and suggest that other aspects of political reform may be at least as important as democratization.

CHAPTER 5

Sinking or Swimming in a Global Capital Pool

We were the trend.

—George Winston in Tom Clancy, *Debt of Honor*

Globalization and liberalization constitute the broadest and most significant transformation of state-capital market relations within and across states since the reforms imposed in response to the economic and financial crises of the Great Depression. The importance of financial globalization and liberalization cannot be overstated. Economists and financial experts marvel at the efficiency gains produced by the development of deep and liquid global capital pools. These markets complement national capital markets and enlarge the set of options for borrowers and lenders by spanning national boundaries. Nevertheless, efficiency is only one criterion for evaluating the changes that fall under the categories of liberalization and globalization. Liberalization and globalization do expand financing opportunities and help all categories of borrowers in absolute costs and access, but the transformation systematically favors some borrowers over others. This has implications for the distribution of wealth, opportunities, and influence in the international political economy as well as within domestic political economies. Systematic variations in access separate haves from have nots. It highlights, creates, and exacerbates potential divisions in societies. In this chapter, I focus upon who accesses the global capital pool and explore systematic variations in such access.

I limit my domain to the global intermediated loan and disintermediated bond markets, as they comprise the vast majority of tractable international borrowing. I divide borrowers by origin into four categories: (1) OECD nations, (2) developing nations, (3) nations that formerly had command economies, and (4) international development organizations (IOs). I do not distinguish private from public borrowers, as the mix of public and private ownership varies across economies and has become a moving target with increasing privatization of public enterprises in many nations. I check for variations in access over time and following unusual events such as financial crises.

Systematic differences in access are a positivist description but one endowed with normative implications for economic growth and the distribution of wealth in the international arena. Capital is a key factor of production, a foundational element in economic growth and development. The recent fascination with globalization probably overstates the role of global capital in economic activity and obscures the centrality of domestic savings and markets to economic enterprise. Domestic savings, investment, and financial markets continue to provide the primary sources of investment capital for borrowers (Feldstein and Bacchetta 1991; Feldstein and Horioka 1980; Frankel 1992). Global capital may offer additional resources to enterprises, but it cannot supplant the central role of domestic savings and investment to the success and well-being of any national economy.

Yet, even without being the primary source of capital for national borrowers, global capital significantly impacts political and economic activity. Systematic differences in access to global capital translate into productive advantages or disadvantages in the global economy. Any investment capital introduced into an economy will have a multiplier effect in terms of economic activity. Globalization and liberalization expand the choices of savers over their surplus capital, enlarge financing options for producers, affect jobs, and influence the competitiveness of national industries and economies. The new international economic order (NIEO) agenda of the 1970s highlighted the importance of capital by targeting the redistribution of capital from northern to southern nations. Systematic differences in capital access have the potential to exacerbate what Krasner labeled structural conflict (1985) regardless of the underlying causes of such differences.

Access to global capital also expands the options and strategies available to politicians. They can sidestep the fiscal discipline of state tax structures by borrowing to fund programmatic goals. Global capital provides politicians with tools to expand programs while pushing fiscal responsibilities into the future. The Mexican peso crisis in 1994 and the Southeast Asian financial crises of 1997–98 show the flip side of this coin, as the flight of global capital imposes harsh constraints on government and domestic societies. At least in the short run, access to global capital may permit politicians to have their cake and eat it too, as they can fund politically desirable programs, help their friends, and co-opt their opponents without imposing politically costly taxes. Expanding the borrowing reach of governments beyond national boundaries allows governments that are evaluated as good risks to constrain the costs of borrowing without necessarily raising the costs of private capital domestically.

Systematic Differences By Category of Borrowers

Changes in various nations' political arrangements and regulatory frameworks shifted the incentives of market participants and opened the door to an expansion of international capital mobility and heterogeneity of financial instruments. Lower national barriers increases the pool of capital available to borrowers and expands the set of choices for investors. Investors and borrowers find greater opportunities within and across national boundaries. Liberalization and globalization may help all categories of borrowers in absolute costs and access, but the transformation systematically favors some borrowers over others.

International borrowing grew across all categories following the rejuvenation of global finance in the 1960s, but borrowers from developed states—private and public—found better overall access to the international markets than did other categories of borrowers. Eyeballing the international bond tables from the *Financial Times* hints at such systematic differences in access (see chap. 1, fig. 2). These tables provide trading information for bonds for which an active secondary market exists. Very few bonds of borrowers from developing nations appear in these tables. Figure 16 confirms this pattern. It shows that borrowers from OECD nations enjoyed the fruits of financial globalization more than those in the other categories of borrowers did. International lending to public and private borrowers from the OECD nations exploded. Aggregate international borrowing of developing states, Eastern European states, and international organizations increased slowly by comparison during the same period. The absolute differences suggest that borrowing by those from developed economies drove the expansion of international borrowing, while borrowing by those from developing nations remained a small portion of the global pie. A more pessimistic interpretation suggests a bifurcation of the global economy wherein globalization describes a select group of nations, borrowers, and investors. Even more perverse, the advent of globalization may enhance the abilities of investors from developing nations to move their capital offshore, potentially disengaging domestic savings from investment in those states.

Variations in national economic size and growth rates may help account for differences in international borrowing across categories. But developing economies, those with the smallest increases in international borrowing, experienced higher average growth rates than the OECD economies did (see

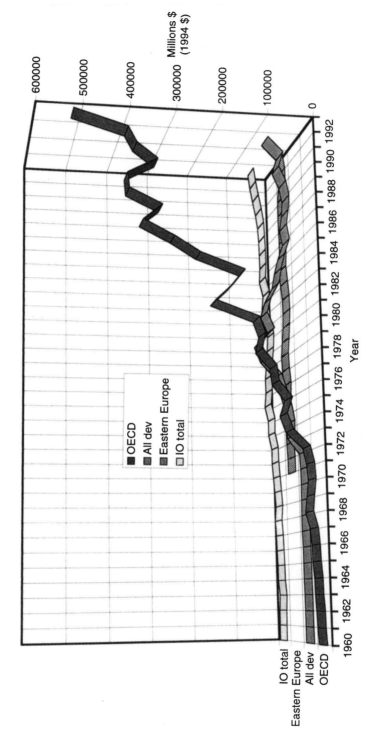

Fig. 16. International borrowing by category of borrower

table 6). International borrowing by those from OECD states expanded faster than that by developing borrowers despite higher average growth rates among developing nations. Of course, the variance in growth rates is greater among developing states, which partly incorporates and reflects the divergent degree of success that developing borrowers experience in accessing global capital. An optimistic and naive interpretation is that a little goes a long way among developing borrowers (i.e., developing borrowers are more efficient in their use of capital).

Disaggregating by financial instrument gives a more detailed picture of the differences in access. Figure 17 shows especially striking disparities across instruments by borrowers. OECD borrowers accessed international markets more than other categories of borrowers did, *and* they took greater advantage of the growing heterogeneity of markets. Looking only at the intermediated markets, one could falsely conclude that the gap separating developed from developing borrowers is shrinking. This narrowing gap in intermediated markets results from developed borrowers shifting to disintermediated strategies not from the success of developing borrowers in accessing global capital markets.

As double-digit inflation swept the industrialized economies in the late 1970s, governments tightened money supplies. They raised the interest rates they charged banks, bought currencies on the open market, and elevated reserve

TABLE 6.   Growth Rates of Industrial and Developing Nations 1972–94 (percentages)

Year	Industrial Nations	Developing Nations
1994	3.0	6.3
1993	1.2	6.1
1992	1.5	5.9
1991	0.8	4.9
1990	2.4	3.9
1989	3.3	3.9
1988	4.4	5.2
1987	3.2	5.7
1986	2.7	4.0
1985	3.4	3.9
1984	4.9	4.1
1983	2.7	2.2
1982	−0.3	−2.1
1972–81	3.0	5.0

Source: International Monetary Fund, *World Economic Outlook,* various years.

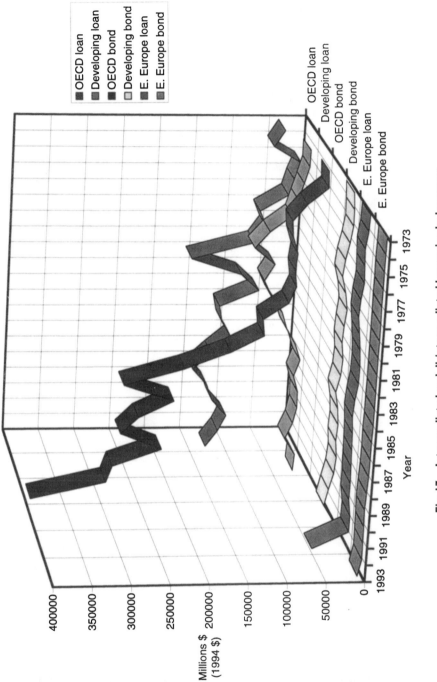

Fig. 17. Intermediated and disintermediated borrowing by borrower

requirements to constrain monetary expansion and inflation. Chapter 3 showed that commercial interest rates, the cost of capital in the commercial loan markets, increased and became more volatile over time. Commercial loan markets became less competitive in comparison with disintermediated instruments. Figure 17 suggests that borrowers from OECD nations responded to such government-driven shifts in economic incentives. They accessed the disintermediated markets with greater and greater frequency over time. Borrowers from developing nations lagged far behind in accessing these more flexible strategies. They continued to borrow predominantly in the intermediated markets instead of switching strategies. Overall, differences in access between developed and developing borrowers in disintermediated markets are greater and growing compared with the intermediated markets.

Further disaggregation by type of financial instrument reveals that discrepancies in access between borrowers from OECD nations and those from developing nations increase as one moves from less to more flexible instruments within the disintermediated markets. Figure 18 compares foreign and international bond issues. Developed borrowers enjoy greater access to the more flexible and less regulated instruments (i.e., those under less national regulatory oversight). As a category, borrowers from developed states access a larger overall international capital pool and choose among a wider range of less expensive, more flexible, and more liquid instruments. Even developing borrowers who do access disintermediated capital will likely find differential barriers by type of financial instrument in those markets. OECD borrowers and lenders generate the trend toward disintermediation and globalization. As globalization is endogenous to the advanced industrialized economies, so is the nature of that globalization.[1] Differences across categories of borrowers must result from differential access, as no rational borrower would consciously choose more expensive and less flexible instruments unless it was denied access to cheaper and more flexible instruments.

Turning to another category, borrowers from the Soviet and Chinese spheres of influence began approaching global capital markets for long-term financing in the 1970s. Détente, political shifts, decaying Communist Party control, democratization of political enterprise, and privatization of economic enterprise affected the attitudes of policymakers toward international capital within these political economies. The shifts also influenced the perceptions of international investors regarding investment in those countries. Many internal and external barriers to the global markets disappeared, or were significantly reduced, for borrowers from these economies. The actual integration of these economies into the global political economy remains limited so far, but the shift

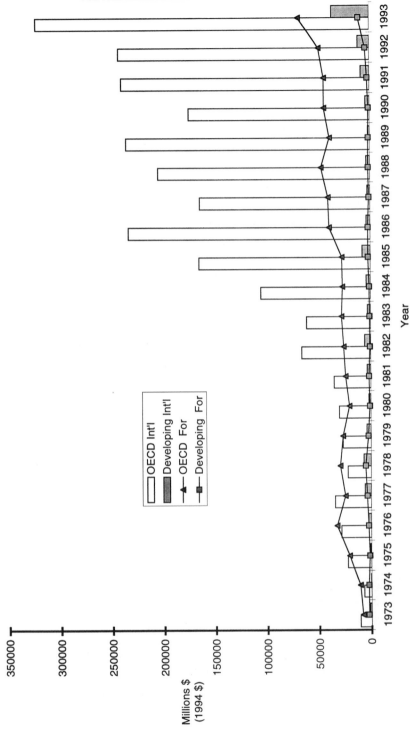

Fig. 18. International and foreign bond issues by borrower

in perspective toward the global political economy by those within these political economies and the potential impact of these nations upon the global political economy are quite dramatic and worthy of attention.

Figure 11 in chapter 3 shows the growth in international borrowing from the Eastern bloc political economies. The relative changes in global borrowing by these nations are impressive despite their small absolute size compared with borrowing from the OECD nations. Latent capital demands apparently existed in those economies for years prior to détente. Barriers, predominantly political, restrained such demand. Shifts in political arenas unleashed that demand. Eastern bloc borrowers also took advantage of the expanding heterogeneity of financial strategies. These borrowers increasingly accessed global capital through disintermediated bond issues. Borrowers from the former command economies appear willing and able to take advantage of the greater flexibility and lower costs of the disintermediated markets.

East and West German political unification supplies a quasi-laboratory setting in which to consider the latent demand for global capital from former Eastern bloc economies and the importance of changes in the domestic political context. East Germany's plight after the revocation of communist rule differs from that of other Eastern bloc states. Eastern bloc states and newly independent states carved out of the former Soviet Union face the task of restructuring state-society relations. Social, economic, and political uncertainty characterizes these transitions. East Germany experienced the political component of such uncertainty for only a short time. With unification in 1990, East Germans shed East German governance mechanisms and came under the umbrella of West German political arrangements. German unification amounted to nothing less than a stunning change in political-institutional arrangements for East Germans. Such large changes in political-institutional arrangements create an opportunity to speculate about the East's latent capital needs by comparing pre- and postunification borrowing. East German capital needs now approach global capital markets under the umbrella of established West German legal and political arrangements and not under the evolving rules and guarantees of a transforming government.

Figure 19 shows a notable increase in aggregate German borrowing following unification. After 1990, aggregate German borrowing expanded well beyond that of previous years and grew dramatically faster than borrowing by other Eastern bloc states. Much of this is attributable to the costs of unification such as converting East German to West German deutsche marks and the large social welfare transfers from West to East Germany that were initiated to cushion the transition. Nevertheless, the weakness in the East German currency and

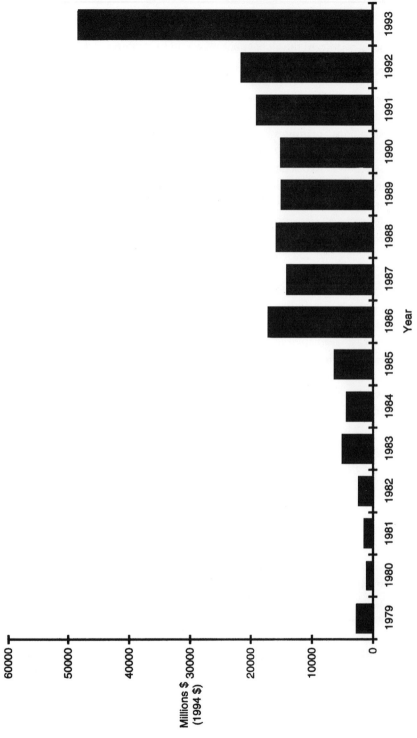

Fig. 19. German borrowing (East and West)

other costs of unification represent a shortfall in capital due to East German needs. Germany was transformed from a net capital exporter to a net capital importer literally overnight as the government accessed global markets to help finance unification and reform of the former East German economy. The political shifts and resulting unification revealed East Germany's latent capital needs, which went unrequited under the previous governing arrangements.

The potential for the former Eastern bloc economies to crowd out other developing borrowers remains ambiguous. Borrowers from the former command economies may compete for the same capital as developing borrowers, but the pool is relatively small and neither group has increased its relative market share of the global pool. In fact, both lost relative market share as the global capital pool expanded. This does not preclude borrowing by the former command economies from taking off and crowding out opportunities in the developing world. The results from the German example suggest that enormous capital appetites may exist within the former Comecon states but remain concealed. East German capital needs were revealed and permitted a shortcut by means of unification. Political unification under West German institutions constitutes a major policy intervention that other Eastern bloc states did not share. If the German case is instructive, then the success of other former command economies in accessing international capital depends upon their building domestic political arrangements that are attractive to international investors.

International organizations such as the World Bank, the IMF, and regional development banks also operate in global capital markets. Many IOs act as financial intermediaries that channel funds to projects in developing nations.[2] These organizations acquire capital for their activities by two paths: membership contributions and borrowing in capital markets. They increasingly access the global capital pool to fund their operations and projects. They have become large and frequent issuers of financial instruments in the global markets. Figure 20 shows that IO borrowing in the international markets increased significantly after the early 1970s. Disaggregating IO borrowing reveals that IOs prefer disintermediated over intermediated instruments. IO borrowing profiles mimicked those of OECD borrowers. IOs find disintermediated markets more accessible than the developing nations they service.

International development organizations appear to perform financial alchemy. They take projects in developing nations that encounter difficulty in accessing global capital, bundle these projects, and issue financial instruments to fund them. These projects leapfrog barriers to entry to attain global capital they cannot access independently. Moreover, the funding for these projects often comes via the less expensive and more flexible disintermediated markets.

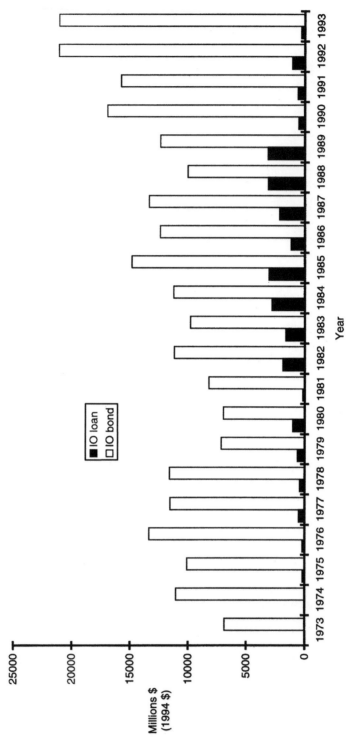

Fig. 20. Borrowing by international development organizations

This is an alternative institutional pathway for enterprises in developing nations to access global capital. By cloaking themselves in the institutional mechanism of an IO, some projects in developing nations obtain capital from global capital markets at a price below that dictated by a market evaluation of their individual cases or obtain capital they would normally find inaccessible. IOs succeed in constraining investors' concerns over the safety of their investments. IO-issued bonds offer interest rates (cost of capital) comparable to those provided by the lowest risk borrowers in OECD nations. This suggests that investors perceive such instruments as being relatively low risk, so issuers do not have to pay more to attract investors. International development banks diversify risk and uncertainty across numerous loans that independently would be viewed as extremely poor prospects by global investors. IOs perform a function for borrowers from developing nations that is similar to what mutual funds do for investors.

Systematic Differences: Crises

What happens during a financial shock? Do the systematic differences in access map into investor behavior following financial distress and crisis? Investor psychology inevitably produces some capital flight following a crisis regardless of a market's long-term stability and economic fundamentals. During a financial crisis, investors seek shelter—safe havens—for their capital. They retreat from markets viewed as risky and uncertain. Invariably this retrenchment originates in the markets that generated the crisis, but sometimes it spreads beyond them. Examining the extent and duration of flight suggests that the systematic variation across developed and developing borrowers becomes even more pronounced under conditions of financial duress. Financial crises damage developing borrowers' access to capital more severely than they damage developed borrowers.

Capital flight varies systematically by category of borrower and instrument following financial crises. Controlling for the source of a crisis, investors flee in greater proportion and for longer periods from developing than from developed borrowers. I use the Third World debt crisis of 1981–83 and the October 1987 market crash as benchmarks. These two crises provide variation across key dimensions: type of borrower and type of market. Threats of default by developing borrowers precipitated the Third World debt crisis in intermediated instruments. The October 1987 market crash began in the industrialized nations' disintermediated markets, which are patronized predominantly by participants from the developed economies. Intermediated markets are generally less volatile than disintermediated markets. Ex ante, this leads to expectations of greater capital flight and dislocation in disintermediated markets during times of financial duress, all else being equal. The opposite occurred, which means all else was not equal.

Figure 16 shows a decline in global borrowing by those from developing nations following the Third World debt crisis. Lenders fled the intermediated markets for developing borrowers and stayed away for a substantial period. Global lending to developing borrowers fell below the precrisis level for almost a decade and recovered only in the 1990s. Some implausible interpretations are that the capital needs of enterprises in the developing economies suddenly declined following the Third World debt crisis or an efficient accumulation of local savings supplanted international borrowing. More plausibly, international investors and financial institutions became reluctant to loan capital to many developing borrowers.[3] Investors continued their international activities, as evidenced in the expansion of global capital markets during this period, but they changed strategies and targets. Lending continued, and increased, to borrowers from OECD states following the Third World debt crisis. The data show that investors embraced global markets, but reallocated their international portfolios to discriminate in favor of the more certain and less risky markets. They adjusted strategies to incorporate their changed expectations about risk and return due to the new information presented by the debt crisis.

Ironically, flight from developing borrowers in the disintermediated markets proved less severe than the reduction in lending to developing borrowers in the intermediated markets. Disintermediated lending declined, regained some volume, fell, and bounced back again in the early 1990s. More flight from intermediated than from disintermediated global markets within the same category of borrower seems odd despite the fact that the intermediated markets were the source of the crisis. Disintermediated markets are generally viewed as riskier and less certain than intermediated markets. Financial institutions limit investors' risks in intermediated markets, but investors incur the full risk of their investments in disintermediated markets. Financial distress increases perceptions of risk and uncertainty for investors in all markets but especially in disintermediated markets where investors incur the full risk of investment and information is more decentralized. If the Third World debt crisis furnished information about developing nations in general, the first impulse is to expect at least as great, and probably greater, flight from disintermediated than intermediated markets during a crisis that undermines investor confidence.[4]

Selection bias helps account for this outcome. The large majority of developing borrowers access global intermediated markets. Only a small portion of developing borrowers issue instruments in disintermediated global markets. Considering the advantages in costs and flexibility of disintermediated borrowing, this suggests that most developing borrowers confront insurmountable barriers to disintermediated capital. Consequently, as concerns international investors, developing borrowers in the disintermediated markets already differ from those in the intermediated markets along important dimensions. Developing borrowers in the global disintermediated markets surpass a threshold of risk and certainty for international investors—a selection bias. Developing borrowers perceived as greater risks and less certain are limited to the global intermediated markets if they can access global markets at all. If the Third World debt crisis prompted international investors to pull back from lending their capital to less certain and more risky ventures in the developing nations, the bulk of such endeavors were already consigned to the intermediated markets.

The October 1987 market crash originated in the NYSE—one of the largest, most liquid, and most advanced disintermediated financial markets of the advanced industrialized nations. The six days of trading surrounding October 19, the center of the crisis, saw a decline in the Dow Jones Industrial Average of 769 points. The Dow fell 508 points, a 23 percent decline, on October 19 alone. It lost approximately a third of its total value or almost $1 trillion. This rivaled the entire U.S. government budget for that year.

Despite the crisis's origins in New York, other major equities markets followed New York's lead and experienced similarly stunning declines as investors fled the major developed disintermediated markets. Prices collapsed on the London (LSE) and Tokyo Stock Exchanges as investors sold into rapidly declining markets (Sobel 1994, U.S. General Accounting Office 1988, U.S. Presidential Task Force 1988, U.S. Securities and Exchange Commission 1988). The Nikkei Dow fell 14.9 percent, the Financial Times Stock Exchange Index in London declined 12.26 percent, Sydney dropped 25 percent, and Hong Kong registered a phenomenal 42 percent downturn. Trading volumes reached record levels as investors panicked and fled. Three times the daily average volume was traded in New York on October 19. The sheer volume of trading swamped computer trading systems and paralyzed information and clearing systems in New York. The TSE stood apart as trading volumes fell far below average, even as price movements on the TSE mimicked those of the other major markets.

The 1987 market crash generated far more intense financial distress in less time than the Third World debt crisis did. Paper losses in the advanced industrialized disintermediated markets exceeded the total value of lending to developing borrowers in the global markets. Despite the extraordinary intensity and speed of the 1987 crash, its effects upon investors appear to have been remarkably ephemeral and less durable than those of the Third World debt crisis. The disintermediated markets in New York, Tokyo, and London proved robust. They recovered far more quickly than the intermediated markets for developing borrowers following the Third World debt crisis. Prices on the TSE reached precrash price levels in less than six months. The NYSE and LSE price indices took about two years to regain their precrash levels (Sobel 1994). Price levels on the NYSE stood fourfold above the 1987 levels within a decade after the crash. A similar trend appears in public stock offerings. New capital issues declined initially and then regained their precrash levels within several years,[5] whereas borrowing levels by those from developing economies took nearly a decade to recover. Trading volumes returned to their precrash levels even faster. The extraordinary trading volumes on the NYSE that characterized the 1987 crash became commonplace within the decade as interest in the disintermediated markets expanded.

The data displayed in figure 16 show that international investors behaved as expected following the 1987 crash. Investors temporarily withdrew from global disintermediated markets, as they did in national disintermediated markets. Capital did not shift to developing markets in the aftermath of the 1987 crash. They shifted to the advanced global and national intermediated markets. Capital flight during periods of duress appears to go in one direction regardless of the source of the crisis. Unlike global intermediated borrowing by those from developing nations following the Third World debt crisis, OECD global disintermediated borrowing recovered quickly following the 1987 crash. Borrowers in developing nations faced greater flight, tighter capital access, and greater obstacles to regaining lost access following financial distress. Investors waited longer to return to the developing markets following the crisis. Developed borrowers found alternatives to disintermediated borrowing as they followed investors to global and national intermediated markets following the crash. Developing borrowers lacked the good fortune of having another, lower-risk, global market to which to turn following the Third World debt crisis.

Distribution and Justice: Equity versus Effort

Markets are one type of preference aggregation and resource allocation mechanism. They aggregate individual choices through a price mechanism to determine how resources will be allocated and distributed. Proponents of markets emphasize that they produce an efficient use of a society's resources, which benefits the community as a whole. This is a claim about the community outcome but not about the condition of any individual in those markets. This is a socially desirable outcome but only one of many. This miracle of markets depends upon underpinning assumptions concerning complete information, frictionless exchange, and competition in the marketplace. Full information, frictionless exchange, and pure competition limit the opportunities for strategic behavior and market manipulation. Relaxing the assumptions that underpin smoothly functioning neoclassical liberal markets creates a potential for strategic behavior and market manipulation. But even if these assumptions hold, markets do not necessarily produce "fair" disaggregated outcomes based upon many measures of distributive justice. This sits at the core of the classic ongoing debate over equity versus efficiency (Okun 1975).

Incomplete information, transaction costs, strategic behavior, and market manipulation subvert the beauty of the price mechanism. Markets will no longer produce the most efficient use of societal sources as per society's wants except as a special case. The societal outcome may be more efficient than many outcomes, but it is no longer likely to be the most efficient outcome possible. The distance from the most efficient outcome constitutes the degree of market failure. Recognizing the inability of imperfect markets to produce the socially efficient outcome, and the resulting inevitability of a suboptimal use of societal resources, begs the question of fairness to individual actors within the community.

How fair or just are the distributional outcomes produced by global capital markets? This question provokes more questions than it asks. Debates over justice and fairness fail to produce convergence on a single set of criteria for evaluating different social outcomes or a definition of what is fair or equitable. Despite the lack of closure and continuing disagreements over notions of justice, posing different notions of justice against each other proves interesting and useful. Comparing the distribution of a resource to the distribution of population constitutes one popular test of just and fair division. Comparing the amount of borrowing in global markets by a category of borrowers as a percentage of total global borrowing to that of the category's percentage of world population provides an egalitarian-based global capital distribution index.[6] In this definition of a just world, a borrower, group of borrowers, or category of borrowers consumes only its fair share of global capital as defined by its share of the global population.

Conceptually, this notion of equity originates from the same principles that underpin one-person, one-vote rules. These are equality rules, but other conceptualizations of justice exist. A utilitarian approach would advance social efficiency as the standard for evaluating whether an outcome is just. A Rawlsian standard would ask whether an individual behind the "veil of ignorance" and not knowing where he or she stands in society—whether the poorest, the richest, or somewhere in between—would find the outcome fair. This is really a maxi-min standard that assesses fairness by the effect upon the worst off in society. Another conceptualization of justice could be based upon "just desserts." This posits that distribution is based upon effort. These are fundamentally different views of justice, and they have different implications for the design of institutions and policies.

Table 7 displays the results for the egalitarian global capital distribution index measured at three different times: 1979, 1985, and 1993. I compare OECD, developing, and Eastern bloc global borrowing. If the ratio produces a global capital distribution index greater than one, those borrowers consume more global capital than their proportionate share of world population. If a category consumes more global capital than its proportionate share of world population, then others must be consuming less since global capital is a finite resource.

The egalitarian global capital distribution index demonstrates that OECD nations consumed a disproportionate share of global capital at all three times measured. By the definition of equity underpinning this index, the Western industrialized nations obtained an "unfair or inequitable" share of the global capital pool. Previous examination revealed this bias, but the degree of unequal distribution appears more pronounced with this measure. The comparison over three periods shows that as the global capital pool expanded from the 1970s to the 1990s the differential in access grew disproportionately. The expansion of global capital markets helped all categories of borrowers in absolute amounts of borrowing, yet it helped OECD borrowers at a disproportionately greater and increasing rate. The precipitous decline in the index from 1979 to 1985 for developing borrowing captures the impact of the Third World debt crisis on capital availability for developing borrowers. The global capital pool expanded dramatically during this period, but a far smaller portion of that pool found its way to developing borrowers in the aftermath of the crisis. Conducting a similar analysis by type of financial instrument—intermediated versus disintermediated—would reinforce the bias.

TABLE 7.   Egalitarian Global Capital Distribution Index

Category	1979	1985	1993
OECD	2.64	4.77	5.19
Command	.35	.23	.14
Developing	.56	.13	.14

A conceptualization based upon "dessert" offers an alternative notion of justice. Here, access to capital should be determined by contribution to economic activity. This notion corresponds to effort. An effort-based global capital distribution index compares the amount of borrowing in global markets by a category of borrowers as a percentage of total global borrowing to that of the category's percentage of global economy. Table 8 displays the effort-based ratios for the same times as the egalitarian measure. This index uses World Bank GDP data at current market prices in dollars. The effort-based index shows the distribution of capital may be fairer than in the picture painted by the equity index, yet the index demonstrates that developed economies still obtain more than their fair share of capital by this notion of fairness. As with the equity-based measure, the fairest distribution occurred in 1979. The later periods, regardless of index, reflect an expanding bias in favor of borrowers from developed nations. Western industrialized nations obtain an "unfair" share of the global capital pool regardless of the notion of justice. Disproportionate access is robust.

The results of the indices also raise questions about whether borrowers from the former command economies of the Eastern bloc threaten to crowd out developing borrowers. Both groups of borrowers consume a smaller portion of global capital than their portion of the world's population, and their proportion of the global capital pool is shrinking. The Eastern bloc economies did relatively better—they obtained a "fairer" share of the global capital pool—before the demise of the communist leadership and the disintegration of the Soviet Union. Absolute borrowing by Eastern bloc borrowers increased, but their per capita share of the global capital pool decreased enough to mirror that of the developing nations. The relative decline in access by these borrowers is even more pronounced when it is compared to their contribution to global GDP—the effort-based index. These categories of borrowers may compete for the same capital in the global pool, but the ratios suggest that neither increased its share of global capital at the expense of the other. Both categories are losing market share to borrowers from the OECD nations. Borrowers from the industrialized nations garner the lion's share of global capital and in increasing propor-

TABLE 8.   Effort Global Capital Distribution Index

Category	1979	1985	1993
OECD	.62	1.09	1.05
Command	.78	.20	.15
Developing	2.02	.56	.69

tions. If crowding out is a concern, then the capital appetites of OECD borrowers should prove more unsettling to borrowers from the former command economies and developing economies than the competition from each other.

Conclusion

Financial globalization and liberalization opened up channels through which borrowers can access an increasingly larger pool of global capital. The results appear to favor all categories of borrowers in absolute capital access but not equally. Borrowers from OECD nations enjoy better access to a variety of global capital mechanisms than other categories of borrowers do. This access improved relatively with the growth of global markets. Borrowing strategies also differ across categories of borrowers. Aside from an overall advantage in capital access, OECD borrowers employ a wider array of strategies. OECD borrowers have shifted toward global disintermediated markets and away from global intermediated markets since the late 1970s. IOs followed the pattern of OECD borrowers as they shifted toward global disintermediated instruments. Borrowers from the former command economies also appear able to gain access to the global disintermediated markets—although it is too soon to draw definitive conclusions.

    Global borrowing from the developing nations differs markedly. Overall opportunities may have increased for many developing borrowers with the decline of many formal national political barriers to global access, but these borrowers still face greater handicaps than other categories of borrowers. To a significant extent, the revitalization of global finance bypasses potential borrowers from developing nations. Despite a great need for investment capital, their global borrowing increased at much slower rates and even declined marginally for a time following the Third World debt crisis. Developing borrowers continued to rely predominantly upon global intermediated markets when other types of borrowers shifted to more flexible and less expensive disintermediated strategies. Global disintermediated borrowing by developing borrowers remained flat through the 1980s even though the global trend shifted substantially toward securitization and disintermediation. Disparities in access between developed and developing borrowers are greater in these markets than in others, and they continue to grow as developed borrowers generate the global trend toward disintermediation. Even those from developing nations able to access global disintermediated markets find differential barriers by type of financial instrument in those markets.

The greater variety of strategies available to developed borrowers exacerbates the differences in capital access between developed and developing borrowers. Assuming that rational borrowers generally prefer greater flexibility and lower costs, systematic differences in access and borrowing strategies constitute more than differences in the needs, preferences, and tastes of the borrower. They reflect supply constraints upon borrowers' options. International investors appear less willing to transfer their surplus to developing borrowers overall, particularly in the more flexible and less expensive disintermediated markets. Developing borrowers enjoy their best success in accessing the more centralized intermediated markets and face the most stringent constraints in the most decentralized markets. In disintermediated markets, lending outcomes emerge from the aggregation of a large number of market decisions by institutional and individual investors. Bankers, financiers, and government officials do not coordinate these outcomes from the "top down," as happens in intermediated markets. Investors build these outcome from the "bottom up."

CHAPTER 6

Risk, Uncertainty, and Borrowing in Global Capital Markets

Global capital access varies by category of borrower and consequently by nationality of borrower. Popular notions of the extent and depth of financial globalization and long-term capital mobility prove misleading when examined closely. Only a select group of borrowers routinely accesses global capital markets despite the demise of formal national barriers to international capital mobility and an increasing openness of national economies to capital flows. In international capital markets, globalization and the free flow of capital systematically favor some borrowers more than others. Access to global capital fails to mirror the global distribution of population or the distribution of economic activity—falling short of equitable or efficient distribution. This bias clearly favors advanced industrialized political economies, but systematic differences also appear within other categories of borrowers.

What explains national variations in access to global capital markets? Proximity to regional markets, domestic market size, local economic appeal, location of physical resources, labor force quality and availability, firms' reputations, and other economic factors contribute to the macro- and microeconomic contexts of prospective borrowers and to their differences in access. But these make up only part of an explanation. They fail to account for the reasons why borrowers from some states prove significantly more or less successful than their geographic neighbors with similar demographic characteristics.

Earlier I emphasized that international borrowers and investors operate in incomplete information environments characterized by an asymmetric distribution of information. Investors assess opportunities in light of their risks and expected rates of return. Some of the risk to investors derives from an inability to fully predict market outcomes regardless of the information environment— a fundamental uncertainty. But information environments exacerbate or ameliorate the dilemmas of evaluating risk by increasing or decreasing information about risk, affecting uncertainty, and encouraging or limiting incorrect assessments of risk. Capital access is a function of lenders' expectations about borrowers and their uncertainty about those expectations.

Evaluating risk under conditions of incomplete information and across national boundaries presents a formidable task, which is further complicated because borrowers know more about their individual cases than investors and can mislead investors about their true nature. Investors attempt to pierce the informational haze surrounding borrowers, but a substantial likelihood exists for suboptimal lending choices.[1] When uncertainty is constrained and borrowing types known, investors will generally prefer to loan their surplus capital to good risks versus bad or at least known versus unknown.[2] Such situations allow investors to more accurately price their risks and limit the opportunity for market failures. Investors face a problem of identifying a borrower's risk type when uncertainty is less constrained. In such situations, investors may loan their capital to good risks but at costs higher than warranted. Or they may loan capital to poor risks at costs lower than warranted. In the worst scenario, markets collapse and good risks fail to obtain capital.

Investors use a variety of tools to limit suboptimal lending and constrain risk in their portfolios.[3] Their primary tools are research and portfolio diversification, which are intricately connected. Investors diversify their portfolios and risks along multiple dimensions—industry sector, geography, time, market, type of financial instrument, and so on. Investors' abilities to assess risk associated with different investment strategies are at the heart of portfolio diversification. They do not simply and randomly throw different types of investments into a portfolio basket. Investors use research to enhance the information environment, improve their ability to evaluate risk, and reduce uncertainty about borrowing types.

Here I focus upon the economic components of lending decisions. I connect assessments of contextual risk and uncertainty about that risk to variations in global capital access. These help to make up the information environment of investors. In testing the connections between contextual risk, uncertainty, and borrowing outcomes, I include population as a proxy indicator for the attractiveness of the domestic market size of borrowers and potential rate of return. This supplies a supplementary economic explanation. Some version of this variable appears in a host of studies examining foreign direct investment (Agarwal 1980; Lizondo 1991). Often, studies employ GNP or GDP as an indicator of potential market size. But investment, growth, and economic size are so highly correlated that using GNP or GDP would be equivalent to including the independent variable on both sides of the equation. Population circumvents this problem. As investors care about expected rates of return in addition to risk and uncertainty, the appeal of accessing potentially large domestic markets may help overcome investors' anxieties about risk and uncertainty. In such cases, potential rate of return outdistances risk and uncertainty about that risk.

The economic components I test here provide a baseline against which to assess the contributions of national political arenas to borrowing outcomes. In the next chapter, I connect variations in borrowing, risk assessment, and the information environment to the political arena. National political conditions influence the information environments of international investors. State policies and institutions help structure these environments. They affect information asymmetries between borrowers and investors, help determine the type and quality of information available to investors, provide information about risks to investments from the state, furnish information about protections against the malfeasance of borrowers, and generally influence investors' expectations about contextual risk to their capital.

I use annual surveys of country credit risk conducted by *Euromoney* and *Institutional Investor*, two financial trade publications, to construct a measure of uncertainty. The measure captures variations in investor uncertainty across different national environs. Next I use the *Institutional Investor* or the *Euromoney* measure of country credit risk, the new measure of uncertainty, and population to account for variations in access to global capital.[4] This provides insight to the impact of national economic contexts upon global capital access, but it is just one component of an investment decision. International investors also consider the individual cases of borrowers—the microlevel characteristics of each borrower—as good and bad risks exist in every nation. I neglect such individual characteristics here. The microcharacteristics of individual borrowers are unspecified, but they remain critical to understanding which borrowers get capital and which do not in any specific nation (intranation variations).

Initially I examine developed and developing nations. Unfortunately for the period examined, *Euromoney* and *Institutional Investor* omitted Eastern bloc nations in their surveys of credit risk due to the lack of information and disclosure.[5] Next I reduce the scope of the study to exclusively examine developing states. This category contains the largest number of observations, maximizes the variance in the data, and offers the greatest lever with which to examine the role of contextual risk, market size, and uncertainty in accounting for variations in global borrowing. Borrowers from developed nations succeed in accessing global capital at relatively higher rates but under conditions of relatively low contextual risk and uncertainty. There is little variation on the variables of interest, which limits our ability to draw inferences.

The initial analyses uncover problems that stem from particularly odd, perverse, and nonparametric distributions of the data. This inhibits inference using standard statistical approaches. As a consequence of the odd structure of the data, standard linear modeling techniques fail to capture the real effects and in this case severely underestimate effects. I begin with a standard linear model to illuminate the problems with the structure of the data and the dilemma of making inferences using a linear model with such structure in the data. I extensively discuss these problems in the body of this chapter and, step by step, work through the strategies used to address these problems and explore the relationships among the variables. I demonstrate the process step by step as these techniques are relatively unusual in political analysis, but very good reasons exist to believe that such data problems are commonplace and typically unaddressed in political science—particularly in the study of international relations and international political economy.

Briefly, the data problems become manageable by breaking the choice of lending into two components consistent with approaches to portfolio risk management, tinkering with the population distributions, and using more appropriate statistical techniques. For investors, managing and constraining risk under conditions of uncertainty involves two stages. First, investors decide whether to lend at all to specific borrowers, and, second, they decide how much to lend. The first decision filters and conditions the second. Deciding how much to loan is conditioned on the prior of making a loan at all. Both of these choices are consistent with investors' calculations and strategies for constraining risk. They allow a natural attack on the question and the data.

Next I use a variety of visualization techniques to learn about the structure of the data, assist in transforming ill-behaved distributions into those that allow probabilistic inference, and evaluate the relationships in the data (Cleveland 1985, 1993).[6] Even by addressing the odd structure in the data and transforming that structure, some portion of the problem persists—albeit dramatically constrained. This inhibits a return to standard linear modeling techniques and compels the use of more robust tools. These are buttressed by visualization strategies that enable inference by means of "interocular traumatic impact" (Berkson 1942).

Constructing a Measure of Uncertainty

International investors can use their own research and analyses to assess risk in different national contexts, but many may reduce their transaction costs and take advantage of specialization in the information marketplace by turning to the cottage industry that has grown up around risk assessment. Investors purchase risk assessment services that specialize in gathering, organizing, and evaluating information. Numerous public and private risk assessments attempt to forecast, analyze, and compare risks across nations. Some assessments evaluate risk broadly, whereas others focus upon particular components such as political risk. Moody's Investors Service, Standard & Poors Ratings Group, the *Economist* Intelligence Unit, Bank of America's World Information Services, Business Environment Risk Intelligence (BERI), *Euromoney*'s annual country risk ratings, *Institutional Investor*'s annual country credit ratings, the International Country Risk Guide, and the Political Risk Services of political scientists William Coplin and Michael O'Leary of Syracuse University are examples of such services. The *Financial Times* markets a standardized compilation of many of the different assessments.

The multiplicity and differences across risk assessments serve as prima facie evidence of the difficulty in assessing risk across national contexts and the uncertainty that plagues such assessments. Competing assessments can only disagree and prosper under conditions of incomplete information. Imagine a situation with relatively complete information. Public contexts are transparent. Investors know fully the macroeconomic context and the position of the state concerning property rights, enforcement of contracts, overseas investors, and its likelihood of manipulating the economy to the detriment of overseas investors' interests. They enjoy full access to information about individual borrowers. Borrowers do not have the advantage or disadvantage of private asymmetric information. This information environment constrains public and private actors from acting strategically, as markets will discipline easily observable transgressions. Products of competing services should converge with only trivial differences.[7] Figure 21 depicts this graphically. Markets will penalize risk assessments that fail to converge, as they clearly offer an inferior product. Among those surviving, price dominates the investor's choice of which risk assessment to purchase, as they are equal on all other important dimensions.

Figure 21 exists in theory, but the empirical world falls short. Providers of risk analyses agree on some cases and disagree on others. Figure 22 compares *Euromoney* and *Institutional Investor* country credit ratings for 1991. It reveals sizable consensus across the two ratings but also more than trivial divergence. These specialists in risk assessment disagree yet remain in business. The market for such services treats both as legitimate and viable, which can only be possible under conditions of incomplete information. This reflects the uncertainty that confronts investors in their attempts to assess the risk of their investments in different national contexts.

I use *Euromoney*'s annual country risk ratings and *Institutional Investor*'s

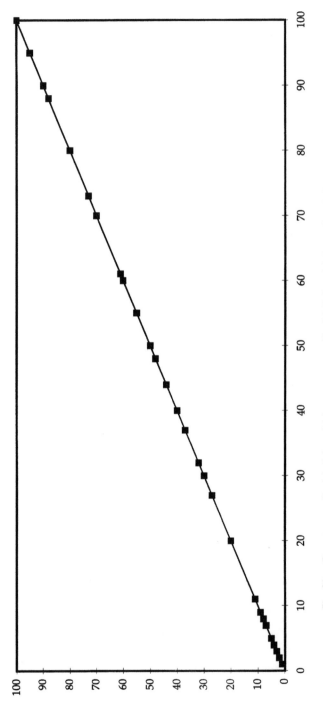

Fig. 21. Country credit risk A (x-axis) by country credit risk B (y-axis) (complete information assumed)

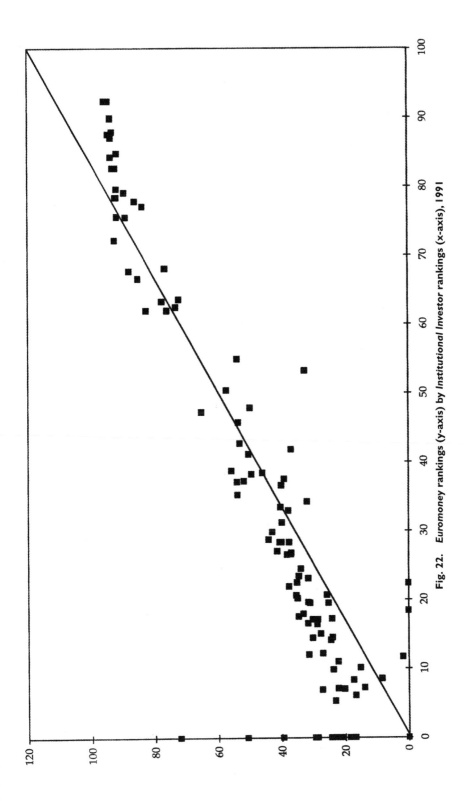

Fig. 22. *Euromoney* rankings (y-axis) by *Institutional Investor* rankings (x-axis), 1991

annual country credit ratings to construct a proxy indicator of investor uncertainty about national arenas. Essentially, I compare across ratings and attribute differences to uncertainty that stems from the incomplete information environment. Why select these two ratings to compare? *Euromoney* and *Institutional Investor* ratings share qualities that make them particularly useful for constructing a measure of uncertainty. First, they address the same audience. As trade publications, they target professionals in the financial services industry. They represent how members of the financial services industry think and act. These publications utilize the skills, knowledge, and perceptions of industry practitioners in corporate finance, institutional investing, commercial banking, and investment banking to construct their country risk ratings. Such practitioners bet real resources on their analyses and evaluations (i.e., they put their money where their mouths are and practice what they preach). Relying upon practitioners limits the introduction of a bias grounded in what social scientists think financial services professionals should do or how social scientists think financial services actors act when considering country risk.

Second, *Euromoney* and *Institutional Investor* conduct their surveys annually and within a relatively close time proximity. The September or October issues contain the results. A narrow time span contains threats to comparison across the measures, which could arise from differences in general and local histories. International or national events could shift a nation's risk assessment. A measure that rates a country prior to a dislocating event could look quite different from a measure constructed after the event.[8] The greater the time separating measures the more likely real events will intervene and create legitimate differences across the ratings—differences that come from real changes in information and circumstance, not from uncertainty. The *Euromoney* and *Institutional Investor* surveys limit this threat by means of their temporal proximity.

Third, *Euromoney* and *Institutional Investor* offer comparable metrics. Their surveys use different methodologies to evaluate nations and produce a weighted score on a zero to 100 scale. I consider these weighted scales as interval-level data, but they also result in an ordinal-level ranking of nations. The interval and ordinal scaling offers a choice of metrics to compare. I use the interval scales to compare the magnitude of disagreement among the surveys, as the ordinal scale may obscure the size of disagreements across the surveys. The interval measures could disagree dramatically across surveys, but if their orderings are similar then the ordinal scales will fail to capture these disagreements.

Fourth, *Euromoney* and *Institutional Investor* conducted their surveys for numerous years. I built a series that spans the years 1982–91. This furnishes an opportunity to examine the impact of risk and uncertainty upon global borrowing nationally, cross-sectionally, and across time. It permits analyses using levels of risk and changes in levels of risk, and it generates future possibilities for examining the relative attractiveness of a national environment to international investors for any particular year, the stability of a nation's rating over time, and changes in risk and uncertainty over time.

Finally, even though *Euromoney* and *Institutional Investor* offer comparable metrics, cross-sectional and cross-time comparisons, temporal proximity, and the perspective of financial service professionals, they employ different methodologies in their construction, which introduces competing methodologies into the mix. This would be irrelevant under conditions of complete information, but in an incomplete information environment competing approaches to risk assessment supply levers to assess uncertainty. *Institutional Investor* asks international bankers to rank countries on a zero to 100 scale, with 100 being those least likely to default. Bankers do not rank their home countries. *Institutional Investor* weights the individual responses to give more importance to bankers with greater international exposure and more sophisticated in-house expertise for evaluating country risk.

Euromoney employs more "objective" data to generate its country risk ratings. Instead of depending solely upon international bankers to assess country risk, *Euromoney* relies predominantly upon analytical indicators, credit indicators, and market indicators to build its assessment. Eighty percent of the *Euromoney* evaluation comes from quantitative measures of access to short-term finance, access to international bond and syndicated loan markets, access to bank finance, credit ratings, debt, debt to default, and so on. But the *Euromoney* evaluation also contains a subjective component. Twenty percent of its evaluation derives from a poll of political risk analysts, risk insurance brokers, and bank credit officers, who rate each nation's risk of nonpayment on a zero to 10 scale.

I partition the data into developing and developed countries and pool observations from 1982 to 1991. I separate developed and developing nations for several reasons. First, the bifurcated results in chapter 5 show that borrowers from developed countries borrow dramatically more global capital than borrowers from developing nations. Any account of such huge differences in access is overdetermined (i.e., such huge differences in access across categories make viable any explanation of differential access that distinguishes between categories). Keeping developed and developing borrowers in the same pool ensures that whichever category one focuses upon the other category will act as an outlier and distort the statistical analysis. Looking at variations within categories provides a more subtle test of the effects of country credit risk, potential market size, and uncertainty upon lending and how such considerations might be weighted differently from developed to developing nations.

Second, the Third World debt crisis occurred during this period. Consistent with Gresham's Law, financial crises can generate capital flight from one market to another. 1982–91 covers a period of rapid expansion in aggregate borrowing in global capital markets but shows a decline or steady state in borrowing by those from developing nations as international investors backed away from their exposure in developing nations. Pooling developed and developing countries obscures this behavior and hides the trends in each category. Conducting analyses for each category allows an examination of the role of country credit risk and uncertainty while controlling for the differential effects of the Third World debt crisis and other category-specific characteristics.

Having separated developed from developing nations and pooling across time, I regress the *Euromoney* country credit ratings upon the *Institutional Investor* country credit ratings to assess how information contained in one measure predicts the other. This controls for unspecified sources of systematic variation. Under conditions of perfect information, taking one measure of country risk and regressing it upon the other measure of country risk should produce a perfect, or near perfect, fit (i.e., the residuals should be zero or near zero). In an incomplete information environment, viable and persistent differences across ratings should appear in the residuals and provide insight into the level of uncertainty in the information environment. Saving the residuals from the regression, squaring them, and taking their square root provides a measure of uncertainty that controls for systematic variations.[9]

Descriptive Statistics for Country Credit Risk and Uncertainty

For developed and developing countries alike, the *Institutional Investor* ratings predict the *Euromoney* rankings fairly well. Table 9 provides summary statistics by country category. The R^2s show that the *Institutional Investor* ratings account for 56.5 and 77.2 percent of the total variance in the *Euromoney* ratings for developed and developing nations, respectively.[10] The model fits substantially better than using the sample means to fit the data. The *Institutional Investor* country credit rating provides information significantly different from zero to fitting the model. This comes as no surprise, as both scales contain information derived from investment professionals who spend substantial time trying to analyze risk and opportunities across national boundaries. Unless such activities are random, we should expect a fairly high correlation. The fit demonstrates a

TABLE 9.   *Euromoney* Country Credit Ratings Regressed on
Institutional Investor Country Credit Ratings

	Developed Nations	Developing Nations
R^2	.565	.772
RMSE	7.681	9.534
Mean	87.119	40.134
N	213	654

strong consensus among investment professionals in their assessments, which suggests that risk assessment will ultimately dominate the role of uncertainty in investment decisions (i.e., it will produce the greatest effect). But the fit also demonstrates that sizable differences, or uncertainty, exist across the competing assessments.

At first glance, differences in R^2 between developed and developing nations suggest more agreement and less uncertainty across the surveys for developing than for developed nations. This contradicts expectations if true. But differences in sample size drive this result, not greater certainty about developing borrowers. The comparison contains three times the number of observations for developing than for developed nations. Larger pools of observations usually provide more information and enable a better model fit. Truncating the pool and eliminating outliers to reduce the number of observations by only a small number shrink the R^2 and fit quite dramatically for developing nations.

This artifact of pool size becomes acutely apparent when descriptive statistics across categories of borrowers are compared. Descriptive statistics in table 10 for the *Euromoney* country credit rating and the uncertainty measure show that developed nations have lower risk and less uncertainty in their overall lending environments than developing nations do. A wide gulf exists between the mean score for developing nations in the *Euromoney* rankings and the mean score for developed nations (high scores reflect less risk). Differences in standard deviations in the *Euromoney* rankings show that the spread around the mean is substantially larger for developing than for developed nations despite the statistical advantages of a far larger sample. This greater dispersion on the *Euromoney* measure reflects the greater diversity in the pool of observations. The descriptive statistics for the uncertainty measure are consistent with those for the *Euromoney* country credit rating. The mean level of uncertainty and the spread around it are far smaller among developed than developing nations. Greater dispersion on the uncertainty measure for developing nations represents greater uncertainty.

TABLE 10.   Descriptive Statistics: *Euromoney* Credit Ratings and Uncertainty, 1982–91

Category	*Euromoney* Credit Ratings	Uncertainty
Developed nations		
Mean	87.170	4.906
SD	11.580	5.878
SE mean	.790	.403
Upper 95% mean	88.726	5.700
Lower 95% mean	85.613	4.112
N	215	213
Developing nations		
Mean	39.880	7.183
SD	19.989	6.253
SE mean	.772	.245
Upper 95% mean	41.396	7.663
Lower 95% mean	38.363	6.703
N	670	654

Testing the Association between Risk, Uncertainty, and Borrowing

Separating developing and developed nations, I pool observations for the period 1982–91 and test a linear model for each category to evaluate the effects of country risk and uncertainty about that risk upon borrowing in global markets. Ideally, this would provide a baseline model for later comparisons, but the results reveal serious problems within the structure of the data. Several of the variables, particularly the dependent variable of borrowing in global markets, are not well behaved. They are not normally distributed; nor are the residuals for any linear model using this dependent variable. This undermines inference based upon normal distributions of the data and forces adoption of more robust strategies. I display the results from these baseline models to demonstrate the dilemmas inherent in the structure of the data before addressing such problems. The initial linear model follows the form

$$y_i = \alpha + \Sigma(\beta_\kappa X_{ki}) + \varepsilon_i,$$

where for each nation i

y_i = global borrowing and

$\Sigma(\beta_\kappa X_{ki})$ is a matrix of vectors such that

β_κ = {credit risk, uncertainty, year, credit risk*uncertainty}.

The dependent variable is the total of foreign and international intermediated and disintermediated borrowing as reported by the OECD and rescaled in 1994 dollars. This excludes equities and private placements. The initial models use the *Euromoney* country credit risk ratings, but *Institutional Investor* country credit risk ratings can be substituted with little effect on the outcomes. Uncertainty is the measure constructed in the previous sections. I include an interaction term, as uncertainty interacts with risk to affect investor calculations, but this ultimately proves unnecessary. The model already contains this interaction, as I used the measures of country credit risk to generate the measure of uncertainty. Uncertainty and country credit risk are not completely independent. Future specifications omit this interaction term. I include a time variable—year—to control for systematic trends in the global markets independent of individual nations.

What are the expectations if a linear model constitutes the correct approach? As country credit risk ratings run from zero to 100 (with 100 the best), the coefficient for country credit risk should be positive—the better the rating the greater the borrowing. The effect of uncertainty should be negative, but this requires taking uncertainty and the interaction term into account. Greater uncertainty interacts with risk and should reduce access to global capital, but a theory of adverse selection explicitly anticipates that some uncertain risks should get more capital than they would under conditions of perfect information and some will obtain less than they should. Ex ante, there is little reason to believe that a bias exists for one condition or the other. Uncertainty benefits some poor borrowers just as it penalizes some good borrowers.[11] Consequently, the signs of the coefficients on the uncertainty and interaction terms are difficult to predict. They could both be negative or one could be negative and one positive, but both should not be positive. Based upon the underlying metrics, the interaction term probably outweighs uncertainty in most cases. Table 10 shows that the mean score on risk for developing countries exceeds the mean score on uncertainty by approximately six times. This suggests that the interaction term should carry a negative coefficient. Finally, the dependent variable is censored. The lower boundary of borrowing is truncated at zero, since no one borrows negative amounts of capital, yet the upper boundary is unbounded. This alone severely biases the effects, confounds expectations, and complicates predictions.

The trend variable proves to be unusual and underscores the rationale for separating developed and developing nations. Capital markets expanded at a rapid rate from 1982 to 1991. This should lead to expectations of a positive coefficient on trend. But chapter 5 shows that borrowing declined or remained flat for developing nations following the Third World debt crisis. Capital fled such markets and stayed away for most of the period in question. Consequently, I expect a negative coefficient on the trend variable for developing nations and a positive coefficient for developed nations.

Table 11 presents the results of the model. The initial results appear promising. An analysis of variance produces F ratios for the developing and developed nations models of 23.915 and 12.370, respectively. The R^2s, or proportions of the variation around the mean accounted for by the models, are .192 for developed and .129 for developing nations. The models fit the data significantly better than they would by chance alone. The developed nations model fits better despite fewer data points. The better means and smaller standard deviations for developed nations detailed in table 10 of the descriptive statistics suggests why. For a substantive interpretation, developed nations enjoy less risk and uncertainty overall and more stable and predictable contexts. This helps account for a better fit despite fewer observations.

The parameter estimates support expectations. Country credit risk imparts the greatest and most significant influence upon capital access. Trend provides a glimpse of Gresham's Law at work, as the signs on the trend coefficient switch from the developed to the developing nations models. Developing borrowers confronted a declining trend in global capital access even as borrowers from the developed nations experienced expanding access. It is highly significant in the developed nations model but not significant in the developing nations model.

TABLE 11.   OLS Models: Economic Determinants of Lending, Developed and Developing Nations Models (nonstandardized coefficients, standard errors)

Variable	Developed Nations Model	Developing Nations Model
Country credit risk[a]	682.655**	25.087**
	(115.858)	(3.085)
Uncertainty	1,420.146**	32.390**
	(402.092)	(12.864)
Country credit risk*	−21.562**	−.731**
uncertainty	(6.294)	(.277)
Year	1,229.050**	−11.718
	(347.191)	(14.695)
Constant	−2.5e + 6**	2,2676.982
	(690,591)	(29,211.4)
N	213	652
R^2	.192	.129
F ratio	12.370	23.915
Prob $> F$	.000	.000

[a]This analysis uses the *Euromoney* measures for country credit risk.
*significant at .05;   **significant at .01

Uncertainty proves to be statistically significant, and it operates much as expected, but the substantive effect appears to be less than expected and dwarfed by the effect of country credit risk. Considering the coefficients on the interaction and uncertainty terms, the underlying metrics for uncertainty and risk, and the mean scores on uncertainty and risk, the combined substantive effects of uncertainty and the interaction term appear relatively small compared to country credit risk. As noted earlier, the sign of the coefficients on both parameters, including uncertainty, were difficult to predict, but a negative overall effect was expected. In the interaction term, uncertainty combines with country credit risk to reduce access to global capital. The coefficient on the interaction term is negative and highly significant for developing and developed nations, but the coefficient on uncertainty alone is positive and highly significant. In general, the combined effect of uncertainty and the interaction term is negative, particularly for the developed nations.

Recognizing and Addressing the Data Problems

At this stage of the analyses, problems within the structure of the data become increasingly evident. These contaminate the results produced by the linear model and misestimate the real relationships among the variables. Scatterplots of the models (see fig. 23a–b) reveal serious truncation and heteroskedasticity problems. Those borrowing less than predicted cannot get less than zero, but those borrowing more than predicted can technically obtain an infinite amount more. If any borrower from a nation accessed the global capital markets even once during 1982– 91, I included observations for that nation for the entire period even if no capital was borrowed during the other years. The developing nations scatterplot suggests that this presents more than a trivial problem. A large number of observations sit at zero—approximately half of them. At a minimum, this skews the distribution. This problem suppresses the slope of the model, biases its coefficients, and underestimates expected effects. If the data distribution is sufficiently ill behaved and skewed, then statistical inference based upon a normal distribution proves to be severely misguided and fundamentally flawed.

The scatterplots provide evidence of problems within the structure of the data, but as an aside they offer some entertainment despite problems with the linear model specification. Cases falling above the confidence interval in the scatterplots consist of those nations that obtain more capital than predicted by the linear model. Observations below the confidence interval in the scatterplot constitute cases that obtain less credit than predicted. Table 12 lists the cases of

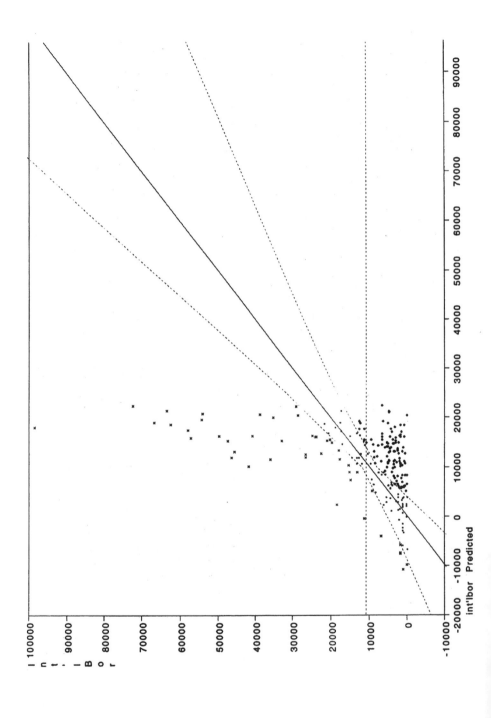

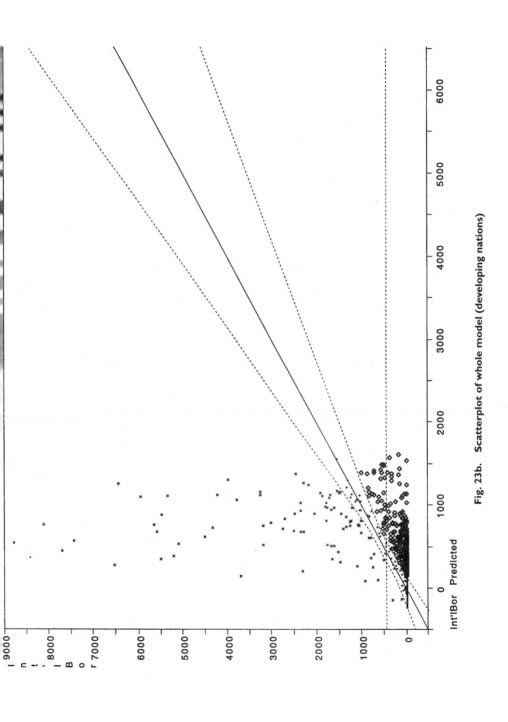

Fig. 23b. Scatterplot of whole model (developing nations)

TABLE 12.　Developing Nations That Borrow Less Than Predicted (by year)

1982	Algeria, India, Gabon, Jordan, Morocco, Pakistan, Dominican Republic, Sri Lanka, Bangladesh, Iraq, Bolivia, Guatemala, Kenya, Nigeria, Panama, Honduras, Mauritius, Turkey, Cyprus, Colombia, Uganda, Kuwait, Syria, Thailand, Singapore, Cameroon, Zambia, Trinidad and Tobago, Israel, Paraguay, Liberia, Ecuador, Zimbabwe, Cote d'Ivoire, Egypt, Uruguay, Tunisia
1983	Morocco, Egypt, Ethiopia, Saudi Arabia, Ecuador, Cameroon, Venezuela, Israel, Thailand, South Africa, Nigeria, Jordan, Trinidad and Tobago, Syria, Dominican Republic, Cyprus, Bangladesh, Panama, Costa Rica, Cote d'Ivoire, Kenya, Turkey, Tunisia, Jamaica, Pakistan, Hong Kong, Zimbabwe, Papua New Guinea, Singapore, Kuwait, Uruguay, Sri Lanka, Paraguay, Taiwan, Bolivia
1984	Jordan, Saudi Arabia, Costa Rica, Angola, Iran, Nigeria, Syria, Cote d'Ivoire, Barbados, Bangladesh, Panama, Pakistan, Zimbabwe, Ethiopia, Gabon, Tunisia, Guatemala, Algeria, Taiwan, Kenya, Congo, Argentina, Morocco, Papua New Guinea, Uruguay, Turkey, Sri Lanka, Ecuador, Singapore, Peru, Cameroon, Egypt, Cyprus, Venezuela, Trinidad and Tobago, Kuwait, Iraq, Colombia, Paraguay, Philippines
1985	Nigeria, Oman, Barbados, Mauritius, Saudi Arabia, Mexico, Kuwait, Kenya, Congo, Taiwan, Hong Kong, Cameroon, Singapore, Indonesia, Gabon, Israel, Tunisia, Papua New Guinea, Syria, Uruguay, Sri Lanka, Venezuela, Jordan, Panama, Trinidad and Tobago, Cyprus, Paraguay, Egypt
1986	Singapore, Nigeria, Syria, Gabon, Mauritius, Trinidad and Tobago, Saudi Arabia, Kenya, Papua New Guinea, Barbados, Morocco, Taiwan, Cameroon, Hong Kong, Colombia, Venezuela, Chile, Tunisia, Cote d'Ivoire, Uruguay, Congo, Zimbabwe, Pakistan, Jordan, Israel, South Africa, Sri Lanka, Cyprus, Paraguay, Iran, Egypt, Tanzania, Argentina, Panama, Oman, Jamaica, Kuwait
1987	Taiwan, Pakistan, Thailand, Barbados, Philippines, Kenya, Malaysia, Brazil, Panama, Cote d'Ivoire, Uruguay, Gabon, Sri Lanka, Egypt, Morocco, Israel, Trinidad and Tobago, Saudi Arabia, South Africa, Mauritius, Chile, Kuwait, Colombia, Oman, Venezuela, Cameroon, Singapore, Hong Kong, Tunisia, Paraguay
1988	Egypt, Swaziland, Cameroon, Argentina, Morocco, Zimbabwe, Taiwan, Israel, Trinidad and Tobago, Gabon, Hong Kong, Cote d'Ivoire, Singapore, Panama, Barbados, Saudi Arabia, Pakistan, Tunisia, Kuwait, Uruguay, Philippines, Kenya, Jordan, Paraguay, Chile, Papua New Guinea, Mauritius, Mexico, Cyprus, South Africa, Sri Lanka, Oman
1989	Dominican Republic, Ecuador, Kenya, Nigeria, Cameroon, Jamaica, Jordan, Morocco, Honduras, Chile, Trinidad and Tobago, Iran, Zimbabwe, Pakistan, Senegal, Bangladesh, Oman, Saudi Arabia, Malawi, Tunisia, Papua New Guinea, Barbados, Cote d'Ivoire, Swaziland, Gabon, Singapore, South Africa, Philippines, Malaysia, Venezuela, Syria, Paraguay, Kuwait, Uruguay, Mauritius, Costa Rica, Guatemala, Cyprus, Israel, Mexico, Sri Lanka, Tanzania

TABLE 12.—*Continued*

1990	Cameroon, Pakistan, Jamaica, Argentina, Jordan, Sri Lanka, Taiwan, Barbados, Brazil, Swaziland, Zimbabwe, Senegal, Bangladesh, Trinadad and Tobago, Iran, Kenya, Paraguay, Papua New Guinea, Morocco, Israel, Nigeria, Gabon, Malawi, South Africa, Colombia, Kuwait, Mauritius, Tanzania, Panama, Singapore, Egypt, Uruguay, Saudi Arabia, Cyprus, Chile, Peru, Costa Rica, Oman, Malaysia
1991	Algeria, Cameroon, Colombia, Iran, Jamaica, Taiwan, Tunisia, Morocco, Pakistan, Barbados, Sri Lanka, Gabon, Mauritius, Philippines, India, Paraguay, Oman, Cyprus, South Africa, Trinadad and Tobago, Uruguay, Swaziland, Costa Rica, Malawi, Senegal, Ecuador, Guatemala, Malaysia, Tanzania, Honduras, Chile, Israel, Kenya, Egypt, Singapore, Zimbabwe

Developing Borrowers That Get More Than Predicted (by year)

1982	Korea, Peru, Philippines, Chile, Argentina, Mexico, Malaysia, Venezuela, Brazil, Indonesia
1983	Mexico, Chile, Korea, Malaysia, Argentina, Indonesia, Algeria
1984	Malaysia, Korea, Mexico, Chile, Indonesia, Brazil
1985	Korea, Malaysia, Philippines, Argentina, Iraq, Colombia, Thailand, Chile, Algeria, Turkey
1986	Indonesia, Korea, Malaysia, Algeria, Thailand, Turkey, India
1987	Mexico, Argentina, Indonesia, India, Korea, Turkey, Ethiopia
1988	Venezuela, Algeria, Indonesia, Colombia, India, Turkey, Korea, Brazil
1989	Colombia, Turkey, India, Hong Kong, Indonesia, Egypt
1990	India, Mexico, Venezuela, Ethiopia, Thailand, Philippines, Turkey, Indonesia, Korea
1991	Argentina, Kuwait, Mexico, Korea, Hong Kong, Saudi Arabia, Turkey, Brazil, Indonesia, Thailand

overestimation and underestimation for the developing nations model. The lists spotlight the problem of adverse selection and suggest why investors became wary of loaning capital to developing nations at the very time when global borrowing expanded at unprecedented rates for developed borrowers. The large Latin American nations that precipitated the Third World debt crisis fall into the overestimation category, usually as distant outliers. At the onset of the crisis, lenders were loaning far more capital to borrowers from these states than was predicted by the model. These outliers regressed toward the mean for several years after the debt crisis struck. On the other side of the mean, borrowers in many African nations had less access than warranted based on the model's predictions.[12]

The scatterplots warn against placing confidence in the results of the linear model. To determine the appropriate modeling strategy requires a more careful

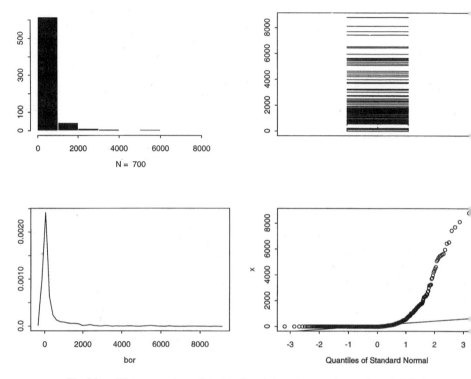

Fig. 24a.   Histogram, box plot, density plot, and normal q-q plot of global borrowing

examination of the structure of the data. From here, I focus exclusively upon the developing nations. Figure 24a-b displays exploratory visualizations of the structure of international borrowing and the residuals from the full economic linear model.[13] These are the key distributions relevant to statistical inference. Classical statistical inference relies upon assumptions that the data are normally, or near normally, distributed and outlier free. The histograms, box plots, density plots, and normal quantile-quantile (q-q) plots in figure 24 reveal whether these assumptions are violated and if so how seriously (MathSoft 1997, 45–46).

The graphs confirm the worst fears about the data's distribution. Starting at the top left corner and moving clockwise, the two sets of graphs show the structure of the dependent variable, international borrowing, and the residuals from the full linear model. The first graph is simply a histogram of the distribution. Already problems with the distribution appear. The second display is a version of Tukey's box plot (Cleveland 1993, 25–27; Tukey 1977). The perverse

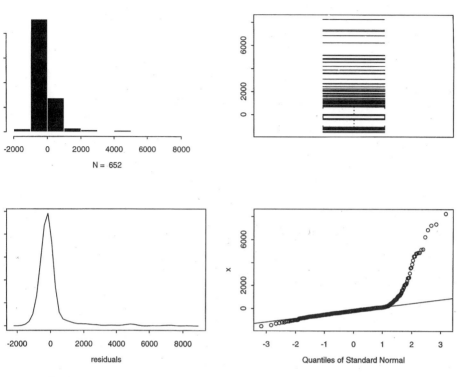

Fig. 24b. Histogram, box plot, density plot, and normal q-q plot of residuals from full economic model

structure of the data complicates reading the box plot. The median of the distribution for international borrowing is near zero according to the box plot—the white bar at the bottom of the plot. Approximately 50 percent of the data fall within the box surrounding the median. The upper and lower ends of the box are the upper and lower quantiles of the distribution. This range gives an indication of the spread of the distribution. In the case of international borrowing, the data are tightly packed around the median. The dashes in the box plot lead to the adjacent values, which supply information about the shape and spread of the distribution by describing the tails of the distribution. The observations falling beyond the adjacent values are depicted individually. These outside values give additional information about the shape and spread of the distribution. Specifically, they describe the very extreme tails of the distribution, or the outliers. There are unusually large numbers of extreme outliers falling beyond the range of the adjacent values.

The third graph is a density plot of the distribution. This provides a view of the data similar to what the histogram shows but smoother. It estimates the probability density curve of the distribution. As with the histograms, the density plots reveal a strong skew to the distribution. In the fourth graph, normal q-q plots compare the quantile distributions of the variables against corresponding quantiles of the standard normal distribution. The line superimposed on the data passes through the upper and lower quantiles of the normal linear distribution and allows comparison of the data with the normal distribution. The distribution of international borrowing and the residuals from the full economic model deviate from linearity. Compared to the normal distribution, the dependent variable is skewed to the right, truncated left, and displays excessive curvature. The histograms, density plots, and normal q-q plots furnish good pictures of the distribution. The box plots and normal q-q plots supply the most information about outlying values. Clearly, by any of the visual explorations in figure 24 a linear model that assumes normally distributed data and residuals is an extremely poor choice of analytical strategy. The results from the linear regressions are fundamentally flawed despite being consistent with expectations.

Initially the data problems appear to be similar to those addressed by Tobin (1958) with the Tobit procedure. In analyzing the consumption of durable goods by households, Tobin noted that households consumed large amounts of durable goods in some years and zero amounts in other years. The dependent variable registered as zero for a significant fraction of the observations. Normal regression approaches fail to compensate for this censoring of the dependent variable—a limited dependent variable. The Tobit procedure corrects for this problem under certain conditions, but it proves problematic for the analysis here for two reasons: one technical and the other theoretical.

Technically, the Tobit procedure is sensitive to heteroskedastic data. The scatterplots in figure 23 and the normal q-q plots in figure 24 show that heteroskedasticity plagues the data. More important though, Tobit is logically and theoretically inconsistent with the substantive explanation being tested. International borrowing is probably different from the truncated measures involved in purchasing a new car, refrigerator, washer, or dryer. In the original manifestation of Tobit, the consumption of durable goods was the decision of the household, not of the retailers of those goods. For international borrowing, most of the zero observations reflect investors' unwillingness to extend capital to borrowers from those nations during those years, not a lack of desire for capital by borrowers from those nations. These are substantively different problems. The former is demand driven, and the latter is constrained by supply.

The technical and theoretical limitations of Tobit warrant an alternative at-

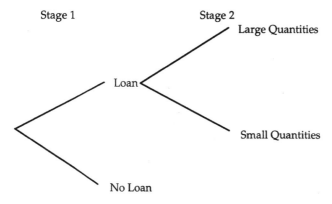

Fig. 25. Two stages of investment decisions and risk management

tack on the problem. I divide investment decisions into two components. Investment decisions involve two distinct and sequential stages (see fig. 25). These coincide with investors' strategies in managing their portfolios as they balance risk, expected rate of return, and uncertainty. First, investors decide whether to lend at all. Second, if investors decide to loan capital, they continue to manage their exposure to risk and uncertainty by calculating how much to lend. These two choices vary across investors according to their particular risk acceptance profiles and current situations. The first stage involves a discrete yes or no choice and the second stage a continuous choice over level of lending. The first stage filters and conditions the second. The second stage contains only those cases in which borrowing is greater than zero. This attacks the truncation problem with an approach consistent with how investors really behave.

I use a logistic model to capture the logic of the first stage—the decision to loan. A discrete variable, loan/no loan, serves as the dependent variable. Given the unusual structure of the data, I compensate and substitute the Huber/White estimator of variance for the traditional estimator in order to obtain robust estimates of variance. This generates robust standard errors. The logistic model takes the form

$$\Pr(\text{Loan}_i = 1) = F[\alpha + \Sigma(\beta_\kappa X_{ki}) + \varepsilon_i] \, ,$$

where for each nation i
$\Pr(\text{Loan}_i = 1)$ is the probability of borrowing and
$\Sigma(\beta_\kappa X_{ki})$ is a matrix of vectors that may include
$\beta_\kappa = \{\text{credit risk, uncertainty, year, population}\} \, .$

The results prove striking. I introduce the economic variables of country credit risk, uncertainty, year, and population into the model step by step. Table 13 details the results from three specifications. Risk, year, and population prove to be extremely significant factors in predicting the likelihood of lending to borrowers from a nation. Uncertainty does not prove significant as an independent effect. This is not unexpected. I used country credit risk to generate the measure of uncertainty. Country credit risk and uncertainty are not independent. Country credit risk already contains much of the information in uncertainty. The addition of uncertainty to the model introduces little new critical information. Apparently, investment professionals build uncertainty into their estimates of risk in a world of incomplete information. All the models strongly reject the null hypothesis that these variables do not matter in decisions to loan. The models account for the variations in the data fairly well and significantly better than the ill-chosen linear regression. The pseudo R^2s range from .331 to .393.

Employing the logistic model to assess the decision to loan or not marks a notable improvement over the problematic linear model. More importantly, the results provide a strategy for censoring the data, which theoretically coheres to the motivations and actions of international investors. The logistic analysis provides a theoretically consistent means of eliminating the zero observations and moving on to assess levels of lending. Once investors decide to lend their capi-

TABLE 13.   First Stage: Logistic Analysis of Economic Determinants to Loan, Developing Nations (odds ratios, robust standard errors estimated with Huber/White)

Variable	Model 1	Model 2	Model 3
Country credit risk[a]	1.116**	1.118**	1.129**
	(.012)	(.013)	(.015)
Uncertainty	1.028	1.011	1.025
	(.019)	(.020)	(.020)
Year	—	.872**	.837**
		(.033)	(.034)
Population	—	—	1.000**
			(3.02e–06)
N	652	652	615
Log likelihood	−302.473	−295.737	−258.617
Pseudo R^2	.331	.346	.393
χ^2	105.79	107.40	110.33
prob > χ^2	.000	.000	.000

[a]These analyses use the Institutional Investor measures for country credit risk.
*significant at .05   **significant at .01

tal to particular ventures, they must decide how much to lend. The first decision filters out many prospective borrowers as part of the investors' portfolios and risk management strategies. The second decision is conditioned on the prior information that a loan will actually be made. This corresponds with managing the degree of exposure of the investor's portfolio to a particular investment. For the second stage of this analysis, I include only those cases of nonzero international borrowing. This eliminates approximately half the cases used in the first stage of the analysis.

Censoring the data by eliminating the zero observations on the dependent variable affects the structure of the data. Ideally, this would jettison the problems in the structure of the data that undermined the use of the linear regression model and limited classical statistical inference. The structure of the data does improve but unfortunately only marginally. The structure of the data still falls far short of approximating a normal distribution. The original problems persist even after severe truncation of the data. This situation improves substantially if the data are transformed by taking the logarithm of nonzero international borrowing. This helps constrain and remove much of the skewness and other problems in the structure of the data but not enough to permit a return to a linear model strategy for the second stage of the analysis.

I ran models with the log of nonzero international borrowing as the dependent variable. I used a χ^2 test to compare the distributions of the log of nonzero international borrowing and the residuals from the models against the normal distribution. The null hypothesis was that the relevant distribution approximated the normal distribution. I was able to accept the null hypothesis for the log of nonzero international borrowing. The log of nonzero international borrowing is approximately normal. But comparing the residuals against the normal distribution forced rejection of the null hypothesis. The residuals for any of the models failed to approximate the normal distribution, but they came close.

Figure 26 presents exploratory visualizations of the three versions of the dependent variable. Moving from left to right and top to bottom are histograms, box plots, density plots, and normal q-q plots for international borrowing, nonzero international borrowing, and the log of nonzero international borrowing, respectively. The histograms, box plots, density plots, and normal q-q plots in figure 26 furnish excellent pictures of the distributions and enable comparisons across the three versions of the dependent variable. This provides important information about the extent of the problems plaguing normal linear models. Using the logarithm of nonzero international borrowing to transform the dependent variable clearly addresses problems in the structure of the data.

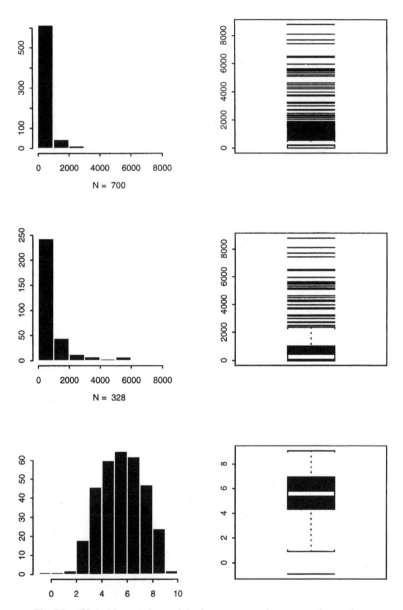

Fig. 26. Global borrowing: original measure and two transformations

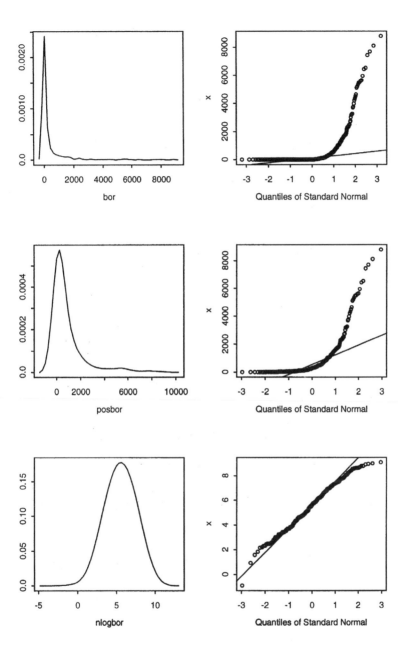

This tempts a return to the linear regression model strategy, but the nonnormally distributed residuals continue to undermine classical statistical inference. This prevents recovering the linear modeling strategy. The data problems force adoption of an alternative strategy for the second stage.

The problems in the data prohibit fitting a model with a well-behaved parametric function. The patterns in the data are too complex. In this case, a simple parametric linear regression underestimates the relationships among the variables despite the relatively successful logarithmic transformation of nonzero international borrowing—the independent variable. Too much information remains underutilized and trapped in the residuals. Loess (or robust, locally weighted regression) offers a nonparametric approach to the data with some valuable statistical properties (Cleveland 1979; Cleveland 1993, 94–101; Fan 1992). The loess model takes the same form as the initial linear regression

$$y_i = \alpha + \Sigma(\beta_\kappa X_{ki}) + \varepsilon_i,$$

where for each nation i

y_i = the log of nonzero global borrowing and
$\Sigma(\beta_\kappa X_{ki})$ is a matrix of vectors such that
β_κ = {credit risk, uncertainty, year, population}.

Loess estimates a separate regression for each observation in the data and then predicts a smoothed value for that observation. Normal linear regression uses all the observations and weights each observation equally, so distant observations can obscure local nonparametric patterns in the data. Loess uses only a limited number of observations near each point to estimate the predicted values. Loess allows specifying this span, or neighborhood. For the analyses here, I specified a span that uses at most 60 percent of the data for estimating each smoothed point. In loess, observations closest to the central point in each regression receive the greatest weighting and those observations further away receive less. As a consequence, loess is extremely local and follows the patterns in the data. Loess also allows a choice between locally linear and locally quadratic fitting. In this case, locally quadratic fitting does substantially better at discerning the patterns in the data. This underscores the nonlinearity and problems within the structure of the data.

Table 14 presents the results of the loess regression analyses for four models that use various combinations of the economic variables. The log of nonzero international borrowing serves as the dependent variable. Coefficients for the independent variables are unavailable due to the local nature and estimation procedures of loess. It is possible to get an idea of the influence of each predictor variable by incrementally adding them to the model. Immediately the results demonstrate the paucity of estimating a normal linear regression with this data. Even the simplest loess model, which uses only one predictor variable, captures more information from the data than the linear regression model with four predictor variables. Adding more of the economic predictors accounts for a substantial amount of the variation in the data. The best fit for the OLS developing nations model accounted for only .129 of the variation around the mean, but the comparable loess model produced a .56 fit—a fourfold improvement! The full loess model results in an R^2 of .61.

Clearly, the loess procedures discover far more information in the data than the parametric linear model. The loess procedures recognize the nonparametric problems in the structure of the data and by using local smoothing techniques can extract that information. The loess results confirm and clarify the important impact of country risk, uncertainty, global trend following the Third World debt crisis, and potential market size upon access to global capital markets. All these variables improve the fit of the model and help account for variations in the data. They demonstrate that cross-country variations in economic context prove critical in understanding variations in access to global capital markets.

Country credit risk and population appear as the most important factors in accounting for the variations in the data. This makes sense. Country credit risk tries to incorporate all threats to investment, which include those arising from uncertainty and the fallout from the Third World debt crisis. The variables

TABLE 14.   Second Stage: Loess Regression Analysis of Economic Determinants of Log of Positive Borrowing, Developing Nations (span = .6; degree of equation = 2, a quadratic polynomial; iterations = 5)

Variable	Economic Model 1	Economic Model 2	Economic Model 3	Economic Model 4
Country credit risk[a]	X	X	X	X
Uncertainty	—	X	—	X
Year	—	X	X	X
Population	—	—	X	X
N	328	322	312	306
Residual SE	1.483	1.451	1.209	1.163
Multiple R^2	.27	.34	.56	.61

Note: An *X* indicates the variable is employed in the model estimation.
[a]These analyses use the Institutional Investor measures for country credit risk.

for trend and uncertainty add some new information to the model, as the incomplete information environment prevents country credit risk from incorporating all contextual threats to investment but country credit risk does contain a substantial portion of the information inherent in these variables. The other key variable, population, attempts to capture the attractiveness of investment environments stemming from the size of the local market. This is the proxy measure that serves as a partial substitute for expected rate of return. Big markets attract investment independent of other factors (i.e., the potential payoffs are worth the risks). Risk and expected rate of return constitute the cornerstones of any investment decision. The results of the models validate the models, as they are consistent with theory and expectations.

Even though the full set of economic variables accounts for .61 of the variation around the mean, much remains unexplained. Under conditions of complete information, country risk assessments should contain all the information about contextual risk to investment. The only risks excluded from such assessments under complete information would be those stemming from the micro-conditions of individual borrowers. Clearly, much contextual information escapes the assessments of country risk that would be useful to investors trying to pierce the information haze surrounding cross-border investment opportunities. This occurs as an artifact of the incomplete information environment. Just as measures of uncertainty and trend provide information that eluded contextual risk assessment, other variables could introduce new and important information. These can correspond to activities in national settings that signal investors about local risks to their investments. Some of these activities fall within the boundaries of national political arenas.

Conclusion

Country credit risk, uncertainty about risk, systemic trends, and potential market size and expected return affect investors' calculations as they evaluate investment opportunities across national borders. Comparing competing measures of country credit risk reveals disagreements in these assessments across nations. Using measures of country credit risk produced by trade publications in international finance, a newly constructed measure for uncertainty, and population as a measure of potential market size, expected rate of return, and demand, I show that these factors systematically affect access to global capital markets and the amount of capital available in those markets for borrowers from specific nations.

National contexts matter. Many different factors contribute to variations in national contexts. Economic, political, social, cultural, geographical, and other factors vary by nation to influence global access. Evaluations of country credit risk already contain information about the influence of these nation-specific threats to investment. Ideally, evaluations of risk would contain all the information affecting the value of an investment. But evaluations of risk capture only some of the relevant information. The information environment is woefully incomplete.

For a political scientist, this begs several questions about the political contributions to risk and lending decisions. First, how embedded is politics in estimations of country credit risk? Does the evaluation of country credit risk capture the full impact of the political arena upon investment choices? Second, if measures of risk incompletely incorporate the impact of the political arena upon investments, does this arena influence investors through other channels? Does the political arena provide investors with information by means of paths and processes ignored, or not fully incorporated, in the assessment of risk?

CHAPTER 7

Political Contributions to Risk, Uncertainty, and Borrowing

I am the law.

—Judge Dredd

Differences in domestic market size, country credit risk, and uncertainty about that risk underpinned a significant portion of global borrowing patterns among developing nations, but a large portion of the variation remained unaccounted for by these factors. Evaluations of the expected rate of return and risk should contain all relevant information about investment contexts under conditions of complete information. All contextual factors affecting an investment's rate of return should be fully incorporated into assessments of risk with the exception of fundamental risk, which entails the difficulty of predicting market outcomes even with complete information. Obviously, investors operate with less than complete information. Incomplete information means imperfect specification of factors contributing to risk and translates into slippage in the assessment of risk.

National political arenas may supply investors with additional information about investment environments that contributes systematically to variations in global borrowing and helps further explain the observed patterns of borrowing. National political arenas impact such economic outcomes by several paths. First, national political arenas contribute some of the same information already embedded in the assessments of risk. They are partly endogenous to contextual evaluations of risk. Assessments of risk attempt to incorporate all threats to investment including those arising from the political arena. Such assessments only partially succeed due to the information environment. Second, national political arenas add new information that helps account for borrowing outcomes independent of assessments of risk. They impart distinct and independent effects. This is only possible and observable under conditions of incomplete information. Otherwise, assessments of contextual risk would fully incorporate such information. Third, the activities of the state can affect global borrowing by different channels. Here I disaggregate the monolithic state to consider two specific components of national political arenas: the participatory and the regulatory state.

Contextual risk includes risk from the political arena, but evaluating political components of contextual risk proves to be more complicated, incomplete, and convoluted than assessing economic components of contextual risk. Economic analysis is more conducive to objective measures, but political analysis is more subjective. Yet considering economic risk without accounting for political risk leaves investment professionals ill equipped to evaluate international opportunities.

> Political risk is 50% of the exercise but inseparable from economic risk.[1]

> Assessing politics is a continuing problem. We are economists, not political analysts. You can't separate the economics from the politics, but the question is, what do the political analysts know that we don't?[2]

An elegant first cut might consider whether differences in state capacity affect who gets capital and how much. Organski and Kugler (1980), Organski et al. (1984), Kugler and Domke (1986), Kugler and Arbetman (1989), Jackman (1993), and Arbetman (1990) employ variations in political capacity to understand differences in social outcomes such as war, birth rates, mortality rates, economic growth, exchange rate fluctuations, and other phenomena. Asserting that capable states better contain the economic risk and uncertainty that threaten investors' interests may prove to be a fair empirical assumption. Yet capacity constitutes a description of the ability to implement policies, not the content of them. A capable state should also be more effective at threatening investors' interests, extracting excessive rents from investors, and implementing policies that depreciate the value of investors' investments.

State capacity may be highly correlated with policies that protect the interests of investors, but ex ante no theoretical argument links capacity to this outcome. Political capacity fails to illuminate or capture the state activities that influence international investors and why. What do states do that encourages or discourages international investment, and affects investors' choices over types of investment strategies? Separating more from less capable states underspecifies the mechanisms that help account for variations in borrowing. Capacity is a necessary but not sufficient condition to attract investment and gain access to global capital markets. Political capacity may offer a baseline, but aggregate assessments of political capacity obscure the fact that states engage in multiple functions, many of which are unrelated to international investment.

National political structures rest on complicated foundations and perform numerous tasks. The state divides into different components by function. There is a regulatory state, participatory state, adjudicatory state, social welfare state, and national security state among others. These differ in their effect upon investments and in the information they provide about risks to investment from national political arenas—within and across states. National political and regulatory structures vary in their protection of investor rights, demand for market transparency, and insulation from political pressures to manipulate the domestic economic arena. A nation's political activities and mechanisms can protect the interests of investors, but they can also damage those interests and perversely affect the value of investments.

I focus upon two specific dimensions of national political arenas and how they concern international investors and affect their calculations. The regulatory state and the participatory state offer distinct views of national political arenas. All governments operate in these dimensions, but they vary in what they do and how. The regulatory state helps define the institutional arena, the rules of the game within which economic life takes place. The participatory state defines who participates, the nature of that participation, who has what rights, the extent of political and civil freedoms in society, and the vulnerability of the regulatory state to political pressures.[3] Both affect investors but by different channels to a large degree.

The Regulatory State: Argument and Measurement

The regulatory state oversees economic exchange. The state defines property rights, contract procedures, and mechanisms of exchange and allocation. It affects the security of these property rights, the transparency of economic relations, and the stability of those contracts. The regulatory state extracts rents from the holders of property rights. These may be in the form of fair and legitimate taxes or perhaps less legitimate taxes such as bribes, sidepayments, or excessive taxation. The regulatory state establishes processes of complaint and adjudication to mediate conflicts between private interests or between those interests and the state. The regulatory state supplies tools to enforce the outcomes of the adjudication process—fair or biased. There is no single means, policy equilibrium, or path by which regulatory states implement and provide these functions. Regulatory states vary in countless ways and achieve varying degrees of success in performing their functions. Markets vary across borders partly due to variations across national regulatory arenas.

Institutions and policies of the regulatory state affect economic growth, development, and domestic and international investment (Clague et al. 1996; Clarke and Maxfield 1996; Cukierman, Webb, and Neyapti 1992; Keefer and Knack 1997; Knack and Keefer 1995; Maxfield 1997; North 1990; Olson 1993; Persson 1988; Rama 1993; Rodrik 1989; Scully 1988). Regulatory functions shape expectations about economic and social activity and uncertainty about those expectations. The activities of the regulatory state affect the rights of a "firm or individual to assets, to the revenue streams generated by assets, and to any other contractual obligations due to the firm or individual" (Keefer and Knack 1997). These are the property rights of firms and individuals over their activities and labor.

Keefer and Knack note that "[property] rights are more secure to the extent that political and legal institutions inhibit unilateral private or public decisions that dramatically or frequently reassign them" (1997). But government rules, regulations, policies, and politicians are targets of distributional competition, which affects the exposure of property rights; monetary, fiscal, and adjudication mechanisms; and other aspects of the regulatory state to political manipulation. The insulation of the regulatory state from such manipulation, or lack of insulation, derives partly from the design and activities of the participatory state.

If regulatory institutions, policymakers, and policies resist pressures and succeed in insulating the economic arena from short-term manipulative pressures from the political arena, then they inject a stickiness that constrains government from unpredictable and seemingly arbitrary activity or from perverse rent seeking and reallocative actions (Keefer 1994; Sobel 1995; Weingast 1993). These impose real costs upon governments, policymakers, and politicians, as they disappoint members of society. Resisting pressures to change represents expensive commitments by governments, and as such they act as commitments and signals to international investors. Stable regulatory institutions and policies provide information that permits investors to price their risks with greater confidence—good or bad. Such institutions and policies constrain the information dilemma confronting investors, help define public sector threats to investment, and provide selective incentives or disincentives to the investor.

Operationalizing the regulatory state to test its effect upon economic activity proves difficult. Knack and Keefer (1995, 207) note that "principally because of data limitations, empirical research into cross-country sources of growth and convergence has been restricted to a narrow examination of the role of institutions." This often leads to studies of regulatory institutions that focus upon specific nations—case studies. Two international risk assessment firms compile data and create measures that capture aspects of the regulatory state. Business Environmental Risk Intelligence and the International Country Risk Guide generate data and measures corresponding to important functions and characteristics of the regulatory state.[4] This enables cross-sectional analyses of the institutional effects of the regulatory state upon economic outcomes.

The BERI indicators include *Contract Enforceability, Infrastructure Quality, Nationalization Potential,* and *Bureaucratic Delays.* Many of the BERI observations date to the early 1970s. Unfortunately, the BERI data span only fifty countries and omit many of the nations included in the last chapter's analyses. The ICRG contains five variables: *Government Repudiation of Contracts, Rule of Law, Risk of Expropriation, Corruption in Government,* and *Bureaucratic Quality.* The ICRG begins in 1982, a shorter series than the BERI data, but it covers more than a hundred countries. It includes all the developing nations examined in the last chapter and for the same period. Consequently, I use the ICRG indicators. Knack and Keefer (1995), Clague et al. (1996), and Keefer and Knack (1997) employ BERI and ICRG data as measures of institutional performance by the state and its effect upon economic performance. They found the BERI and ICRG variables interchangeable without significantly altering their results. Their results were robust regardless of whether they were using individual BERI or ICRG variables, an additive index built from those variables, or different weightings of such variables (Knack and Keefer 1995, 212). This attests to the measures' reliability, if not their validity, as they appear to capture similar information.

Government Repudiation of Contracts attempts to capture the "risk of modification in a contract taking the form of a repudiation, postponement, or scaling down due to budget cutbacks, indigenization pressure, a change in government, or a change in government economic and social priorities" (Knack and Keefer 1995, 226). This supplies information about contract enforcement in public-private and private-private relations. If a government respects its contracts and commitments, then by extension that government will be more likely to enforce contracts among private contracting parties. Conversely, if a government fails to respect its contract obligations, then it is probably less likely to fairly adjudicate and enforce contractual obligations among private parties. This variable scores on a scale of one to ten with higher scores for lower risks (i.e., greater contract stability and safety).

Rule of Law represents "the degree to which the citizens of a country are willing to accept the established institutions to make and implement laws and adjudicate disputes" (Knack and Keefer 1995, 225). Higher scores on a zero to six scale reflect a greater likelihood of resorting to peaceful measures for adjudicating disputes. Higher scores indicate "sound political institutions, a strong court system, and provisions for an orderly succession of power" (225). Low scores reflect an increased likelihood of reliance upon physical force or some activity outside the formal legal boundaries to settle disputes. Like *Government Repudiation of Contracts*, *Rule of Law* addresses expectations about the stability and security of property rights and contracts.

Risk of Expropriation measures risk of "outright confiscation or forced nationalization" (Knack and Keefer 1995, 226). This assesses the most blatant and extreme threat to private property rights from the state—the absolute denial of such rights. The scale runs from one to ten, with higher scores indicating lower risks as with the other ICRG variables. Together with the previous two, this variable builds an overall picture of the state's respect for private property and provides information about the likelihood that the state will infringe on private property rights. Is the state a threat to investments or the return on those investments of international investors? More implicitly, the measure furnishes information concerning the vulnerability of state mechanisms to myopic manipulation.

Corruption in Government considers whether "high government officials are likely to demand special payments" and whether "illegal payments are generally expected throughout the lower levels of government in the form of bribes connected with import and export licenses, exchange controls, tax assessment, policy protection, or loans" (Knack and Keefer 1995, 225). This supplies evidence about the competence, character, and insulation of the bureaucracy; its rent-seeking proclivities; and the likelihood a government may show favoritism based on some criteria other than merit. Corrupt states will more likely infringe upon property rights and arbitrarily change the rules of economic interaction. They are less likely to impartially enforce contracts. These introduce greater risk and uncertainty. States scoring poorly should have difficulty making credible commitments about refraining from corrupt behavior. High scores on a zero to six scale indicate lower threats from the regulatory state.

Bureaucratic Quality indicates "autonomy from political pressures and strength, expertise to govern without drastic changes in policy or interruptions in government service, and the presence of an established mechanism for recruiting and training" (Knack and Keefer 1995, 225). *Bureaucratic Quality* incorporates many of the same qualities included in *Corruption in Government*. Governments with bureaucratic competence and a professional civil service developed through established recruitment procedures are more likely to display consistency in decision making, follow merit criteria for the awarding of government services and contracts, enhance transparency in the policy environment, protect property rights, resist myopic political pressures, and adjudicate contracts fairly. Again, high scores on a zero to six scale represent a state environment with lower risk to the international investor.

These five ICRG variables overlap in what they measure. They are not mutually exclusive. This introduces a problem of multicollinearity if used as distinct explanatory variables. I additively combine the five ICRG variables into an index to produce a single measure for the regulatory state. This additive index includes all the effects and information from the separate ICRG measures, yet it avoids problems of multicollinearity across those individual variables. This index provides a lever with which to evaluate the contribution of the regulatory state to estimations of country credit risk and patterns in global capital access.

The Participatory State: Argument and Measurement

Governments do far more than function as regulatory thermostats of social and economic life. They affect economic and social expectations by paths and activities in addition to those of the regulatory state. Governments and their societies interact through the participatory mechanisms of political life. Governments and their policies, even the most authoritarian, reflect a structure of distributional interests in domestic society, competition among those interests, and shifts in those interests. Governments may reflect the interests of a pluralist majority, a partition of elite interests, a shifting coalition of interests, or some other division in political and civil society. Distributional interests in society can be mobilized or latent, active or passive, represented or repressed. Governments, politicians, and policymakers may be more or less susceptible to pressures arising from such distributional interests in society—however organized. These activities occur within the participatory domain of the state.

The liberty and ability to participate in political life defines the boundaries of the participatory state. At one boundary of this dimension resides perfectly representative democracy, where members of society operate with perfect information, voting imposes no costs, no vote trading exists across issues, and strategic manipulation is impossible. Members of this society exercise choice and affect decisions and institutions of governance. The voting rules of this participatory state translate the wishes of society perfectly and without perversion of the collective choice. At the other extreme sits a lone policy dictator who controls the tools of coercion in society and acts independently of others' preferences in society. Only one member of society chooses. The policy dictator could benignly impose the collective preference of society if by some idiosyncratic chance the preferences of the underrepresented society align perfectly with the preferences of policy dictator, but this occurs as a special case among an infinite range of outcomes. These boundary conditions exist only in theory. All empirical cases fall between these boundaries with varying degrees of participation. Participatory states range from those fairly representative of societal interests to others that are perversely representative of a few at the expense of society. Increasing participation or democratization involves expanding access to state policymakers by members of civil society. Political violence, elections, party politics, and lobbying constitute ways to expand or limit the political franchise.

Activities in the participatory sphere spill over to affect the regulatory state and economic activity. Regulatory states arise within the context of participatory states. Tension exists between the stability of rules conducive to economic activity and pressures upon the participatory state from domestic society to change such rules. Within fragmented and contentious polities, responsive participatory institutions may impose hurdles to constructing and maintaining stable regulatory institutions that resist pressures to change. This does not preclude stable regulatory institutions in democratic societies. The successful regulatory states of the advanced industrialized economies arose within highly participatory political arenas. Yet democracy may exact an economic price upon society or impose costs upon political actors seeking to promote a stable regulatory environment. Long-term gains arising from a stable regulatory arena may easily dwarf such costs, but getting to this point can prove tenuous, involve foregoing short-term myopic gains, and impose career risks upon politicians and policymakers. Governments, political actors, and diverse interests in democratic societies can opt to constrain themselves and adopt a stable regulatory structure conducive to economic exchange. In such situations, states and societies strike bargains to limit pressures from the participatory arena upon the regulatory arena. These bargains are cast in the design of institutions and policies, which buffer the regulatory state and constrain the ability of dissatisfied interests in society to employ the participatory state to change the regulatory state.[5]

The connections between political liberty and economic outcomes remain controversial, ill defined, and circumspect. Despite normative biases and preferences, substantial debate and disagreement surrounds this issue. Theoretically and empirically, the evidence seems mixed. States with restricted liberties such as China, Singapore, Korea, Taiwan, and Malaysia have displayed rapid economic growth. Yet the most advanced industrialized economies have successfully combined stable political rights and liberties with economic growth. A long succession of scholars since Adam Smith have linked political freedoms to economic growth. Implicitly, this assumes that choice on one dimension correlates positively with choice on other dimensions and that no conflict exists between them. In their approaches to modernization, Rostow (1960) and Lipset (1960) suggest that democracy and economic growth are mutually reinforcing. Wittman (1989, 1995) argues that democratic institutions can be efficient as political markets and promote economic growth. Leblang (1997) uses pooled cross-sectional and time-series evidence to demonstrate a positive empirical connection between democracy and economic growth. Pastor and Sung (1995) describe a positive connection between democracy and private investment in developing nations.

Yet others speculate that political demands in democratic societies lead to redistribution, which restrains economic growth. In this vein, Olson (1982) argues that democratic political institutions are particularly vulnerable to rent-seeking interest groups. Such group demands lead to policies that reduce wealth, constrain growth, and eventually generate a sclerosis in modern democracies. Alesina and Rodrik (1994) conclude that substantial inequality within democratic frameworks will lead to political demands for redistribution. These demands result in policies that shift resources from investment to consumption, which retards economic growth. Persson and Tabellini (1994) make a similar case. Nordhaus (1975) suggests that partisan competition in democratic systems produces excessive and destructive manipulation of growth rates. Buchanan and Wagner (1977) warn that expanding government in democratic societies will curtail economic growth. Barro (1994) and Helliwell (1994) also found negative associations between democracy and economic growth.

Other studies produced mixed results. Sirowy and Inkles (1990) in a review of thirteen empirical studies found inconsistent results linking democracy and economic performance. Przeworski (1991) recognized the interdependence of political and economic transformations in Eastern Europe and Latin America, yet he noted an ongoing tension in this interdependence, with less than optimistic expectations. Przeworski and Limongi (1993) in a review of a large number of studies found mixed results. They suggest that a selection bias favoring the economic performance of authoritarian states undermines estimates of the effect of democracy upon economic growth. Burkhart and Lewis-Beck (1994) found no relationship between democracy and growth. Keech (1995) found that democracy can negatively impact economic performance but such costs were relatively modest and nonsystematic. Clague et al. (1996) speculate that authoritarian states may protect property rights better in the short term than nascent democracies do, but the scales shift when considering political succession and regime change over time. They found that long-term representative democracies appear to protect property rights and contracts across successive leaders whereas authoritarian states with limited political liberties protect such property rights and contracts only during the tenure of the leader. Przeworski, Alvarez, Cheibub, and Limongi (1996) suggest that economic performance can sustain democracy but democracies do not emerge as a consequence of economic development. Societies above an economic threshold will be more likely to sustain a democratic regime than societies falling beneath that threshold.

Clearly, determining the relationship between the participatory state and economic performance is difficult to assess and demands continued research. Some have attempted to consider the impact of the participatory state upon economic activity by using measures of political stability based upon the incidence of political violence such as coups, assassinations, and revolutions (Balkan 1992; Barro 1991). These inadequately specify the participatory state. They generalize from a particular and narrow type of participation—disruptive and violent. Kormendi and Meguire (1985) and Grier and Tullock (1989) took a broader tack and used indicators of political and civil liberties based on the Gastil indices (1983, 1987) as proxies for political stability and the participatory state. Bollen (1993) finds that these measures correlate highly with other available alternatives. I view these as more balanced indicators of the relationship between the government and those governed. I follow this path and use Freedom House data to construct a measure for the participatory state.

Freedom House's Comparative Survey of Freedom provides annual evaluations of freedom that cover almost all nations and territories since the 1970s. The Comparative Study of Freedom divides freedom into two categories: political rights and civil liberties. Table 1 (chap. 1) shows that the Freedom House measures correlate highly with the Polity III measures of democracy (Jaggers and Gurr 1996). The Comparative Survey of Freedom attempts to provide a stable metric for comparing the political and civil liberties of individuals across nations over time. Freedom House generates rankings based not on expressed "government intentions or constitutions but on the real world situations caused by governmental and nongovernmental factors" (Freedom House 1995–96). The survey defines *freedom* as "the chance to act spontaneously in a variety of fields outside the control of government and other centers of potential domination" (ibid.).

The political rights dimension of the Comparative Study of Freedom evaluates the ability of people to "freely participate in the political process . . . by which the polity chooses the authoritative policymakers and attempts to make binding decisions affecting the national, regional, or local community. The civil liberty dimension assesses the freedoms to develop views, institutions, and personal autonomy from the state" (Freedom House 1995–96). Freedom House uses checklists to evaluate these two dimensions. I include them in appendix B. Freedom House uses these checklists and the survey team's judgments to generate scores for political rights and civil liberties on a scale of one to seven, with one being the most free and seven the least. A high correlation between the measures produces problems of multicollinearity similar to those that plagued the ICRG variables. Consequently, I use both scales to construct an additive index, which becomes the measure for the participatory state.

Empirical Tests

I use the indicators of the regulatory and participatory state to assess *how* different aspects of national political arenas impact risk and global lending. I constrain the analyses to the same developing nations included in the last chapter and for the same period (1982–91). I limit the analyses to developing nations, as the advanced industrialized nations exhibit little variation in the economic and political measures of interest—no variation on the independent and dependent variables. All advanced industrialized nations score well on regulatory context, political rights, civil liberties, risk, and uncertainty. This offers little leverage with which to evaluate the effects of these characteristics upon economic outcomes such as global borrowing patterns. Developing nations exhibit far more variation on the dependent and independent variables, which enhances our ability to test whether national arenas affect international borrowing outcomes and, if so, how.

I begin by testing associations across the different measures. Do the participatory and regulatory measures of the political arena capture the same phenomena and information? Freedom House began conducting an annual Survey of Economic Freedom in 1995 to accompany its Freedom in the World Survey on political and civil liberties. Comparing these surveys produces an extremely high correlation of approximately .90. From this vantage point, the regulatory and participatory states should supply international investors with almost the same information concerning risk and uncertainty in the environment, all else being equal. Yet all else is not equal. First, the activities of the participatory state may be more visible to outsiders than the activities of the regulatory state. This alone can elevate the importance of the participatory state as a signaling mechanism to international investors and endow it with an independent influence. Second, the Survey of Economic Freedom departs dramatically from *Euromoney* and *Institutional Investor* ratings. The Survey of Economic Freedom fails to capture the same information as the *Euromoney* and *Institutional Investor* ratings do. The *Euromoney* and *Institutional Investor* ratings overlap extensively, and I use them to generate the uncertainty measure.

Table 15 displays correlation coefficients for the major variables using only developing nations. Consistent with the previous chapter's findings, I expected country credit risk and levels of borrowing to produce a positive correlation, as the country credit rating ranges from bad to good risk on a scale of zero to one hundred. Higher scores for the regulatory state measure indicate states that are more stable and predictable, less corrupt, less threatening to contracts and private property rights, and more professional. These characteristics should impose lower risks on investments. Consequently, I expected the regulatory state to correlate positively with risk and levels of borrowing. The participatory state measure is scaled inversely to the other variables. Higher scores indicate less freedom. If greater democracy and participation contributes to access and lowers risk, then I expected a negative correlation between the participatory state measures and those of country credit risk and borrowing based upon their metrics.

Table 15 confirms these expectations. The coefficients are signed correctly based on the underlying metrics. To begin, country credit risk positively correlates with borrowing. This was already clear from the results in the previous chapter. But table 15 introduces substantial and important new information. First, the participatory and regulatory measures of the political arena show an association of −.331. Despite their overlap, this correlation coefficient demonstrates that a significant lack of association also exists. Two-thirds of what they measure are independent. The measures for the regulatory and participatory state contain information that reflects different aspects of the political sphere.

Second, the results reveal differences in the relationship between the different components of the political arena and the economic variables. The .587 correlation between the regulatory state and country credit risk exceeds the −.190 correlation between the participatory state and country credit risk by more than three times. The correlation between borrowing and the regulatory

TABLE 15.   Correlations

Variable	*Euromoney* Rating	International Borrowing	Regulatory State
International borrowing	.358	—	—
Regulatory state	.587	.240	—
Participatory state	−.190	−.120	−.331

state more than doubles the strength of the association between borrowing and the participatory state. From these correlations, the regulatory state appears to be far better connected to assessments of economic risk and levels of global borrowing than the participatory state. The regulatory state appears deeply embedded and endogenous to assessments of country credit risk, which strongly relate to borrowing outcomes.

Taking the analysis one step further illuminates the relationship between the political variables and assessment of country credit risk. Four linear regressions test the endogeneity of the different components of the political sphere to country credit risk: (1) country credit risk by the regulatory state, (2) country credit risk by the regulatory state and year, (3) country credit risk by the participatory state, and (4) country credit risk by the participatory state and year. These allow comparison across the different activities of the political arena. The second and fourth models include the year as a control for any systematic trends in the data unrelated to the predictors. Table 16 displays the results.

First, the signs go as expected. The trend variable was statistically significant in one equation but contributes only marginal improvements in accounting for the variation around the mean of country credit risk. Both measures of the state prove to be statistically significant in all models, but the similarity ends there. Consistent with the results in table 15, the regulatory state accounts for far more variation around the mean of country credit risk than the participa-

TABLE 16. OLS Models: Evaluating the Endogeneity of Regulatory and Participatory Components of National Political Arenas to Country Credit Risk, Developing Nations (nonstandardized coefficients, standard errors)

Variable	Model 1	Model 2	Model 3	Model 4
Regulatory	2.122**	—	2.167**	—
	(.109)		(.108)	
Participatory	—	−1.166**	—	−1.188**
		(.206)		(.207)
Year	—	—	−.846**	−0.382
			(.221)	(.260)
Constant	.629	48.464**	1,680.494**	807.844
	(2.110)	(1.840)	(439.633)	(516.362)
N	624	650	624	650
R^2	.379	.047	.393	.050

Note: This analysis uses the *Euromoney* measures for country credit risk.
*significant at .05   **significant at .01

tory state. The size of the difference stands out. In the base models, the regulatory and participatory states produce R^2s of .379 and .047, respectively. The models controlling for trend attained only marginally different results—R^2s of .393 and .050 for the regulatory and participatory states. The regulatory state accounts for eight times more of the variation around the mean of country credit risk than the participatory state. The participatory state makes a relatively small real contribution to estimates of country credit risk compared to the regulatory state. The regulatory state is far more endogenous to estimations of country credit risk. The measure for country credit risk already incorporates much of the information in the regulatory state measure but little of the information in the participatory state indicator.

The construction of the *Euromoney* country credit ratings makes these results especially noteworthy. *Euromoney* explicitly includes a subjective component in its assessment, part of which is dedicated to political risk. This component constitutes 20 percent of the evaluation and derives from a poll of political risk analysts, risk insurance brokers, and bank credit officers who gave each nation a score on a scale of one to ten of the risk of nonpayment. This means that up to 20 percent of the *Euromoney* ratings explicitly attempt to capture political risk. The impact of the participatory state measure falls far short of this 20 percent, but the regulatory state measure almost doubles this expectation. The participatory state measure fails to capture aspects of the political arena that *Euromoney* tried to include in its assessments. Conversely, the regulatory state measure is far more deeply endogenized in contextual risk than expected in the *Euromoney* methodology.

Politics influences estimations of country credit risk, but the regulatory component of the state exercises this influence far more than the participatory component. This poses a normatively uncomfortable finding if investors actually care little about the nature of the participatory regime, whether democratic or authoritarian. These results fail to support such pessimism. First, the regressions only assess the endogeneity of different components of the political arena to assessments of country credit risk and not their impact on access to global capital. Table 15 shows that investors prefer more democratic contexts, at least on the margins.

Second, the results reflect only developing nations. I excluded advanced industrialized societies due to their lack of variation on key variables. All advanced industrialized nations score highly on the measure of the regulatory state and with small variations. Their domestic political economies all display stable institutional arrangements that protect contracts, ensure property rights, limit corruption, constrain risk of expropriation, encourage the rule of law, and insulate political leaders from excessive myopic behavior that could damage the interests of investors. All advanced industrialized nations score well on the measure of the participatory state. Their citizens enjoy significant political rights and civil liberties. Finally, borrowers from the advanced industrialized states prove to be extremely successful in accessing global capital. The disproportionate success of borrowers from these societies in obtaining global capital poses a substantive dilemma for a claim that democracy does not matter, or worse, inhibits lending.

Does adding political measures to the models improve their ability to account for the variations in borrowing, and if so how? As demonstrated earlier, the data display a stubborn and perverse structure. The original dependent variable, global borrowing, is nonnormally distributed, as are the residuals from the linear models. I present linear models with political and economic predictors for comparison, but the nonnormal distributions contaminate these results and prevent inference based upon normal parametric distributions to the data and the residuals. The data's structure leads to severe underestimation of the effects. The linear models miss important information present in the data. The residuals from those models still contain systematic information.

Consequently, I repeat the two-step analytic strategy adopted in the last chapter but with the addition of the political measures. First this strategy considers the decision of whether to lend by attacking the data as a logistic model with loan or no loan as the dependent variable. Second, if investors accept the risk to lend, then how much will they lend? The prior information from the first stage conditions this one. The second stage uses the first to filter the data and includes only those cases in which borrowing exceeds zero. This eliminates a large number of observations that bias the analysis. It examines only those attaining global capital and assesses their level of borrowing as a function of the predictor variables. Investors may decide to lend but constrain their risk by limiting the amount of investment. The log of nonzero borrowing becomes the dependent variable for the second stage. It is normally distributed. Unfortunately, the persistence of nonnormally distributed residuals prevents recovering a linear modeling strategy for the analysis. I continue with the loess, or locally weighted, regression strategy adopted in the last chapter.

The linear regressions tickle the appetite given that the problems within the structure of the data lead to underestimation of effects. I begin with an economic model from chapter 6 as a baseline and incrementally introduce the political measures into the baseline model. The linear model follows the form

$$y_i = \alpha + \Sigma(\beta_\kappa X_{ki}) + \varepsilon_i \, ,$$

where for each nation i
y_i = global borrowing and
$\Sigma(\beta_\kappa X_{ki})$ is a matrix of vectors.

Table 17a-b displays the results of the linear models. First, the coefficients are signed properly. Second, the regulatory state imparts no significant effect by itself or as part of an interaction term. The regulatory state barely improves the fit of the models. This follows given its high multicollinearity and endogeneity to country credit risk. The inclusion of the regulatory state measure adds little new information. Country credit risk already contains much of the information

TABLE 17a.   OLS Models: Economic and Political Determinants of Lending, Developing Nations, Models 1–3 (nonstandardized coefficients, standard errors)

Variable	Economic Model	Political-Economic Model 1	Political-Economic Model 2	Political-Economic Model 3
Country credit risk[a]	25.087***	23.178***	25.067***	24.191***
	(3.085)	(4.215)	(3.408)	(4.330)
Uncertainty	32.390***	28.277*	30.764**	29.672*
	(12.864)	(14.913)	(13.585)	(15.174)
Country credit risk *uncertainty	−.731***	−.548	−.645**	−.566
	(.277)	(.343)	(.319)	(.355)
Regulatory	—	5.340	—	3.382
		(9.949)		(10.623)
Country credit risk *regulatory	—	—	—	—
Participatory	—	—	−12.382	−16.885
			(11.879)	(13.242)
Country credit risk *participatory	—	—	—	—
Year	−11.718	−12.118	−12.515	−11.351
	(14.695)	(16.113)	(15.069)	(16.484)
Constant	22,676.982	23,447.902	24,362.836	22,067.565
	(29,211.4)	(32,018.5)	(29,962.8)	(32,753.7)
N	652	616	632	599
R^2	.129	.132	.134	.139

[a]This analysis uses the *Euromoney* measures for country credit risk.
*significant at .10   **significant at .05   ***significant at .01

offered by the regulatory state predictor. The participatory state produces a different result. In relative terms, it substantially improves the models' fit. The fit improves by more than 10 percent over the baseline model when the participatory state is included in an interaction term. Incorporating both political measures as independent and interaction terms improves the fit by almost 20 percent—.024 in real terms.

Even more tantalizing are the channels through which the political variables exercise their influence. The regulatory state contributes endogenously to the estimation of economic risk and consequently endogenously to borrowing outcomes. The participatory state imparts the most additional information independent of estimations of country credit risk. Being more or less democratic

TABLE 17b.   OLS Models: Economic and Political Determinants of Lending, Developing Nations, Models 4–6 (nonstandardized coefficients, standard errors)

Variable	Political-Economic Model 4	Political-Economic Model 5	Political-Economic Model 6
Country credit risk[a]	29.871***	39.599***	53.323***
	(8.408)	(6.660)	(11.857)
Uncertainty	30.421**	29.309**	30.786**
	(15.096)	(13.538)	(15.233)
Country credit risk			
*uncertainty	−.627*	−.633**	−.656*
	(.354)	(.318)	(.362)
Regulatory	18.509	—	19.799
	(17.432)		(18.511)
Country credit risk			
*regulatory	−.305	—	−.419
	(.331)		(.358)
Participatory	—	51.590*	70.008**
		(27.864)	(30.269)
Country credit risk			
*participatory	—	−1.819**	−2.464***
		(.717)	(.778)
Year	−12.153	−16.574	−16.087
	(16.115)	(15.089)	(16.443)
Constant	23,261.758	31,896.79	30,427.173
	(32,023.2)	(29,981.3)	(32,653.4)
N	616	632	599
R^2	.133	.143	.153

[a]This analysis uses the *Euromoney* measures for country credit risk.
*significant at .10   **significant at .05   ***significant at .01

or more or less repressive affects investment choices and generates a proportionately significant improvement in accounting for the variations in borrowing. The nature of the participatory state improves model fit mostly as an independent and exogenous effect. Evaluations of country credit risk mistakenly omit the information in the measure of the participatory state.

Turning to strategies to address the difficulties in the data proves to be analytically and substantively rewarding. Following the attack on the data adopted in chapter 6, I begin with a logistic model. This captures the first stage of investors' decisions whether to loan or not. A discrete variable, loan or no loan, serves as the dependent variable. Given the unusual structure of the data, I use the Huber/White estimator of variance in place of the traditional estimator. This generates robust estimates of variance and robust standard errors. The logistic model takes the same form as in the last chapter but with the addition of political variables representing the regulatory and participatory state:

$$\Pr(\text{Loan}_i = 1) = F[\alpha + \Sigma(\beta_\kappa X_{ki}) + \varepsilon_i],$$

where for each nation i

$\Pr(\text{Loan}_i = 1)$ is probability of borrowing and

$\Sigma(\beta_\kappa X_{ki})$ is a matrix of vectors that may include

β_κ = {credit risk, uncertainty, year, population, regulatory state, participatory state}.

Table 18 presents the results from the logistic models. The economic model serves as a baseline, and then I add the regulatory and participatory state predictors one at a time. With the sole exception of uncertainty, the economic variables are very highly significant and influential in affecting the likelihood of lending. They impose the largest effects. This follows logically. First, lending is above all an economic decision. Second, in a full information environment evaluations of risk—an economic variable—should include all the political factors affecting lending. Incomplete specification of country credit risk means investors can improve upon their evaluations by looking at other factors such as the regulatory and participatory state. Uncertainty proved to be nonsignificant in the baseline economic model, but the addition of the political variables elevated the impact of uncertainty on the likelihood of lending. Ironically, the addition of only the participatory state decreases the model's fit even though its impact is highly significant.

The regulatory state contributes the most information to improve model fit beyond the baseline economic model. Yet the regulatory state barely exceeds

TABLE 18.   First Stage: Logistic Analysis of Economic and Political Determinants to
Loan, Developing Nations (odds ratios, robust standard errors estimated with White/Huber)

Variable	Economic Model	Political-Economic Model 1	Political-Economic Model 2	Political-Economic Model 3
Country credit risk[a]	1.129***	1.115***	1.122***	1.115***
	(.015)	(.017)	(.015)	(.017)
Uncertainty	1.025	1.044**	1.035*	1.047**
	(.020)	(.021)	(.019)	(.021)
Year	.837***	.839***	.822***	.833***
	(.034)	(.038)	(.035)	(.038)
Population	1.000***	1.000***	1.000***	1.000***
	(3.02e–06)	(3.63e–06)	(3.24e–06)	(3.72e–06)
Regulatory	—	1.060*	—	1.040
		(.034)		(.035)
Participatory	—	—	.931**	.927**
			(.033)	(.036)
N	615	583	595	566
Log likelihood	−258.617	−236.213	−251.511	−232.142
Pseudo R^2	.393	.416	.390	.408
χ^2	110.33	113.51	114.45	111.33
Prob $> \chi^2$	.000	.000	.000	.000

[a]These analyses use the *Institutional Investor* measures for country credit risk.
*significant at .10   **significant at .05   ***significant at .01

a relatively generous significance threshold in one model and fails to surpass
that threshold in another. The participatory state is highly significant whenever
it is included, but it does not seem to add as much new information as the regulatory state despite levels of significance. Overall, the addition of the political
variables improve model fit by 3 to 5 percent. This is a good improvement for
what fundamentally constitutes an economic decision, but it is a limited improvement.

Clearly, at this first stage investors overwhelmingly weight economic context. But the political variables do improve model fit and generate statistically
significant independent effects. Moreover, the regulatory state is heavily endogenous to the economic variable of country credit risk. Tables 15 and 16 reveal that country credit risk and the regulatory state overlap by approximately
40 to 60 percent. Politics is far more embedded in lending decisions than the independent effects of the participatory and regulatory states suggest. The declining statistical significance of the regulatory state with the addition of the
participatory state captures the overlap between the regulatory and participa-

tory state. Much of the information provided by the regulatory state measure is redundant to information already contained in the participatory state and country credit risk measures.

Once investors decide to lend, they must decide how much. Investors manage their risk exposure by deciding upon whether to lend and the amount of investment. The information from the first decision conditions the second. The first stage justifies reducing the truncation problems in the data and dropping observations from the analysis. The second stage includes only cases in which borrowing exceeds zero. This eliminates a large number of observations that bias the analysis and suppress effects. Even so, the variable of nonzero borrowing remains ill behaved and heavily skewed. This is readily apparent in figure 26. It inhibits the straightforward use of nonzero borrowing as the dependent variable for the second stage. As before, I use the transformed log of nonzero borrowing as the dependent variable for the second stage. It approximates a normal distribution. Unfortunately, a linear model generates residuals that are nonnormally distributed. This prohibits returning to a linear model for this stage and warrants a more robust analytical technique.

The loess, or locally weighted, regression strategy adopted in the last chapter provides a consistent and robust approach for the second stage. Least trimmed squares robust regression (LTS) offers an alternative robust approach. I experimented with LTS and report the results in appendix B.[6] The loess model takes the form

$$y_i = \alpha + \Sigma(\beta_\kappa X_{ki}) + \varepsilon_i,$$

where for each nation i
y_i = log of nonzero global borrowing and
    $\Sigma(\beta_\kappa X_{ki})$ is a matrix of vectors such that
β_κ = {credit risk, uncertainty, year, population, regulatory state,
    participatory state}.

Table 19 displays the results of four quadratic loess models using only the data for developing nations. I begin with an economic baseline model. This is the concluding model from chapter 6 and includes the full set of economic factors—country credit risk, uncertainty, year, and population.[7] This model already demonstrates an extraordinary improvement over the linear parametric regression. Next I incrementally introduce the political variables.

The political variables contribute new information. They capture more of the information embedded in the structure of the data and account for more of the variation around the mean. The full economic and political model produces a multiple R^2 of .64. The political variables improve the model fit from 5 to 9 percent. This is a very conservative estimate of the impact of these components due to the endogeneity of politics to country credit risk. A thought experiment furnishes some leverage in assessing the real impact of politics. A loess model using the same data and with only country credit risk as a predictor achieves a multiple R^2 of .27 (table 14). As country credit risk and the regulatory state overlap by approximately 40 to 60 percent (tables 15 and 16), the combined embedded and independent contributions of the regulatory state explain between 16 to 25 percent of the variation around the mean. Far less endogenous to country credit risk than the regulatory state, the participatory state nevertheless contains some of the same information contained in country credit risk. This further underestimates the real impact of national political arenas upon access to global capital markets. Even with conservative estimates, these components of national political arenas make a substantial difference in accounting for variations in borrowing.

Visual diagnostics buttress, substantiate, and reinforce the results in table 19. Figure 27 displays the fit of the model, which incorporates all the specified political and economic effects. Given the original nonparametric problems in the structure of the data, the scatterplot of the fitted model against the log of nonzero borrowing is rewarding. The two-stage approach to evaluating lending, the resulting transformations of the dependent variable, and the use of ro-

TABLE 19.   Second Stage: Loess Regression Analysis of Economic and Political Determinants of Log of Positive Borrowing, Developing Nations (span = .5; degree of equation = 2, a quadratic polynomial; iterations = 5)

Variable	Full Economic Model	Political-Economic Model 1	Political-Economic Model 2	Political-Economic Model 3
Country credit risk[a]	X	X	X	X
Uncertainty	X	X	X	X
Year	X	X	X	X
Population	X	X	X	X
Regulatory	—	—	X	X
Participatory	—	X	—	X
N	273	273	273	273
Residual SE	1.207	1.067	1.042	1.071
Multiple R^2	.59	.62	.64	.64

Note: An *X* indicates that the variable is employed in the model estimation.
[a]These analyses use the *Institutional Investor* measures for country credit risk.

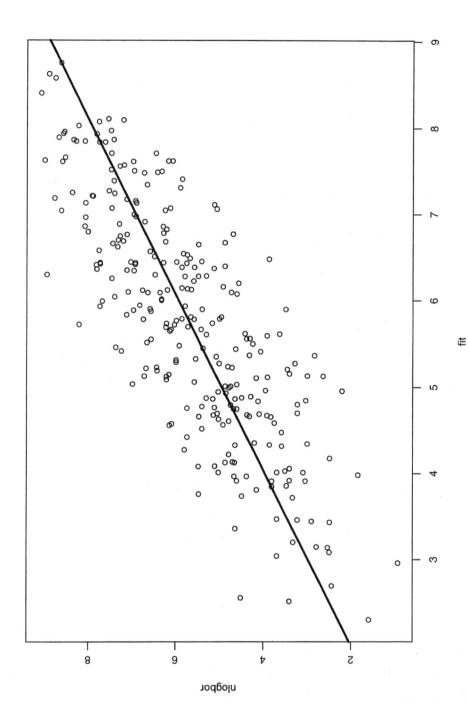

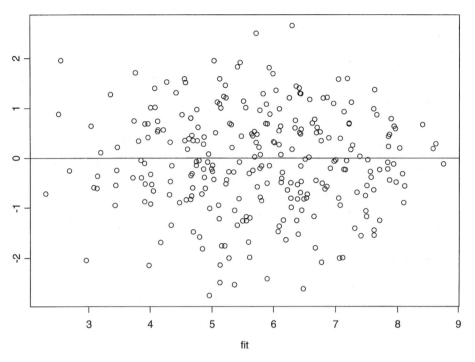

Fig. 28. Residuals plotted against full fitted political-economic loess model (model 3)

bust estimation techniques tease a substantial amount of information from the data. Visual examination of the scatterplot in figure 27 shows that the model fits well. The truncation and heteroskedasticity problems that plague the scatterplot of the linear parametric model in figure 23b disappear. These problems no longer threaten interpretation or undermine inference.

Figure 28 plots the residuals from the full political and economic loess model against the fitted model. Again, the visual diagnostics prove comforting. There is no apparent systematic pattern to the distribution of the residuals in figure 28. Very little systematic information remains in the residuals that is related to the predicted effects. The logistic model provided a theoretically consistent means of eliminating the truncation problem, the log of nonzero borrowing constrained some of the heteroskedasticity dilemma, and the loess techniques adjusted to the remaining stubborn nonparametric problems in the structure of the data. The loess analysis gathered far more information from the data than comparable parametric techniques did. Figure 29 takes this visual ex-

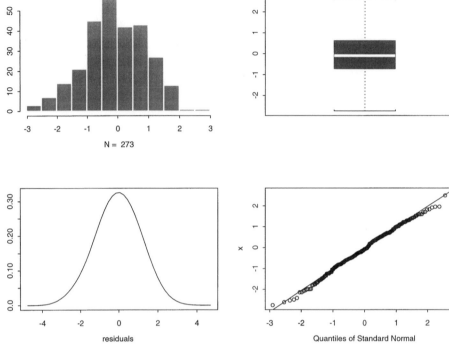

Fig. 29. Histogram, box plot, density plot, and normal q-q plot of residuals from full political-economic model

amination of the residuals a step further by displaying their structure. The histogram, density plot, and normal q-q plot reveal that the distribution of the residuals closely approximates the normal distribution. This is amazing given the initial problems. The box plot and normal q-q plots show the absence of outliers that might disproportionately bias an analysis. The residuals are well behaved.

The qualities that make loess a superb robust approach to ill-behaved data distributions impose a shift in typical strategies for evaluating and comparing the impact of individual factors. Loess furnishes overall model fit but precludes regression coefficients from summarizing the effect of individual variables. I add explanatory factors incrementally to the analysis and experiment with different combinations of those factors. This experimentation allows insight into the weightings across explanatory factors by considering the resulting shifts in the multiple R^2s. Visual exploration with conditioning plots, or coplots, provides a powerful way to circumvent the absence of regression coefficients and reveals information that regression coefficients might obscure (Cleveland 1993, 184–87). Coplots are visual tools used to examine the relationship of individual factors to the level of borrowing in global capital markets.

Figure 30 explores the dependence of the log of nonzero global borrowing upon the participatory state (lib) given economic factors included in the loess estimation and the regulatory state. Figure 31 does the same for examining the dependence of the log of nonzero global borrowing upon the regulatory state given economic factors included in the loess estimation and the participatory state. I use a summary measure for the economic predictors: ecopredict. The values on ecopredict are simply the predicted values from the full economic loess model in table 19, which uses country credit risk, uncertainty, year, and population as the predictors. They encapsulate the information in the economic model before the addition of political predictors.

In figures 30 and 31, the panels at the top and right are the given panels; the panels nestled between the given panels are dependence panels. The rectangles on the given panels represent intervals of the values of the given variable. In these analyses, I specified an overlap of .333 for the given intervals. The given panel at the top of both graphs is ecopredict. From left to right, the intervals on ecopredict range from poor to better economic conditions. In figure 30, the given panel at the right side of the graph gives intervals of the regulatory state. From top to bottom, the intervals of the regulatory state go from good to bad regulatory state conditions. In figure 31, the given panel at the right side of the graph gives intervals of the participatory state. Here, due to the scaling of the Freedom House measures, the intervals from top to bottom represent poor to good participatory state conditions.

On the dependence panels in each graph, the 3 x 3 array located between the given panels, the log of nonzero borrowing is graphed against one of the state measures given the interval conditions for that particular dependence panel. The three dependence scatterplots in any row have the same conditioning interval of values of the given panel on the right side of the graph. The three dependence scatterplots in any column have the same conditioning interval of values of the given panel on the top of the graph. Each dependence scatterplot has the data plotted and a line fitted to the data to aid visualization.

The coplots reveal very interesting information. First, slicing the data into different intervals and examining the dependence of the log of nonzero borrowing upon activities of the state, given other factors, underscores the quirkiness in the data. The dependence relationship shifts across the different panels: sometimes the relationship is flat, sometimes positive, sometimes negative, and sometimes shifting between positive and negative. This reaffirms the problems

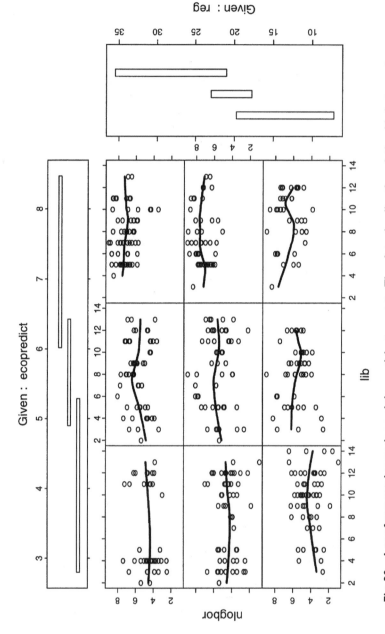

Fig. 30. Log of nonzero borrowing and the participatory state. The plots visualize the relationship between borrowing and the participatory state, controlling for economic conditions and the regulatory state.

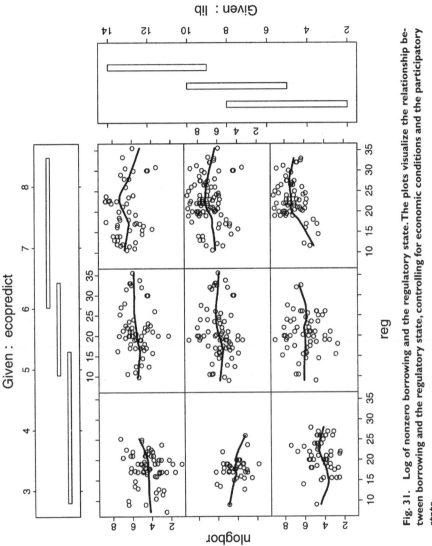

Fig. 31. Log of nonzero borrowing and the regulatory state. The plots visualize the relationship between borrowing and the regulatory state, controlling for economic conditions and the participatory state.

of using linear regression with parametric assumptions. Many of the oddities in the data will mediate each other and obscure the real relationships. This is particularly apparent when comparing outer rows or columns in the graphs.

Second, comparing rows in figure 30 immediately demonstrates the key importance of the regulatory state. Each row constitutes a different interval of values on the regulatory state; good to bad values going from top to bottom. The very level of borrowing changes from interval to interval and in a systematic direction. Borrowers in good regulatory states obtain more global capital than those from states with less successful regulatory apparatus.

Third, figure 30 provides insight into the debate over the effect of the participatory state upon economic investment and growth. The dependence of the log of nonzero borrowing upon the participatory state is fairly flat in the top two rows. This means that, given an assortment of economic conditions and relatively good to fair regulatory state conditions, differences in the participatory state impose fairly small effects upon borrowing. The effects are marginally positive in these two rows, which means it is somewhat better to be more democratic than less, but not dramatically so. The strongest effect in these two rows appears in the dependence plots with the best economic condition interval (far right column). Here the number of observations clearly favors borrowers from more democratic regimes.

The bottom row shows the strongest relationship between borrowing and the participatory state. In this row, the regulatory state is the weakest, most unstable, and least conducive to investors. In such states with fair to good economic conditions, being more democratic clearly correlates positively with improved access to global capital markets. The slopes of the fitted line in those dependence plots trend downward. Evidently, democratic regimes provide information that assuages international investors even under perverse regulatory conditions as long as some attractive economic conditions exist. Interestingly, the lower left dependence plot reveals a convex relationship between borrowing and the participatory state given poor economic and regulatory conditions. The relationship reverses. This again demonstrates of the odd structure of the relationships in the data. In this plot, it appears better to be somewhat less democratic but not too much so. Substantively, investors want some stability in such environments, which may be provided by less democratic regimes, but they do not want a completely unrestrained authoritarian regime that can arbitrarily attack investor interests without some constraint from society. None of the dependence panels suggests that extremely repressive states do better than less repressive and more democratic states.

In general, good regulatory states enjoy an overall positive association with good participatory states.[8] If a tradeoff exists between declining levels of the regulatory state and the importance of the participatory state for global borrowing, then that tradeoff tends to favor being more respectful of political and civil liberties. This contradicts the arguments that authoritarian regimes can provide more stability conducive to economic arenas in cases in which the regulatory state is weak. The exceptions, and they are highly conditioned, are cases in the direst of economic and regulatory straits. These are fringe cases and are only good borrowers compared to those omitted from the analysis during the first stage—those unable to access global markets. Once again, ecopredict also contains information about the regulatory and participatory states. As a consequence, the given panels cannot fully control for the consequences of the different components of the state. The slippage actually underestimates the effects of good participatory and regulatory states as they correlate positively with improvements in economic context.

Figure 31, which displays the dependence of the log of nonzero borrowing upon the regulatory state given economic and participatory state conditions, reinforces some of the results in figure 30. Again, economic conditions and the embedded political effects in those conditions clearly exert the greatest influence upon borrowing levels. Next, the level of borrowing tends to be positively associated with improving regulatory conditions—the slopes are either flat or increasing. Only in one dependence plot is the trend persistently negative, and this is heavily influenced by limited observations and strong outliers.

This graph also reinforces the subtle relationship between the regulatory state and borrowing given different intervals of the participatory state and economic conditions. The bottom row represents states with the most democratic participatory regimes. In the interval with the least attractive economic conditions, borrowing tends to improve with improvements in the regulatory state. In the most democratic interval with the best economic conditions, the strongest trend appears in the data. Here, the payoff for improvements in the regulatory environment produces the largest proportional gains in market access. The top row constitutes the most repressive observations on the participatory measure. In the top row, repression increasingly penalizes borrowers from states with good economic conditions even as the scores on the regulatory state climb. Generally, a more effective regulatory state improves an investment environment, but in this case the slope actually decreases. Perhaps investors who generally like effective regulatory state mechanisms are wary of them in the hands of a highly repressive participatory state. Given fair to good economic conditions (middle and right columns), the average level of borrowing in fair to good participatory states exceeds the level of borrowing in repressive states.

Unpacking the distribution and slicing it into plots based upon different conditioning variables reveals a wealth of information. Repeated interocular examination reveals more and more of the subtleties disguised by standard approaches to the data.

Conclusion

The results connect national political and economic characteristics in developing political economies to global capital access by their borrowers. After adjusting analytical strategies to compensate for the problematic structure of the data, economic and political differences in national contexts account for a substantial portion of investors' behavior. Data transformations, logistic regressions, and loess regressions turned ill-behaved nonparametric data, which defied statistical inference and interpretation, into manageable structures with very strong statistical findings. The scatterplots of the model fit in figure 27 and the diagnostic plots of the residuals in figures 28 and 29 provide strong evidence that this approach captured much of the information in the data related to the specified model. This model easily outperforms a straightforward linear parametric regression, which obscures the real relationships in the data.[9]

A borrower's nationality counts for political and economic reasons independent of a borrower's proposed enterprise. Furthermore, the regulatory and participatory components of the state influence investors by separate paths. The regulatory state exercises its greatest influence endogenous to calculations of country credit risk, whereas the participatory state operates exogenously to estimations of country credit risk. Evaluations of country credit risk overlap extensively with estimations of the regulatory state. They incorporate much of the same information. Assessments of country credit risk should reflect any contextual influence to an investment under conditions of complete information. This includes political factors. This overlap between the regulatory state and country credit risk essentially conforms to such an expectation, but with some slippage due to incomplete information. For the same reason, the small overlap between the participatory state and assessments of country credit risk is particularly noteworthy. The participatory state exercises influence relatively independent of country credit risk and the regulatory state. Evaluations of country credit risk contain little of the information included in the participatory state measure.

In the end, democracy matters. Borrowers from developing countries with more democratic regimes generally find equivalent or greater opportunities in global capital markets than borrowers from less democratic regimes.[10] Unfortunately, the analysis reveals exceptions to this statement. The conditioning plots reveal oddities in the relationships, particularly at the extremes. These are the source of the problems in the data structure that inhibit parametric techniques and inference. Borrowers from democratic states with more reliable regulatory mechanisms almost always find better access to global capital than others. Yet borrowers from states with extremely unreliable regulatory mechanisms may find better access under a less democratic participatory regime, at least in the short term. Stable expectations remain central to investment calculations. Weak and unpredictable regulatory states constitute the worst case for investors. In such cases, more authoritarian and repressive regimes might provide investors with sufficient signals about the stability of an investment environment to entice investment. In reality, the number of cases matching these criteria are extremely small. Such states score poorly on all the economic criteria, let alone the political measures. The likelihood of any substantial lending to borrowers from such states is extremely limited even with an authoritarian regime that might impose some predictability.

CHAPTER 8

Conclusion

Obviously politics, policies, and political institutions count. Social actors invest significant amounts of time, effort, money, and other resources in affecting the content of politics, policies, and political institutions. But, this tells us little about *how* they count and operate to affect social behavior. In this book, I examine how activities in the public sphere, specifically public policies and political institutions, influence the choices and activities of private actors in global capital markets.

Public policies and institutions affect the incentives and calculations of private actors. They contribute to contexts in which private actors make choices. They help delineate the broad rules of political, social, and economic interactions. Other factors help structure and affect social interactions such as exchange in global capital markets, but public policies and institutions supply an important set of social constructs and channels through which we can understand and explore behavior. In the case of global capital markets, public policies and institutions rarely dictate a specific outcome or equilibrium, but they do make some outcomes more likely than others. Governments cannot produce global capital markets independent of the choices of private market actors, but governments can generate conditions more conducive to global markets. As policies and institutions shift, the incentives for private actors change. Such shifts can create necessary conditions for new individual behavior, but private actors must still make those choices. These private choices and actions aggregate to produce the outcomes we observe daily, monthly, and yearly in global capital markets.

This project targets a limited set of factors that affect behavior, but other factors remain important. Undeniably, the history of the particular borrower influences the calculations of international investors. The results demonstrate that politics and institutional components of national political arenas account for significant variations in global capital access. These effects vary by category

193

of borrower and by component of the political arena. National contextual factors account for more of the variation in capital access for borrowers from developing nations than for those from developed nations. The importance of national context recedes for investment decisions in developed nations, or at least it fades in conscious deliberations. In these nations, stable national institutions and polices conducive to exchange are accepted as given (i.e., there is no variation on this independent variable).

Global capital markets provide an excellent arena in which to study the effects of national policies and institutions. The aggregation and allocation of surplus capital underpin economic growth and development. These are core functions in modern political economies. Financial markets and other capital aggregation and allocation mechanisms, such as the state, form the backbone and infrastructure of any modern economy. Understanding how such mechanisms operate and the relationship between politics and economics in this domain presents an imposing and important task. The formation of modern financial infrastructures, which include effective banking systems and capital markets, sits near the top of the agenda for policymakers from developing and transitional economies. Capital markets constitute the vehicle for privatizing state-owned industries in the developing and former socialist economies.

Institutionalists argue that institutions are key to economic growth, development, the distribution of resources in society, and who wins or who loses. This emphasis underpins the rise of the new institutional economics and the resurgent study of institutions in political science. Kindleberger (1993) places capital market mechanisms ahead of institutions in their importance for many of the same questions. In reality, both institutions and capital markets affect the distribution of resources in society, who wins, who loses, the type of growth and development, and the very nature of social interaction. They are intricately intertwined, as this study demonstrates.

Capital markets operate within arenas structured by government policies and institutions. Such policies and institutions provide market actors with information about the fairness of markets and the threats to their market activities. They instill confidence and contribute to the expansion of credit when successful and feed wariness and constrict capital when not. Successful institutions and capital markets are mutually reinforcing. Symbiotically, capital markets provide policymakers with resources that expand and subsidize policy boundaries and flexibility, but they also restrict policymakers by providing market actors with channels through which they can register their disagreements with government activities and potentially subvert the intentions of government policies.

Global capital markets are one category of markets, and they have some un-usual characteristics. They span national boundaries and formal regulatory arenas. Public oversight mechanisms are inherently more ambiguous for mar-kets that operate in gray areas outside national regulatory arenas. Instead of a single set of national regulatory rules and mechanisms governing behavior, pri-vate actors must consider the protections and rules of multiple political juris-dictions. Investors must look across regulatory jurisdictions to determine rules, their protections, and the effect of such contexts on their risk exposure. National governments of borrowers convey information to international investors about their protections and exposure to risks from the local context, independent of the particular histories of the borrowers. Borrowers with successful regulatory and participatory state mechanisms achieve greater success in accessing global capital markets. This translates into global pressures upon societies for effective state mechanisms. Rather than undermining the nation-state, the possibility of investing across national boundaries empowers governments. Globalization and global capital access depend heavily upon national foundations.

Over the past thirty years, financial markets in general and global finance specifically have undergone significant change. Concurrently, national policies and the institutions that affect such markets have undergone great changes. These shifts overlap, temporally and causally. Trying to understand relation-ships in a stable, unchanging arena proves to be inherently problematic. An en-vironment displaying significant shifts in outcomes and potential causes pro-vides an opportunity to test explanations. The reemergence of global finance after the 1960s yields substantial variation on the dependent variables—global finance and capital access. Shifts in public regulatory structures and state-soci-ety relations represent shifts in possible explanatory mechanisms. This creates a laboratory in the real world complete with changes in the independent (pub-lic policies and institutions) and dependent (private behavior in global capital markets) variables. Threats to explanation remain, as variation occurs in many more independent variables than is accounted for by the analyses in this book.

I described four major and ongoing transformations in global finance dur-ing the 1960–90s that grew out of policy and institutional reforms in a handful of states. The expansion of international capital mobility; the increasing securitization and disintermediation of finance, which feed capital's growing heterogeneity; the advent of financial derivatives, which create linkages across financial markets; and the introduction of new participants to global markets grew from an interaction of public and private and domestic and international. These shifts revived global finance, transformed international and national cap-ital markets, altered relations between investors and borrowers, and generated new demands upon the regulatory state. The transformation of the global arena affects governments and national economic arenas the world over, but it does not affect all of them equally.

What began as endogenous to the policy arenas of the United States and a few other influential states spilled over to transform the international political economy. Similar public policy choices in less influential states could not produce such dramatic transformations in the international political economy independent of policy choices in the more influential states. This transformation then imposed exogenous pressures upon all nations, including those that had initiated the transformation as an endogenous process. This highlights the ability of actions in key nations to transform the international context, but it also recognizes that actions endogenous to a few can later become exogenous to all. All governments react to pressures originating from financial globalization, but some governments help unleash such pressures.

Rather than a dichotomous outside-in or inside-out approach to financial globalization and its impact upon nations and global processes, this refinement describes a dynamic interaction between public and private, domestic and international, and macro- and microbehavior. This dynamic interaction includes a feedback loop to start the cycle anew. It is continuous, a dialectic. Public policies and institutions produce contextual shifts that affect the calculations of individuals and can lead to changes in their behavior. If the new behavior of individuals aggregates to alter the context, they in turn rearrange the demands upon public policies and institutions. States differ in their abilities to intervene and temper those pressures, producing the different faces of globalization.

State choices and actions have been fundamental to the reawakening of global finance and its transformation since the 1960s. Yet such choices and activities furnish only a partial explanation. Policy and institutional changes may be necessary conditions, but they are not sufficient for the revival and transformation of global finance. Private investors and borrowers dominate the action in global capital markets. Absent changes in private activity, global markets would have remained stagnant. Interactions between public shifts and the activities of private actors serve as critical steps.

Policy and institutional changes such as the IET and the VFCR Act, Eastern bloc decisions to open themselves to the West, Western choices to relax relations with the Soviet sphere, and shifts in central banking policies affected the benefits and costs of private activity. They altered conceptions of risk and rates of return. Private actors perceived shifts in their estimated risks, gains, and costs. Shifts in constraints and expected gains assailed investors with opportunities to reevaluate their strategies and invent new ones. In no way deterministic, shifts in the public context merely supplied opportunities and incentives for private individuals to alter their behavior. Nothing had to change, nor does such description encourage predictions about the particular content of private reactions ex ante.

Independent of the origins of globalization, what does the transformation of global finance mean for state-society relations? Casting globalization and international economic change as exogenous forces suggests that the transformation of global finance significantly limits the role of the state, weakens the policy autonomy of state policymakers, and recasts state-society bargains. Even though globalization emerged from processes endogenous to a few states, it now operates exogenously to all states and could affect the ability of state actors to manipulate domestic economic arenas. Some strains of speculation posit that financial globalization constrains governments, disciplines their fiscal transgressions, and disadvantages less mobile factors of production by enhancing the ability of investors to vote with their feet.

Yet the evidence contradicts such predictions and expectations about the diminishing role of the state as a consequence of expanding international capital mobility and increasing interdependence. The relationships are far more nuanced. Instead of downplaying the role of the state, the results in this book highlight the continued importance of the state. Differences in state capacities and activities help account for variations in global capital access. Like other substantive arenas where interdependence and sovereignty intersect, financial globalization and national autonomy exist in tension, but they also share a complementarity. What governments do vis-à-vis their economic and political spheres proves critical in explaining variations in global capital access. A nation's borrowers find access to global capital improved by a bureaucratically competent, professional, capable, fair, judicious, effective, and democratic state. In many ways, globalization empowers states and domestic institutions. Governments gain responsibilities and hence leverage in their relations with private actors and markets, domestically and internationally.

Developing countries provide the clearest view of the importance of the state. In this category, a broader range of variations in state activities across countries covaries with investors' behavior. Among developed nations' borrowers, the importance of national context declines as variations in state activities that affect investors occur over a more narrow range. Governments in developed nations are all above threshold in activities that influence international investors. Concerns about government activities retreat into the background and allow investors to consider primarily microeconomic threats to their investments. Investors accept the government component as nonthreatening and conducive to international investment.

As the evidence demonstrates, governments play important roles in access to global capital markets, but some state activities appear to influence international investors more than others and by different paths. Effective regulatory states that nurture economic activity and limit the temptation of public and private actors to cheat or defect on their obligations appear more critical than participatory states that encourage political participation, political rights, and civil liberties. The regulatory state is heavily endogenous to evaluations of country credit risk. Borrowers with governments that encourage bureaucratic professionalism, limit corruption, increase transparency and accountability, protect property rights of investors, resist extracting excessive rents, work to maintain a stable currency, avoid financial repression, and encourage stability discover greater access to global capital than borrowers whose governments fail to provide such public environments. Citizens of successful regulatory states are better positioned to take advantage of economic globalization. Many reforms associated with liberalization and deregulation address these particular activities of the state. Interpretations that see liberalization and deregulation as the dismantling and pushing back the boundaries of the state are misleading.[1]

Despite normative preferences, international investors seem less affected by democratic ideals, political rights, and civil liberties than with the stability of the investment environment and the activities of the regulatory state. Yet the participatory state still exerts important pressures upon international investors. The connections between borrowing outcomes and the participatory state are subtle. On average, and all else being equal, borrowers from more democratic states among the developing nations find better global capital access than borrowers from less democratic regimes in the same category. The notable systematic exception occurs in situations with extremely weak, corrupt, and perverse regulatory states. Apparently an authoritarian participatory state might stabilize investor expectations sufficiently in those cases when the regulatory state fails to provide even the smallest amount of insurance and stability for investors. But drawing the conclusion that authoritarian regimes contribute to global capital access in these cases proves to be inaccurate. These constitute a small number of cases. Most cases that fall in this category fail to attain any capital.

In the short term, international investors may prefer a politically repressive regime over a newly democratizing regime if democratization increases the responsiveness of governments to short-term pressures, which introduce greater variability and uncertainty into the investment context. In the long term, stable democratic governments develop mechanisms, institutions in the regulatory state, to shield policymakers from such pressures and reduce short-term variability in the policy arena. Add the advanced industrialized political economies to the mix and borrowers from the more democratic states prove to be far more successful in borrowing global capital. The participatory state affects international investors by different channels than the regulatory state. Whereas the regulatory state is heavily endogenous to estimations of country credit risk, the participatory state operates exogenously to those estimations. The participatory and regulatory components of the state provide international investors with different information about the safety of the investment environment and by separate routes.

Alternative Channels and Strategies

What can good, sincere borrowers in developing nations, who are burdened with costly national factors and a dilemma of adverse selection, do to distinguish themselves as good risks and obtain global capital? What can they do to signal international investors of their creditworthiness and to separate themselves from less capable and reliable borrowers in a muddy information environment? Merely asserting good creditworthiness is insufficient. All strategic borrowers will make similar claims, whether they are true or not. This exacerbates and confuses an already complicated information environment. Turning the problem around, how can investors constrain the risks generated by confusing national contexts?

An obvious, and facile, first response is to advocate and construct national regulatory institutions and policies that protect property rights, ensure contracts, improve the transparency of the investing environment, and impose sanctions upon those who misrepresent their true conditions. Public and private accounting standards, disclosure requirements, transparency rules, conflict of interest regulations, and compliance and adjudication mechanisms distinguish nations with successful domestic capital markets whose nationals find lower barriers to international capital. These regulatory fixes help pierce the veil of information engulfing borrowers in capital markets. Self-enforcing restraints that limit the state's ability to threaten the interests of investors also characterize such environments. Private consultants and international organizations such as the World Bank and the IMF advise governments undergoing economic reforms to develop regulatory institutions and frameworks amenable to market exchange.

The path to developing constructive institutions and policies includes at least several imposing obstacles to successful implementation. First, developing institutions that are stable and conducive to exchange is easier said than done. North (1990) notes that stable institutions conducive to economic growth and development took centuries to evolve in Europe. Such institutions vary dramatically across those states. A variety of institutional arrangements can perform the same functions and produce similar results. Rational institutional design by experts insulated from political realties inaccurately describes the process and history in the advanced industrial states. Even if governments and societies intentionally attempt to design such institutions, the likelihood and extent of success varies.

Institutional design presents tremendous problems and pitfalls. Policymakers have mixed motives and agendas in designing institutions. They encounter political pressures in their design. Many regulatory institutions overseeing financial markets emerged following financial crises that revealed weaknesses in previous arrangements. Economic crisis necessitated political response. Policymakers had to appear responsive regardless of the content of their responses. They may have sought long-term rational solutions that addressed the problems underpinning the crisis, but they also perceived institutional changes as tools to ameliorate political costs and as means of limiting public fear of markets. On top of all these problems, design is rife with potential for unintentional consequences.

Second, institutions and policies impose costs and allocate advantages. Negotiations and debates over their design are inherently competitive and potentially very contentious. Everyone in a society may prefer institutions and policies that create stable expectations, reduce uncertainty, and separate good from bad risks; but numerous arrangements may fulfill such a criteria. Debate and deliberations over which set of institutions and policy arrangements amount to a competition over the distribution of costs arising from the different arrangements—even if the net gain is positive for all. If enough alternatives exist that impose differential costs across mobilized interests in society, then institutional and policy design can cycle or be blocked. The resulting instability can reinforce rather than constrain a problematic information environment. Even with the best intentions, institutional and policy fixes prove tricky and difficult to achieve. This is a classic "social trap," wherein social structure leads actors to select strategies that produce suboptimal social outcomes (Miller 1992, chap. 1).

Third, the prescription for developing "good" institutions and policies implicitly assumes that governing elites wish to fix the problem and improve access to global capital for their nationals. A nation's governing elite may be comfortable with institutional and policy arrangements that penalize good economic risks in their ability to access overseas capital and produce economically suboptimal societal outcomes. Government decision makers may find inefficient, unstable, and perverse institutional arrangements and policies consistent with their narrow self-interests—at least in the short term. Such institutions and policies could fulfill the myopic needs of powerful interests in a society. Normatively and prescriptively uncomfortable for outside observers, a governing elite could be comfortable, and might even enhance their political survival in the short term, with institutions and policies that discourage international investors.

Political markets are imperfect. Questions of who gets represented, best accesses government decision makers, mobilizes for political activity, wins, and loses underpin political economy and political science. Imperfect political markets open the gates to strategic political action, which can advance particular interests at the expense of societal interests. International investment and economic growth may redistribute resources in domestic society and empower groups and individuals at the expense of the status quo. Institutions and policies that stabilize expectations to promote economic growth and development are good societal outcomes, but specific interests may prefer institutions and policies with different distributional characteristics, which redistribute resources to those specific interests regardless of the societal outcome. Global capital composes only a minor portion of the investment capital in any society. Most investment capital in any nation arises from domestic savings. A potential exists for rules and policies that create incentives for local capital accumulation and investment but impose disincentives on overseas capital.[2]

Considering the construction and design of institutions and policies only in the economic context of efficiency neglects the political microconditions and constraints surrounding their construction, the time horizons of the parties designing the institutions, and the foundations of a political economy that can lead to stable and socially suboptimal arrangements. Politically efficient outcomes can, and usually do, diverge from economically efficient outcomes. Clearly, government institutions and policies supply the most effective solution for good borrowers and international investors penalized by national contexts that nurture dilemmas of incomplete information and adverse selection. If successful, the overarching character of such policies and institutions limits variations in type and quantity of information. This simplifies the search routines of international investors by reducing ambiguities introduced by national context. But, if such public institutions and policies prove problematic due to (1) the difficulty of designing and implementing good policies and institutions, (2) the potential for producing suboptimal or unstable institutions and policies despite the best intentions of policymakers, or (3) the preferences of powerful organized interests in society to maintain suboptimal social outcomes and their ability to manipulate the political market, then can good borrowers and international investors find alternative strategies to constrain threatening national contexts?

Foreign direct investment (FDI) and joint ventures between local and overseas capital afford alternative channels to accessing overseas capital. FDI and joint ventures are distinct from local borrowers raising capital in global markets. With FDI and joint ventures, international capital becomes an integral part of the firm's operating management, not just as equity shareholders or creditors. This could exclude local ownership or occur as a mix of overseas and domestic ownership. By obtaining ownership or partial ownership of an economic enterprise, international investors can bypass some of the dilemmas presented by uncertain political institutions and policies. FDI and joint ventures help bypass some of the threats that arise from transparency, information, uncertainty, property rights, and contractual dilemmas in the public arena by resolving those dilemmas internal to the firm. Hierarchy and organization within a firm can limit risks arising from contracting problems and incomplete information that may plague local borrowers and unsettle international investors operating in a regulatory climate with inadequate disclosure, transparency, and contractual regulation (Miller 1992).

Effectively, FDI and joint ventures provide private institutional solutions to the some of the problems that effective public institutions and policies address. Many threats from the political arena can be sidestepped by private contractual arrangements and industrial organization, but some threats to international investors remain and cannot be negated by private institutional arrangements independent of an effective regulatory state. These continue to impinge upon FDI and joint ventures. Foreign owners and overseas capital must still consider the possibility of government actions that affect the value of their investments independent of private solutions to contracting, disclosure, and market transparency problems. Tax policy, monetary and exchange rate policies, differences in national treatment, controls restraining the outflow of capital, and the possibility of governments expropriating excessive shares of the firm still burden investment decisions.

A joint venture may contain such threats by pairing local with foreign interests,[3] but this depends on the standing of the local interests. Private solutions, which rely on the internal arrangements of a firm to compensate for threats to investment from the public arena, cannot resolve all those dilemmas from the public arena without taking into account the firm's interaction with the local authorities. The interaction between public and private is key even for private institutional solutions, depending upon the nature of the threat to investors. Empirical evidence suggests that FDI and joint ventures do furnish alternative pathways to garner overseas investment. Table 20 shows that foreign direct investment in developing countries nearly tripled from 1989 to 1994. The growth in FDI far exceeds the growth in global borrowing by nationals from developing nations over this same period. In fact, global borrowing by nationals from such nations stagnated during this period.

For most FDI and joint ventures, investors usually lend to multinational firms from developed economies. These firms enjoy established reputations. They have already proved successful and reliable. Despite the physical location of plants and operations, most MNCs are headquartered in states with effective regulatory mechanisms. Investors have recourse to regulatory and adjudication mechanisms of the state where the physical investment is located and to the state that hosts the headquarters the established industry. The established firm's home state extends a regulatory and adjudicatory umbrella that protects investors even if the site of physical operations is located elsewhere.

International development organizations (IDOs) furnish another alternative for borrowers in developing states. IDOs provide low-risk investment vehicles for international investors and a relatively low-cost source of capital for borrowers in developing nations. An IDO pools a variety of risky investments and projects from developing nations into one financial vehicle to borrow global capital. The IDO backs that instrument with its reputation and resources, but it also uses the pooled reputation and resources of its membership to assuage international investors. IDO membership usually includes developed as well as

TABLE 20. Foreign Direct Investment in Developing Nations

Year	Dollars (millions)
1989	28,622
1990	34,689
1991	40,889
1992	54,750
1993	73,350
1994	84,441
1982–86 (annual average)	19 billion
1983–88 (annual average)	19 billion
1987–91 (annual average)	31 billion

Source: UNCTAD 1995, annex table 1, 391–96.

developing nations. Pooling and diverse membership constrain lenders' risks, shroud an IDO in the reputation of its most reputable members, and allow it to borrow at terms equal to those received by the best credit risks. There is little chance of IDOs reneging on their obligations. Even if one member government fails to protect IDO capital, other member governments will act to guarantee the safety of the IDO instrument.

IDOs are capital sources of last resort for risky and uncertain borrowers. As such, they act as informal financial rating services. Private investors look at IDOs' willingness to provide capital as a market signal about contextual risk in a nation. Borrowers and countries that fail to obtain IDO assistance or, worse, renege on an IDO obligation, bear the stigma of being labeled an unacceptable risk in the capital market of last resort. Consequently, governments and borrowers that want to maintain the possibility of accessing global markets avoid rejecting IDO obligations. Their ability to define public reputations furnishes IDOs with informal enforcement power, which enables them to solicit guarantees and government policies as a condition of their assistance. IDO conditions may be politically unpopular, but failing to agree to them sends negative signals to private capital markets.

Yet IDOs fail to supply a wide-ranging remedy for borrowers burdened with national contexts or investors seeking higher rates of return in riskier instruments. Borrowers seeking IDO capital encounter fairly strict limitations. First, IDOs often limit their lending to government borrowers and particular types of projects. Their loans usually concentrate on government projects that develop infrastructure—physical or human. These can help stabilize national political-economic contexts and improve the attractiveness of such contexts for international investors, but private borrowers must rely predominantly on access to private capital markets—local or global. Second, IDO resources are extremely limited. Despite their ability to borrow at some of the lowest risk premiums in global markets, the size of such borrowings remains relatively small compared to the capital needs of those in developing nations. Third, IDO capital often carries a cost for local governments. IDO loans may act as a signal of creditworthiness, but they often carry externally imposed policy demands and protections that infringe upon national sovereignty.

The Future

The reemergence of global finance, the explosion in international capital mobility, increasing diversification and heterogeneity of global lending markets, and increasing interconnectedness of financial markets have ushered in a rapidly changing era of global economic relations. Technological and economic change contribute to these changes, but politics is integral to lowering national boundaries and unleashing technological and economic forces across borders. Unfortunately, everyone does not share the same capacity to participate and take advantage of these changes or engage the opportunities and risks they present to participants in local and global economies. Such changes produce a bifurcation in global capital access. This surely has implications for international tensions and the distribution of wealth, advantage, and power in the global arena.

This emerging bifurcation, or differential access to global capital, results not from conspiracy, hierarchical manipulation, or discrimination by the rich and powerful against the poor and weak. Instead, differences in access emerge from the bottom-up aggregation of decentralized decisions by investors in diverse global capital markets. International investors evaluate investment opportunities, looking to increase their returns within individually defined levels of acceptable risk. They consider contexts and the individual characteristics of borrowers in an environment of incomplete information. Local arenas, defined to a substantial extent by state arrangements, play fundamental roles in such evaluations. Variations in those local arrangements can lead to different global outcomes. Global outcomes are rooted in local activities.

Perhaps not the most important factors, national political arenas contribute significantly to who accesses global capital markets and by what instruments. This affects the availability of capital for economic growth and development, costs of capital, public well-being, and ultimately the competitiveness of nations' private and public economic enterprises. A monolithic approach to the state and its effects upon national context and the incentives for international investors is insufficient. Dismantling the state into several components reveals that international investors react most strongly to the regulatory state, internalizing it in their evaluations of country credit and economic risk. The participatory state influences international investors' assessments of contextual risks and uncertainty by alternative routes—almost independent of established appraisals of country credit risk.

Much remains unanswered and subject to future research. Limiting the domain to international commercial loans and bonds neglects other types of capital and channels through which borrowers access global capital for their economic enterprises. Capital is far more diverse than what has been presented here, but disaggregating international borrowing into bonds and loans reveals interesting differences in borrowing and the impact of governments. National differences affect not only who borrows but the strategies under which they borrow.

A future agenda should include further disaggregating capital to consider the relationship between different types of capital and public and private behavior. International and domestic capital markets are not converging into a single global capital market with a single price mechanism. Instead, capital markets are becoming increasingly diverse. What are the relationships between this growing diversity of capital markets and public-private arrangements? How do different types of capital constrain or expand the boundaries of state actors? Are some forms of capital more relevant to policymakers than others? Various pathways exist by which borrowers can access capital. What is the relationship between state arrangements and choice among those pathways? If capital markets serve as referenda on government activities, then what does this imply for notions of representation and democracy as these markets become larger, more influential, and their participants increasingly international? Who gets represented, or votes, in such referenda, and what are the implications for public policy?

Finally, the focus upon global markets in international political economy detracts attention from national markets. Domestic capital aggregation and allocation mechanisms continue to supply the bulk of investment capital in every nation. Even those economies most integrated into the global economy rely upon national markets for the vast majority of investment capital in society. A national bias exists in almost every investment portfolio. How does the interaction of public and private arenas affect such biases? Domestic and international markets need to be viewed as a comprehensive pool of capital, not as distinct pools. Borrowers and lenders can select among markets and instruments, depending upon their particular needs, or be limited in their selection depending upon their particular conditions. Why access international versus domestic capital? Are price and access the reasons for borrowing in one market rather than another, or might borrowers have others reasons? Similar questions apply to investors and their choices over where to place their surplus capital. The international portion of capital constitutes just the tip of the iceberg, but it is an expanding and ever more complicated iceberg.

APPENDIX A

Filling in the Gaps

Other important regulatory and political-institutional shifts encouraged private entrepreneurs and market participants and added impetus to the transformation of global finance.[1] Here I focus on three key political economies—those of the United States, Japan, and the United Kingdom. By the 1970s, regulatory arrangements overseeing financial sectors in industrialized nations were under full assault. In particular, rules in investment banking sectors and the regulatory boundaries that segment national financial markets had come under heavy scrutiny and pressures. The pressures resulted in intense policy competitions, leading to dramatic revisions in regulatory approaches and market operations. Table A1 chronicles many of these revisions.

Much of the public regulatory framework for financial sectors traces back to the Great Depression. Governments responded to the economic crises of the 1920s and 1930s by insulating and protecting the financial sectors of their national economies (Sobel 1994; Vietor 1987, 24, n. 66). Policymakers in the industrialized economies designed regulatory structures to address concerns raised by the failures of financial markets and firms during that era. The resulting regulations produced boundaries that advantaged some and disadvantaged others (Sobel 1994). This created incentives for diffuse actors with shared interests to organize for public policy ends and engage in political activities. Organized interests coalesced and formed coalitions to protect or attack the status quo. Following the 1960s, the balance began to shift from those favoring the status quo to those advocating, or at least more amenable to, change.

Prior to the Great Depression, the U.S. government took relatively little notice of investment banking activities specifically and the financial sector in general. This absence of federal oversight changed with the Depression. The stock market crash of 1929, banking crises of the 1930s, and misconduct by financial agents contributed to its severity and longevity. The public lost confidence in capital markets as financial firms, market institutions, and financial agents

TABLE A1. Chronology of Market Liberalization and Opening Reforms, 1966–94

Year	United States	United Kingdom	Japan
1966	Automated computer quotation system	Negotiable certificates	
1967	Foreign membership	1967–71 money market funds certificates	
1968	Centralized depository and clearing		
1969	Official repurchase market		
1970	Public ownership of members Warrants SIPC		
1971	NASDAQ computer quotation		
1972	IMM		
1973	Options introduced on CBOE Demise of IET and VFCR		Overseas stock listing
1974	Money market funds certificate		
1975	Deregulate commissions (May Day)		
1976	DOT computer quotation		Official repurchase market
1977	Treasury bond futures on CBOT		
1978	ITS	Options market	
1979		TALISMAN centralized clearing (1979–93) Relaxation of Foreign Exchange controls	Bond rating system Negotiable certificates
1980	NYFE opens		Relaxation of Foreign Exchange controls
1981			Warrants

Year			
1982	NYSE composite index futures ITS and NASDAQ link	LIFFE futures market Treasury bond futures	CORES, automated quotation, 2d section
1983	NYSE composite index option NYSE composite index futures option Standard & Poor's index option		
1984			Centralized depository and clearing Commercial paper and foreign issue
1985	AMEX and Toronto link	ITS, SEAQ International	Treasury bond futures Money market funds certificates Negotiable banker's acceptances Foreign membership
1986		Financial Services Act Public ownership of member firms Deregulate commissions Foreign membership SEAQ automated quotation Insider trading regulation Negotiable banker's acceptances Commercial paper	
1987	Stock market crash	Gilt warrants Stock market crash	Stock Futures 50 Stock market crash
1988	Coordinated circuit breakers installed 30 banks allowed to affiliate with securities firms for underwriting NYSE opens London office		TOPIX stock index future Nikkei stock index future
1989	Treasury bond futures on NYFE		
1990	Trade date + 1 requirement for completion of transactions		Insider trading regulation

(continued)

TABLE A1.—*Continued*

Year	United States	United Kingdom	Japan
1991	First off-hour trading sessions		Agreement to create SEC clone
1992			Ministry of Finance bill amends 16 laws, allowing increased crossover of commercial and investment banking
1993			3 commercial banks allowed to establish securities subsidiaries Securities houses allowed to establish trust bank subsidiaries
1994			Deregulate commissions (?)

Note:

AMEX	American Stock Exchange
CBOE	Chicago Board Options Exchange
CBOT	Chicago Board of Trade
DOT	Designated Order Turnaround System
IMM	Chicago International Money Market
ITS	Intermarket Trading System
LIFFE	London International Financial Futures Exchange
NASDAQ	National Association of Securities Dealers Automated Quotation
NYFE	New York Futures Exchange
NYSE	New York Stock Exchange
SEAQ	Stock Exchange Automated Quotation
SIPC	Securities Investors Protection Corporation
TOPIX	Tokyo Price Index

abused the public interest to advance private interests. Bankers and financiers were vilified. They came under populist attacks as elitists profiteering at the expense of the common man. The federal government developed a keen interest in financial markets with the increase in public pressure following the apparent abuse of privilege by financiers.

With Franklin Roosevelt's political campaign charge of "let in the light" in 1932, the incoming Democratic Congress and president targeted the financial services industry for reforms. Federal legislation of the 1930s defined the modern playing field for American financial services. The Securities Act of 1933 imposed regulatory requirements upon the primary issue market by specifying disclosure rules for the issuance and registration of securities. The 1933 Glass-Steagall Act forced banks to choose between commercial and investment banking. The Securities Exchange Act of 1934 extended the 1933 protections to secondary markets and required the registration of brokers, dealers, and national exchanges. The act created the Securities and Exchange Commission to regulate securities dealings, securities exchanges, and over-the-counter securities markets.

Primary oversight responsibility for commercial banking falls upon the Federal Reserve and the Comptroller of the Currency, which date to the Federal Reserve Act of 1913 and the National Bank Act of 1864, respectively. The National Currency Act of 1863 and the National Bank Act of 1864 provided a legal framework for federal supervision of commercial banks and for the chartering of national banks by the federal government. The Federal Reserve Act significantly broadened federal oversight of commercial banking and, more importantly, addressed the constraint of inelastic currency, which threatened private banks during periods of financial distress. When depositors doubted the safety of their banks, they withdrew their funds. If such behavior was widespread, then banks exhausted their cash reserves quickly and would try to liquidate their positions in loans and investment. This placed severe constraints upon lending and could act as a brake upon commercial activities. The Federal Reserve Act established a set of mechanisms to ensure outside cash reserves and protect against a liquidity crunch during a financial crisis. The Department of the Treasury; the Federal Deposit Insurance Corporation, which was established by the Banking Act of 1933; and, until the late 1980s, the Federal Savings and Loan Insurance Corporation shared major oversight responsibilities for commercial banking with the Federal Reserve and the Comptroller of the Currency. The Department of Justice, Securities and Exchange Commission, and Federal Trade Commission have some limited regulatory responsibilities in the commercial banking sector.

The McFadden Act of 1927 and the Banking Act of 1933 limited U.S. banks from establishing full service branches in more than one state. Ironically, the McFadden Act excluded some foreign banks from its provisions. They could open full service branches in more than one state. The Banking Act of 1935, Investment Advisors Act of 1940, Bankruptcy Act of 1938, and Public Utility Holding Company Act of 1935 rounded out the major legislation from this era. The Depression and the resulting banking legislation led to the end of "free banking" in the United States and harkened the onset of more oversight, more restrictive charting of banking institutions, more investor protections, and a more segmented financial environment. Ironically, the statutory changes left intact and even reinforced the noncompetitive practices of cartelization and price-fixing that had dominated U.S. investment banking since the Buttonwood Agreement in 1792 established the core principles for the NYSE.

In 1971, commercial bankers and institutional investors, long weary of the lack of price competition for investment banking services and after years of failed efforts, convinced the SEC to require negotiated commissions for large block trades. Commercial bankers and institutional investors lobbied unsuccessfully for decades to end the noncompetitive practices of the NYSE and to deregulate aspects of the investment banking arena. The coalition of commercial bankers and institutional investors finally succeeded, partly due to a mixture of events beyond their control (Sobel 1994). On May 1, 1975, May Day, all commissions became exposed to price competition. May Day touched off a revolution in U.S. investment banking.

Discount brokerage houses offering limited trading services appeared following the demise of fixed commissions with the May Day reforms. By not providing services such as research and investment advice, they reduced their fees. They charged commissions far below those charged by all members of the NYSE prior to May Day. Easy, lucrative commission earnings ceased. Many small research-oriented firms disappeared, and the industry underwent a shakeout that produced greater concentration among a limited number of firms. Investment banks shifted their efforts beyond serving as agents and brokering trades. Firms increasingly focused upon invention of financial instruments and strategies, underwriting, and dealing for their own accounts or portfolios. During this period, the NYSE approved public ownership of member firms. This allowed firms to expand their capital bases through public offerings, which increased their capital for underwriting and trading for their own accounts.[2]

Prodded by President Nixon, Congress repealed the Interest Equalization Tax and the Voluntary Foreign Credit Restraint Act in 1974. The end of these informal capital controls allowed more U.S. dollars into the global markets. This enhanced international capital liquidity and mobility. The United Kingdom and Japan soon followed, eliminating their capital controls in 1979 and 1980, respectively. By the early 1980s, most advanced industrialized nations had lifted their capital controls—removing national barriers to the richest, deepest, and most liquid markets.

Commercial bankers and institutional investors fought hard for further deregulation of investment banking, but interest groups also lobbied for reforms and deregulation in other parts of the financial arena. The Financial Institutions Regulatory and Interest Rate Control Act of 1978 provided regulators with additional powers and tools to attack anticompetitive concentrations of bank ownership and control. The International Banking Act of 1978 removed the special exemptions for foreign banks permitted under the McFadden Act of 1927. It leveled the playing field for foreign and domestic banks in the United States. Foreign banks exempted under the McFadden Act now had to adhere to the same branching and reserve requirements that applied to domestic institutions. The International Banking Act espoused a standard of national treatment for all banks located in the United States, foreign or domestic. All banks were to receive equal, nonpreferential treatment regardless of nationality. This constitutes a principle of nondiscrimination. The act encouraged competitive equality in U.S. markets, hoping that American banks would be afforded national treatment in their overseas operations.[3] The act rejected reciprocity as a guiding principle for international financial arrangements and signaled U.S. expectations for national treatment as an international standard. But reciprocity as a core principle did not die easily. It resurfaced several times, often implicitly aimed toward the Japanese.

The Depository Institutions Deregulation and Monetary Control Act of 1980 abetted the reregulatory trend in American markets. It created uniform reserve requirements across all depository institutions, phased out interest rate ceilings on savings and time deposits, expanded the arena for savings and loan associations, made Federal Reserve services available to all deposit-taking institutions, and permitted new financial instruments. The Garn–St. Germain Depository Institutions Act of 1982 continued the expansion of the lending and investment powers of federal thrift institutions begun in the Depository Institutions Deregulation and Monetary Control Act. Garn–St. Germain allowed competitive deposit accounts at financial institutions and increased the ceiling on national bank lending to individual borrowers. This proved to be a recipe for the savings and loan (S&L) crisis, which struck later in the decade.

The S&L crisis provoked several legislative responses. The Competitive Equality Banking Act of 1987 allocated resources to refinance the thrift insurance fund, which had been depleted by S&L failures. The act placed the full faith and credit of the United States behind insured deposits in bank and thrift institutions. It enlarged the emergency acquisition powers of the government to take over failing banks and thrifts and tightened some of the regulatory provisions that previous reforms had eased. The Financial Institutions Reform, Recovery, and Enforcement Act of 1989 provided more financing to ease the S&L crisis, legislated tougher regulatory and capital standards for thrift institutions, created a new regulatory structure for thrifts, increased deposit insurance premiums to protect against future capital inadequacies in the depositor insurance programs, and allowed bank holding companies to procure savings associations. The 1987 and 1989 acts imposed tougher standards and more federal oversight. They sought to rebuild confidence, ward off a banking crisis, and enhance competitive banking. The reforms contributed to a deepening of American financial markets.

As policymakers shifted market boundaries and constraints with their reforms, aggressive participants invented strategies to take advantage of the changing playing field. Markets in junk bonds and mortgage-based securities exploded in the 1980s. Trading stock portfolios (standardized baskets of stocks) in a single execution began on the NYSE in 1989. The October 1987 market crash proved to be a temporary hiccup, as American investment markets expanded rapidly. Jealous of rapid and lucrative growth in the investment banking sector, other segments of the American financial industry intensified their attacks on the regulatory walls dividing U.S. financial services.

Beginning in the 1960s, policy entrepreneurs gradually found greater success in attacking the regulatory constraints that enforced separation in the American financial services. Critics assailed government-enforced market segmentation as anticompetitive, as damaging to American financial institutions, and for imposing costs upon American consumers. Supporters of deregulation argued that government restraints on competition within American markets threatened the competitive posture of American financial institutions in global markets. Commercial banking interests employed the threat of international competition to push for reforms. This international threat routinely appears in the rhetoric supporting repeal of the Glass-Steagall Act. Incremental reforms have chipped away at the foundations of Glass-Steagall.

Japanese securities markets date to the Stock Exchange Ordinance of 1878, but investment banking remained a weak sector compared to Japanese commercial banking until the 1970s. Investment banking markets existed as primarily speculative outlets. They grew slowly and were undercapitalized compared to commercial banking. Most funding for capital investment came through formal business networks called *zaibatsu*. *Zaibatsu* were industrial groups that included firms from different economic sectors. Group linkages facilitated lending between members, preferential contracts, and close consultation. Commercial banks sat at the center of the *zaibatsus*' capital allocation mechanisms and consequently exercised tremendous influence over which industries received capital and at what price. As the capital demands of heavy industry increased in the interwar years, companies began to bypass their *zaibatsus* and seek capital directly from the public through stock and bond issues. Following World War II, American occupation authorities promoted this trend as they sought to democratize ownership and dilute the influence of the prewar aggressive military-industrial elite. U.S. occupation authorities outlawed *zaibatsus*. The Japanese flattered their occupiers through mimicry by adopting the Securities and Exchange Law in 1948, which enforced the separation of investment and commercial banking.[4]

Despite U.S. efforts to reform Japanese financial services as part of a democratization scheme, the Japanese financial sector remained highly protected, hierarchical, and centralized. Where the Americans had been unsuccessful, time and Japanese initiatives began to succeed. Starting in the 1970s, the Ministry of Finance (MoF) began enacting policies that dismantled national barriers to capital flows, blurred market boundaries, relaxed constraints on competition, and deepened the Japanese financial infrastructure (Horne 1985; Moran 1991; Rosenbluth 1989; Sobel 1994; Suzuki 1987). Banks and investment houses introduced new instruments as MoF decisions removed constraints and generated opportunities. The innovations brought commercial and investment banking sectors into increasing competition. With the reduction of barriers to exit and entrance, Japanese capital increasingly sought opportunities overseas, and foreign capital began flowing into Japanese markets. Japanese financial firms stepped up their overseas activities, and foreign financial firms sought increased access to Japanese domestic markets.

In 1971, the government permitted yen-denominated foreign bond issues called samurai bonds. In November 1974, the MoF allowed Japanese corporations to issue corporate bonds overseas. This enabled Japanese borrowers to access the euro markets and evade high domestic issuance costs. The yen-denominated offshore bond market exploded. With high domestic issuance costs, all but a small minority of private Japanese bond issues shifted to the euro markets. Japanese investors followed Japanese corporate borrowers. This pumped capital into the euro markets. The government approached the bond market with large offerings beginning in 1975. This fed a threefold expansion in that market over the next decade. In April 1979, a new block trading system for government bonds reduced trading costs and stimulated institutional interest. In the same month, the MoF permitted nonresidents to trade *gensaki* bonds, or repos.[5]

The 1971 Law on Foreign Securities Firms allowed foreign investment houses to participate in securities trading through branches in Japan. The government then lifted a ban on Japanese investment in foreign securities and initiated a book entry clearing system to simplify transactions. In April 1973, the Tokyo Stock Exchange began listing samurai bonds, and in December it opened the Foreign Stock Section with six foreign listings. In December 1980, revisions to the Foreign Exchange and Foreign Trade Control Law ended capital controls and allowed Japanese securities firms to engage directly in foreign exchange transactions with foreigners. This removed a major obstacle to cross-border capital movements. Japanese participation in the euro markets received another large boost.

Amendments to the Securities and Exchange Law in June 1981 allowed commercial banking institutions to trade public bonds. The introduction of new bond funds in October 1981 and medium-term bonds in January 1985 combined with other regulatory changes to encourage further expansion of the government bond market. Jumbo investment funds[6] appeared in July 1982 and interest reinvestment funds in November. Banking institutions began publicly selling long-term government bonds in April 1983, and securities houses began lending money from the sale of government bonds in June. The changes provided investors with more options, blurred the boundaries separating the investment and commercial banking sectors, and created increased competition. Liberalization and the deepening of the Japanese bond markets coincided, not surprisingly, with increased deficit spending by the government. Increased depth and liquidity in these markets attract investors.

Japanese policy entrepreneurs used foreign pressures, or *gaiatsu,* as a strategic tool to push for liberalization of Japanese financial markets. At the November 1983 Tokyo Summit, President Reagan and Prime Minister Nakasone established the Yen/Dollar Working Group to examine the yen/dollar exchange rate, internationalization of the yen, treatment of foreign financial institutions in Japan, and the liberalization of Japan's financial markets (Frankel 1984). In April 1984, foreign securities firms became eligible to participate in government bond underwriting syndicates and currency swaps. The government lifted restrictions limiting conversion of borrowed foreign capital into yen, and foreigners obtained the right to issue and lead manage Euro-yen bond offerings. Also that month the MoF permitted securities houses to sell foreign certificates of deposit (CDs) and commercial paper. Securities houses gained access to the domestic CD market in June 1985, which blurred the boundaries separating commercial and investment banking further and generated more competitive pressures across segments of the Japanese financial services industry.

Other shifts also helped liberalization. In May 1984, the Diet created a central depository and book-clearing system to replace the physical transferal of securities certificates. These mechanisms reduce delays in transferring certificates of ownership, which enhances market efficiency and encourages participation. In April 1985, the TSE revised its commission rate structure downward. In August 1985, the MoF allowed foreign currency–denominated foreign bonds and soon after permitted dual-currency bonds. The TSE amended its rules to permit foreign members in April 1982. The first foreign members were admitted in February 1986. New efficiencies, changes in national barriers to entry, new instruments, and new participants attracted capital from more traditional savings mechanisms, some of which found the offshore markets.

Japanese reforms and expansion continued. The Diet amended the Securities and Exchange Law in June 1985 to allow financial futures—more than ten years after their introduction in the United States. Revisions in the Securities Exchange Law in 1988 imposed new insider-trading and transparency regulations as of April 1, 1989. These reforms elevated insider trading to a criminal offense, required greater disclosure of insider transactions, and increased market surveillance. The statutes separating commercial and investment banking, Article 65, are under an attack similar to that upon Glass-Steagall in the United States. In the latter half of 1995, the Bank of Japan reduced already low interest rates and the MoF further reduced the remaining barriers to moving funds offshore. A Japanese big bang on April 1, 1998, introduced more major reforms as this book went to press.

The third major international financial center, the United Kingdom, also has had a history of segmented financial services. Like most industrialized states the United Kingdom emerged from World War II with restrictive controls on cross-border capital flows.[7] But this was a notable change from London's history as a major financial center. A private club environment characterized British financial services and regulation for centuries. A small clique of insiders policed and protected British financial markets. The government relied heavily upon informal self-regulation, which took advantage of small group size, frequent interactions among a small core of influential financial institutions, and jointly held beliefs concerning acceptable behavior. The Bank of England assisted these insiders in exercising self-regulation. Violating the informal standards carried threats of within-group sanctions or exclusion from dealings with other members of the club. British global financial predominance had emerged by the 1800s. The United Kingdom had advanced well down the road of global finance by the turn of the nineteenth century, and approximately 50 percent of British savings were invested overseas in 1913 (Nomura Research Institute 1986, 54).

The 1929 crash encroached little upon the informal British regulatory approach. But the postwar election of a Labour government brought important changes when the government issued securities to fund nationalization of some industries. This stimulated government securities markets. After World War II, the Capital Issues Committee limited the issue of corporate securities. This permitted more government influence over private investment during postwar rebuilding. These restrictions amounted to practicing industrial policy through credit allocation mechanisms. They also afforded the government a market advantage in issuing its securities by limiting alternatives for investors. Capital shifted back into the private corporate securities markets with the demise of these restrictions in 1959. The Prevention of Fraud Investments Act of 1958 provided a loose framework for investor protection in such securities dealings.

London began experiencing major changes with the euro market expansion in the 1960s. As U.S. MNCs sought capital in overseas markets American financial institutions followed their industry clients and established branches in London to initially issue dollar-denominated securities in euro markets. London became the center of these markets. Other important changes soon followed. In 1976, the Restrictive Trade Practices Order benignly assigned oversight responsibilities for the London Stock Exchange to a consumer watchdog agency, the Office of Fair Trading (OFT) under the auspices of the Department of Trade and Industry (DTI). The OFT filed a complaint with the Restrictive Practices Court in 1978, claiming that many LSE practices were restrictive and noncompetitive. The complaint focused upon fixed minimum brokerage commissions, the single-capacity system separating brokers and jobbers, and membership restrictions. Government and LSE lawyers compromised in 1983. The LSE would end minimum commissions and the government removed the LSE from the Restrictive Trade Practices jurisdiction. In April 1984, fixed commissions on government and overseas securities ended. Price competition hit the rest of the market with Big Bang in October 1986.

Changes in financial services and regulation in the period preceding the Big Bang contributed to the forces driving it. In 1979, Prime Minister Thatcher lifted controls on cross-border capital movements and competition from overseas financial firms. Foreign firms' competitiveness in London improved immediately. The end of fixed commissions and the lowering of restrictions upon foreign financial firms revealed the capital inadequacies of British financial institutions. U.S. firms enjoyed a tremendous capitalization advantage over most U.K. firms. This provided advantages in underwriting issues, acting as dealers, market making, and dealing with large institutional traders. Before April 1982, rules limited nonmembers' capital participation in LSE member firms to 10 percent. This limit jumped to 29 percent in April and 100 percent in March 1986. Financial institutions that had been excluded from the LSE positioned for Big Bang by purchasing smaller LSE firms. Competition became less restrained.

The changing financial services sector exposed shortcomings in the investor protections provided by the Prevention of Fraud Investments Act of 1958. Many financial innovations that had occurred since 1958 fell outside the boundaries of the 1958 act. The act covered dealings in securities, but it neglected futures, investment management, and financial management outside of securities. Many investors unexpectedly found themselves unprotected against institutional failures and the negligence of firms. Financial failures highlighted these gaps, undermined public confidence, and precipitated a financial crisis.

In 1981, the Department of Trade and Industry appointed a law professor, L. C. B. Gower, to review financial regulation. Gower proposed sweeping reforms of the financial regulatory framework. In January 1985, the government released a separate but similar report. Parliament responded and passed the Financial Services Act (FSA) of 1986. The FSA provided for a new regulatory structure that moved dramatically away from the old informal regulatory system and back room self-regulation. Financial service activities became far more formally regulated than before. The new framework looks more like that of the United States than the framework it replaced.

The FSA attempts to balance investor protection and efficient markets. These two goals sometimes conflict. The FSA establishes more explicit protections for investors and casts a regulatory net over all investment-related activities. It protects against criminal activity, requires that those in investment businesses be "fit and proper," and extends protections into noncriminal areas such as incompetence and negligence. It specifies requirements for disclosure, advertising, solicitation, compensation, business-client relations, clients' interests versus firms' interests, contractual arrangements, segregation and protection of investors' capital, complaint and arbitration procedures, and record keeping. The system imposes new reporting requirements upon financial firms, but the greater transparency and disclosure requirements reduce uncertainty and barriers to entry for investors.

The FSA constrains investor uncertainty and provides selective incentives to investor participation by formalizing the regulatory structure, establishing a skill and competency threshold for those engaged in the investment business, and requiring greater disclosure of information. British reforms and liberalization attacked the old hierarchy, enhanced market transparency, provoked competitive pressures, and opened national doors to capital flows and foreign firms. Regulatory changes improved foreign access to the London markets and provided assurances that the markets were fair. With London already a major center of euro market trading, the reforms reinforced its position as a major international financial center and provided added impetus to increasing globalization.

Data Appendix

Figure B1a-b, table B1, and table B2 follow this discussion. Figure B1 supplies histograms, box plots, density plots, and normal q-q plots for most of the independent variables. I discuss these techniques in chapter 6, where I present similar explorations of the dependent variables and residuals from the linear model. These techniques offer powerful visualizations of the structure of these variables. These are insightful given the problems within the structure of the data that complicate the analyses in this book. Simple descriptive summary statistics of the distributions fail to convey the richness obtained by the interocular traumatic impact of these visualizations (Berkson 1942). Table B1 contains many of the data used in the analyses. I include only data for developing nations. This category has the greatest variation on all the variables and consequently provides the greatest leverage. The transitional economies are almost as interesting, but data are unavailable for some of the variables.

Table B2 reports least trimmed squares robust regression results for two models using the same variables as the loess regression analyses in chapter 7. I present the results for the sake of comparison. Note that the loess results substantially outperform the comparable least trimmed squares models. These differences underscore the remaining oddities in the structure of the data. The loess regression uses only a specified portion of the observations surrounding each point to produce a predicted value. The technique weights most strongly those observations closest to the point being estimated and then with decreasing weight on observations moving away from the point being estimated. The least trimmed squares approach uses all the observations and weights most strongly those observations closest to the point being estimated. Obviously, including all the observations to predict each point obscures shifts in the data and hides information.

The data on international borrowing, the foundation of the dependent variable throughout the book, are OECD data. These were originally released as part of the *OECD Financial Statistics Monthly*. After spending much time compiling and entering these data by hand, the OECD released them on diskette as part of a longer historical series. In this appendix, I include only the variable for total international borrowing, which includes all intermediate- to long-term bond issues and commercial loans. These include only debt instruments, not equity placements or private placements. The historical series and the *OECD Financial Statistics Monthly* present a breakdown by instrument and nationality of borrower. For more information on these data, consult the *Methodological Supplement to the OECD Financial Statistics Monthly*.

The measures for country credit risk come from surveys conducted by *Institutional Investor* and *Euromoney*. These financial trade publications target investment and financial professionals. They publish these measures as part of annual surveys of country credit risk. The measures use similar metrics but different methodologies in their construction. The measure for uncertainty used here is constructed from the two measures of country credit risk. Chapter 6 supplies a thorough discussion of the measures of country credit risk and the methodology used to construct the measure of uncertainty.

I include the measure for the participatory state in this appendix. Unfortunately, I must omit the measures for the regulatory state. I purchased the ICRG variables used in the construction of the regulatory state measure from Political Risk Services of Syracuse, New York. It holds proprietary rights for these data. These data are relatively inexpensive. I constructed the participatory state measure from data made available from Freedom House in its surveys on political rights and civil liberties. For those seeking an alternative to the Freedom House measures, Polity III furnishes a similar set of measures (Jaggers and Gurr 1996). These correlate highly with the Freedom House measures.

The current Freedom House surveys and a description of their methodologies are available at www.freedomhouse.org on the World Wide Web. I additively combine the scores on the political rights and civil liberties surveys to produce a single index for the participatory state. I only include the additive index and not its components. Freedom House uses checklists to evaluate political rights and civil liberties. The current political rights checklist includes the following questions:[1]

1. Is the head of state and/or head of government or other chief authority elected through free and fair elections?
2. Are the legislative representatives elected through free and fair elections?
3. Are there fair electoral laws, equal campaigning opportunities, fair polling and honest tabulation of ballots?

4. Are the voters able to endow their freely elected representatives with real power?
5. Do the people have the right to organize in different political parties or other competitive political groupings of their choice, and is the system open to the rise and fall of these competing parties or groupings?
6. Is there a significant opposition vote, de facto opposition power, and a realistic possibility for the opposition to increase its support or gain power through elections?
7. Are the people free from domination by the military, foreign powers, totalitarian parties, religious hierarchies, economic oligarchies or any other powerful group?
8. Do cultural, ethnic, religious and other minority groups have reasonable self-determination, self-government, autonomy or participation through informal consensus in the decision-making process?

The survey may include two additional discretionary political rights questions:

1. For traditional monarchies that have no parties or electoral process, does the system provide for consultation with the people, encourage discussion of policy, and allow the right to petition the ruler?
2. Is the government or occupying power deliberately changing the ethnic composition of a country or territory so as to destroy a culture or tip the political balance in favor of another group?

The civil liberties checklist includes:

1. Are there free and independent media, literature and other cultural expressions? (Note: In cases where the media are state-controlled but offer pluralistic points of view, the Survey gives the system credit.)
2. Is there open public discussion and free private discussion?
3. Is there freedom of assembly and demonstration?
4. Is there freedom of political or quasi-political organization? (Note: This includes political parties, civic associations, ad hoc issue groups and so forth.)
5. Are citizens equal under the law, with access to an independent, nondiscriminatory judiciary, and are they respected by the security forces?
6. Is there protection from political terror, and from unjustified imprisonment, exile or torture, whether by groups that support or oppose the system, and freedom from war or insurgency situations? (Note: Free-

dom from war and insurgency situations enhances the liberties in a free society, but the absence of wars and insurgencies does not in itself make an unfree society free.)

7. Are there free trade unions and peasant organizations or equivalents, and is there effective collective bargaining?

8. Are there free professional and other private organizations?

9. Are there free businesses or cooperatives?

10. Are there free religious institutions and free private and public religious expressions?

11. Are there personal social freedoms, which include such aspects as gender equality, property rights, freedom of movement, choice of residence, and choice of marriage and size of family?

12. Is there equality of opportunity, which includes freedom from exploitation by or dependency on landlords, employers, union leaders, bureaucrats or any other type of denigrating obstacle to a share of legitimate economic gains?

13. Is there freedom from extreme government indifference and corruption?

TABLE B1. Variables

Nation	Year	Institutional Investor	Euromoney	Borrowing (mil. 1994 $)	Participatory State	Uncertainty	Population (thousands)
Algeria	1982	54.7	55	131.4	12	9.18	19,862
Algeria	1983	55.4	68.3	1,714.9	12	3.44	20,495
Algeria	1984	53.5	66.8	239.9	12	3.79	21,173
Algeria	1985	53.3	60.05	1,449.7	12	2.76	21,848
Algeria	1986	50.4	55	1,344.3	12	4.98	22,497
Algeria	1987	43.8	37	471.5	12	16.54	23,124
Algeria	1988	39.1	49	795.4	12	0.05	23,758
Algeria	1989	39.5	42	397.1	11	7.34	24,374
Algeria	1990	38.4	—	0	10	—	25,003
Algeria	1991	34.2	31.9	61.4	8	12.27	25,680
Angola	1982	16.4	25.5	0	14	1.3	7,990
Angola	1983	13.9	19.5	8.7	14	4.86	8,202
Angola	1984	13.4	33.5	12.1	14	9.63	8,400
Angola	1985	13.7	25.55	91	14	1.39	8,605
Angola	1986	13.6	26	0	14	1.94	8,841
Angola	1987	11.1	16	0	14	5.62	9,084
Angola	1988	11.2	19	4.9	14	2.72	9,334
Angola	1989	11.9	23	0	14	0.6	9,590
Angola	1990	13.5	25.6	115	14	1.63	
Angola	1991	14.5	24	75	14	0.94	
Argentina	1982	36.7	37.5	1,516.4	11	9.11	29,089
Argentina	1983	28.2	43	1,750	11	4.69	29,507
Argentina	1984	23.2	18.5	0	6	14.93	29,921

(continued)

TABLE B1.—*Continued*

Nation	Year	Institutional Investor	Euromoney	Borrowing (mil. 1994 $)	Participatory State	Uncertainty	Population (thousands)
Argentina	1985	22.7	23.35	3,700	4	9.6	30,331
Argentina	1986	24.9	29	17	4	6.09	30,737
Argentina	1987	25.1	31	2,305	3	4.29	31,139
Argentina	1988	23.2	30	14	3	3.43	31,536
Argentina	1989	19	28	0	3	1.34	31,931
Argentina	1990	18.3	33.3	0	3	4.65	32,322
Argentina	1991	20.2	34.9	750	4	4.39	
Bangladesh	1982	15.2	31.5	0	7	5.87	90,725
Bangladesh	1983	12.6	34.9	0	10	11.81	92,804
Bangladesh	1984	13.9	32.5	0	11	8.14	94,929
Bangladesh	1985	16.3	19.4	0	11	7.3	97,100
Bangladesh	1986	18	18	0	10	10.36	99,294
Bangladesh	1987	18.2	22	0	9	6.55	101,509
Bangladesh	1988	17.6	28	0	9	0.03	103,744
Bangladesh	1989	18.4	38	0	9	9.25	106,000
Bangladesh	1990	17.8	39.3	128	8	11.14	108,275
Bangladesh	1991	16.4	28.7	0	10	1.9	110,564
Barbados	1982	—	52	0	2	—	251
Barbados	1983	—	86.9	0	2	—	252
Barbados	1984	30.9	44	0	2	3.05	253
Barbados	1985	31.9	50	44.2	3	8.07	253
Barbados	1986	33.2	51	99.8	3	7.8	254
Barbados	1987	33.7	43	45.5	2	0.68	255
Barbados	1988	34.3	61	40.1	2	16.73	256

Barbados	1989	38.2	56	25	2	7.92	257
Barbados	1990	38.3	56.3	57.9	2	8.13	—
Barbados	1991	38.2	49.4	20	2	1.32	—
Bolivia	1982	14.9	28	0	12	2.67	5,878
Bolivia	1983	10.2	31.1	0	5	10.35	6,030
Bolivia	1984	7.7	9.6	0	5	8.71	6,185
Bolivia	1985	7.3	10	0	5	7.91	6,342
Bolivia	1986	8	16	0	5	2.6	6,502
Bolivia	1987	8.1	13	0	5	5.7	6,665
Bolivia	1988	9.7	21	0	5	0.74	6,831
Bolivia	1989	9	25	0	5	5.43	7,000
Bolivia	1990	13.2	28.3	0	5	4.63	7,172
Bolivia	1991	15	27.7	0	5	2.27	7,347
Brazil	1982	52.2	45.3	7,429.4	7	16.44	126,962
Brazil	1983	37.6	—	4,628.5	6		129,853
Brazil	1984	29.7	30.1	6,520.6	6	9.68	132,730
Brazil	1985		20	0	6		135,564
Brazil	1986	35.2	35	350	5	10.15	138,357
Brazil	1987	31.7	38	0	4	3.73	141,105
Brazil	1988	28.4	40	5,200	4	1.49	143,803
Brazil	1989	27.8	32	100	5	5.92	146,449
Brazil	1990	26.5	45	0	4	8.34	149,042
Brazil	1991	26.5	38.2	1,479.6	5	1.54	151,428
Cameroon	1982	35	24.6	20.7	12	20.35	9,205
Cameroon	1983	37.3	26.5	166.5	12	20.7	9,457
Cameroon	1984	35.8	41.7	0	12	4.03	9,710
Cameroon	1985	37.7	30.85	46	13	16.74	9,969

(continued)

TABLE B1.—Continued

Nation	Year	Institutional Investor	Euromoney	Borrowing (mil. 1994 $)	Participatory State	Uncertainty	Population (thousands)
Cameroon	1986	38.4	36	0	13	12.27	10,244
Cameroon	1987	36.7	42	100	12	4.61	10,536
Cameroon	1988	33.6	38	0	12	5.59	10,846
Cameroon	1989	31.1	40	0	12	1.15	11,175
Cameroon	1990	27	37	100	12	0.14	11,524
Cameroon	1991	23.1	31.6	0	12	1.74	11,881
Chile	1982	49.4	53.3	1,244	11	5.71	11,516
Chile	1983	32.8	67.3	1,401.1	11	24.5	11,714
Chile	1984	26.4	9.1	780	11	27.46	11,917
Chile	1985	24.6	11.6	1,085	11	23.2	12,122
Chile	1986	25.1	21	0	11	14.29	12,329
Chile	1987	26.3	20	0	11	16.46	12,538
Chile	1988	28.1	54	151	11	15.78	12,748
Chile	1989	33.6	41	0	9	2.59	12,961
Chile	1990	37.8	54.4	285	7	6.71	13,173
Chile	1991	41.1	50.3	0	4	0.61	13,386
Colombia	1982	56.1	66.2	618.9	5	0.65	27,703
Colombia	1983	51	37.9	459	5	22.67	28,301
Colombia	1984	44.9	58	364.3	5	3.38	28,896
Colombia	1985	38.4	55.7	1,052	5	7.43	29,481
Colombia	1986	39.2	42	240	5	7.05	30,058
Colombia	1987	39.2	39	136.6	5	10.05	30,627
Colombia	1988	37.9	52	1,000	5	4.22	31,189
Colombia	1989	36.9	37	1,641	5	9.81	31,746

Country	Year						
Colombia	1990	33.7	45	0	7	1.32	32,300
Colombia	1991	36.6	40	200	7	6.51	32,841
Congo	1982	16.8	29.8	127	13	2.61	1,748
Congo	1983	17	21	27	13	6.38	1,811
Congo	1984	17.1	40.8	13.1	13	13.32	1,847
Congo	1985	16.7	31.75	0	13	4.66	1,938
Congo	1986	15.8	33	0	13	6.79	2,003
Congo	1987	15.9		0	13		2,069
Congo	1988	14.8		0	13		2,136
Congo	1989	13	27	0	13	3.52	2,205
Congo	1990	14	27.4	0	13	2.95	2,276
Congo	1991	14.1	24.5	0	12	0.05	2,350
Costa Rica	1982	14.2	25.4	0	2	0.75	2,425
Costa Rica	1983	12.4	48.5	215	2	25.61	2,498
Costa Rica	1984	14.6	29.6	0	2	4.56	2,570
Costa Rica	1985	15.7	19.95	0	2	6.16	2,642
Costa Rica	1986	17	22	0	2	5.38	2,713
Costa Rica	1987	17	23	0	2	4.38	2,784
Costa Rica	1988	17.9	27	0	2	1.26	2,854
Costa Rica	1989	18.4	33	0	2	4.25	2,924
Costa Rica	1990	21.1	35	0	2	3.62	2,994
Costa Rica	1991	22.5	35.1	0	2	2.35	3,064
Cote d'Ivoire	1982	38	53.7	491.1	10	5.82	8,777
Cote d'Ivoire	1983	35.3	55.7	20	10	10.45	9,076
Cote d'Ivoire	1984	29.4	37.4	0	10	2.09	9,399
Cote d'Ivoire	1985	26	19.2	152.5	11	16.97	9,755
Cote d'Ivoire	1986	27.5	27	0	11	10.63	10,141

(continued)

TABLE B1.—*Continued*

Nation	Year	Institutional Investor	Euromoney	Borrowing (mil. 1994 $)	Participatory State	Uncertainty	Population (thousands)
Cote d'Ivoire	1987	26.5	31	0	11	5.66	10,552
Cote d'Ivoire	1988	25.3	40	0	11	4.52	10,985
Cote d'Ivoire	1989	22	41	0	12	8.74	11,438
Cote d'Ivoire	1990	19.6	25.2	0	11	4.72	11,902
Cote d'Ivoire	1991	17.2	24.2	0	10	3.38	12,360
Cyprus	1982	34	71.2	70		27.22	645
Cyprus	1983	35.3	85.5	0		40.25	653
Cyprus	1984	33.1	52.4	10		9.3	660
Cyprus	1985	38.6	63.15	27		14.68	666
Cyprus	1986	39	52	99.7		3.14	673
Cyprus	1987	40.4	51	89.6		0.78	680
Cyprus	1988	43.1	70	11.9		17.14	687
Cyprus	1989	46.3	67	37.9		11.02	695
Cyprus	1990	46.3	70	10.2		14.02	702
Cyprus	1991	45.7	53.6	120		1.8	710
Dominican Republic	1982	20.5	26.2	0	5	4.6	5,982
Dominican Republic	1983	15.2	33.2	0	3	7.57	6,129
Dominican Republic	1984	13.5	8.6	0	3	15.37	6,275
Dominican Republic	1985	13.9	16.55	0	4	7.81	6,416
Dominican Republic	1986	14.5	23	0	4	1.94	6,554
Dominican Republic	1987	15.5	22	0	4	3.92	6,688
Dominican Republic	1988	15.3	24	0	4	1.72	6,820
Dominican Republic	1989	17.1	35	0	4	7.52	6,948
Dominican Republic	1990	17	28	0	4	0.62	7,074

Dominican Republic	1991	17.1	28.6	0	5	1.12	7,197
Ecuador	1982	43.1	43.9	64.2	4	8.96	8,588
Ecuador	1983	28.2	58.7	441.1	4	20.39	8,826
Ecuador	1984	25	12.5	0	4	22.69	9,067
Ecuador	1985	26.4	11.25	200	4	25.31	9,309
Ecuador	1986	26.7	30	220	5	6.85	9,553
Ecuador	1987	24.1	20	32	5	14.31	9,798
Ecuador	1988	21.4	28	0	5	3.68	10,046
Ecuador	1989	17.8	31	0	4	2.84	10,295
Ecuador	1990	17.6	30	0	4	2.03	10,547
Ecuador	1991	19.6	31.6	0	4	1.68	10,782
Egypt	1982	35.7	60	498.4	11	14.36	43,036
Egypt	1983	33.5	9	149	10	34.49	44,169
Egypt	1984	32.7	56.5	47.9	10	13.79	45,330
Egypt	1985	32.7	46.55	157.7	8	3.84	46,511
Egypt	1986	29.5	43	0	8	3.42	47,694
Egypt	1987	23.5	29	0	9	4.73	48,879
Egypt	1988	23.1	31	0	9	2.34	50,064
Egypt	1989	24	38	500	9	3.78	51,246
Egypt	1990	22.4	39.6	0	9	6.95	52,426
Egypt	1991	23.4	34.5	0	9	0.87	53,602
El Salvador	1982	7.1	23.1	0	10	5.38	4,617
El Salvador	1983	6.2	19.6	0	9	2.76	4,649
El Salvador	1984	6.3	6.2	0	9	10.74	4,687
El Salvador	1985	6.5	4	0	8	13.13	4,739
El Salvador	1986	7.4		0	6		4,846
El Salvador	1987	8.1		0	7		4,934

(continued)

TABLE B1.—Continued

Nation	Year	Institutional Investor	Euromoney	Borrowing (mil. 1994 $)	Participatory State	Uncertainty	Population (thousands)
El Salvador	1988	9.2	20	0	7	0.23	4,967
El Salvador	1989	9.8	27	0	6	6.64	5,065
El Salvador	1990	10.9	25.7	0	7	4.27	5,172
El Salvador	1991	11	22.2	0	7	0.67	5,278
Ethiopia	1982	9.6	23.7	0	14	3.54	39,776
Ethiopia	1983	9	37.8	0	14	18.23	40,859
Ethiopia	1984	8.4	30.2	0	14	11.21	42,040
Ethiopia	1985	8.5	6.8	0	14	12.29	43,350
Ethiopia	1986	10.8	16	0	14	5.33	44,769
Ethiopia	1987	8.9	15	100	14	4.48	
Ethiopia	1988	7.8	20	0	13	1.6	
Ethiopia	1989	7.4	25	0	13	6.99	
Ethiopia	1990	8.1	19.3	306.7	14	0.6	
Ethiopia	1991	7.2	13.9	0	14	3.92	
Gabon	1982	35.3	42.7	33.2	12	2.55	875
Gabon	1983	36		0.4	12		916
Gabon	1984	36.6	41.9	0	12	4.61	957
Gabon	1985	40.2	34.55	60	12	15.48	997
Gabon	1986	40.4	43	0	12	7.22	1,023
Gabon	1987	34.5	35	50	12	9.46	1,050
Gabon	1988	33.3	37	0	12	6.29	1,077
Gabon	1989	30.2	40	0	12	0.27	1,105
Gabon	1990	27.7	35.8	0	11	2.03	1,136
Gabon	1991	26.8	36.9	0	8	0.05	1,168

Country	Year						
Guatemala	1982	14.9	30	0	12	4.67	7,315
Guatemala	1983	13		0	12	9.99	7,524
Guatemala	1984	11.8	32.3	0	12	6.94	7,740
Guatemala	1985	12.6	16.15	0	11	0.67	7,963
Guatemala	1986	13.2	23	0	8	2.89	8,194
Guatemala	1987	12.4	20	0	6	0.15	8,434
Guatemala	1988	14.4	25	0	6	7.06	8,681
Guatemala	1989	14.5	32	0	6	1.29	8,935
Guatemala	1990	16.9	26	0	6	6.73	9,197
Guatemala	1991	17.5	34.6	0	7		9,467
Haiti	1982		23.1	0	13		5,546
Haiti	1983		8.6	0	13		5,648
Haiti	1984	8.4	9.5	0	13	9.49	5,754
Haiti	1985	9.2	14.3	0	13	5.47	5,865
Haiti	1986	9.6	16	0	13	4.16	5,980
Haiti	1987	9.8	20	0	9	0.36	6,099
Haiti	1988	7.9	20	0	11	1.5	6,221
Haiti	1989	7.3	24	0	12	6.09	6,346
Haiti	1990	8.2	23.2	0	12	4.41	
Haiti	1991	8.3	17.4	0	8	1.49	
Honduras	1982	14.1	27.1	0	6	2.55	3,941
Honduras	1983	10.4	21.4	0	5	0.46	4,089
Honduras	1984	9.9	17.5	0	6	2.95	4,237
Honduras	1985	11.2	16.35	0	5	5.37	4,383
Honduras	1986	12.9	13	0	5	10.38	4,528
Honduras	1987	21.1	18	0	5	4.6	4,672
Honduras	1988	14.5	23	0	5	1.94	4,815

(continued)

TABLE B1.—*Continued*

Nation	Year	Institutional Investor	Euromoney	Borrowing (mil. 1994 $)	Participatory State	Uncertainty	Population (thousands)
Honduras	1989	14.6	32	0	5	6.96	4,959
Honduras	1990	13.8	26	0	5	1.74	5,105
Honduras	1991	14.4	30.2	0	5	5.35	5,259
Hong Kong	1982	75.2	86.8	1,559.9		2.61	5,202
Hong Kong	1983	70.8	72.8	821.1		7.1	5,285
Hong Kong	1984	64.3	68.7	1,117		4.85	5,370
Hong Kong	1985	69.2	83.75	165.8		5.42	5,456
Hong Kong	1986	69.4	75	848		3.53	5,524
Hong Kong	1987	68.5	78	322.8		0.35	5,581
Hong Kong	1988	69	82	482.5		3.86	5,627
Hong Kong	1989	69.4	70	1,604.9		8.53	5,686
Hong Kong	1990	64.6	71.2	1,254.8		2.64	5,705
Hong Kong	1991	63.6	72.3	1,495.2		0.57	5,755
India	1982	46.6	72.6	559.3	5	16.33	718,426
India	1983	46.2	72.6	779.1	5	16.72	734,072
India	1984	46.9	68.5	1,049.2	5	11.93	749,677
India	1985	49.4	58	837.6	5	1.01	765,147
India	1986	50.7	69	1,795.4	5	8.72	781,893
India	1987	49.7	74	2,358.7	5	14.7	798,680
India	1988	48.4	74	2,482.4	5	15.97	815,590
India	1989	47.9	67	2,047.5	5	9.46	832,535
India	1990	46.2	58.7	1,242.2	5	2.82	849,515
India	1991	38.4	45.9	225.6	5	2.37	866,499
Indonesia	1982	56	72.1	1,690.7	10	6.65	154,245

Indonesia	1983	51.6	67.4	2,341.7	10	6.24	157,157
Indonesia	1984	49.7	73.9	1,759.6	10	14.6	160,075
Indonesia	1985	49.6	63.95	481	11	4.75	163,036
Indonesia	1986	47.6	59	1,343.5	11	1.75	166,015
Indonesia	1987	43.8	59	1,770.1	11	5.46	168,990
Indonesia	1988	42.9	61	1,008.2	11	8.34	171,994
Indonesia	1989	45.3	62	2,701.5	10	6.99	175,063
Indonesia	1990	48	65.6	5,461.5	10	7.96	178,232
Indonesia	1991	50.4	57.3	5,638.5	11	2.68	181,305
Iran	1982	12.8	23.1	0	12	0.18	41,813
Iran	1983	15.7	9.9	0	12	16.21	43,242
Iran	1984	18.7	10.4	0	12	18.64	44,757
Iran	1985	18.1	14.45	0	11	14.01	46,374
Iran	1986	19.3	10	0	11	19.63	48,087
Iran	1987	18.3	17	0	11	11.65	49,889
Iran	1988	19	23	0	11	6.34	51,778
Iran	1989	21.3	33	0	11	1.42	53,744
Iran	1990	24.1	33.8	0	11	0.51	55,779
Iran	1991	28.3	40.5	0	11	2.09	57,727
Iraq	1982	35.2	23.1	0	13	22.05	13,885
Iraq	1983	24.4	52.6	620	13	17.99	14,344
Iraq	1984	19.3	46.8	0	13	17.17	14,821
Iraq	1985	19.1	15.75	628	14	13.68	15,319
Iraq	1986	18.2	20	0	14	8.55	15,836
Iraq	1987	15.3	9	0	14	16.72	16,372
Iraq	1988	14.9	21	33.3	14	4.33	
Iraq	1989	16.8	28	45	14	0.81	

(continued)

TABLE B1.—Continued

Nation	Year	Institutional Investor	Euromoney	Borrowing (mil. 1994 $)	Participatory State	Uncertainty	Population (thousands)
Iraq	1990	17.8	18.4	0	13	9.76	
Iraq	1991	11.7	1.9	0	14	20.31	
Israel	1982	33.6	26	110	4	17.59	4,031
Israel	1983	31.7	26.9	152.1	4	14.83	4,105
Israel	1984	30		0	4		4,159
Israel	1985	28.8	37.4	22	4	1.5	4,233
Israel	1986	30.9	41	40	4	0.05	4,299
Israel	1987	33.1	52	104	4	8.9	4,369
Israel	1988	34.6	66	89	4	21.44	4,442
Israel	1989	35	56	120	4	11.05	4,518
Israel	1990	36.4	49.9	119	4	3.58	4,660
Israel	1991	35.2	53.8	0	4	8.65	4,946
Jamaica	1982	17.7	24.5	0	5	3.57	2,185
Jamaica	1983	15.7	43.4	12.6	5	17.29	2,211
Jamaica	1984	14.3	24.6	0	5	0.15	2,236
Jamaica	1985	14.9	20.3	0	5	5.03	2,260
Jamaica	1986	14.9	30	0	5	4.67	2,282
Jamaica	1987	14.5	21	30	5	3.94	2,302
Jamaica	1988	16	26	0	4	0.41	2,321
Jamaica	1989	18	36	0	4	7.64	2,339
Jamaica	1990	19.8	39	0	4	8.88	2,356
Jamaica	1991	20.6	35.3	30	4	4.4	2,376
Jordan	1982	37.5	53.4	35.9	12	6.01	2,353
Jordan	1983	37	68	309.4	12	21.1	2,446

Jordan	1984	37.3	59	308.4	12	11.8	2,543
Jordan	1985	38.7	58.05	235.9	10	9.49	2,644
Jordan	1986	37.7	53	20	10	5.41	2,744
Jordan	1987	35.7		220	10		2,846
Jordan	1988	34.5	49	165	10	4.54	2,948
Jordan	1989	31.4	39	0	11	2.44	3,056
Jordan	1990	26.6	31	0	10	5.75	3,278
Jordan	1991	20.7	25.7	0	10	5.29	
Kenya	1982	32.7	45.5	0	9	2.79	18,011
Kenya	1983	28.1	38.7	0	10	0.48	18,744
Kenya	1984	26.7	37.8	0	10	0.95	19,490
Kenya	1985	29.5	18.75	0	11	20.83	20,241
Kenya	1986	29.8	38	58.3	11	1.88	21,000
Kenya	1987	29.8	26	0	11	13.88	21,769
Kenya	1988	30.2	46	0	12	5.73	22,550
Kenya	1989	29.9	43	111.6	12	3.03	23,346
Kenya	1990	31.6	43	9.1	12	1.37	24,160
Kenya	1991	28.3	37.5	0	12	0.91	25,006
Korea	1982	57.2	65.2	3,770.1	11	1.42	39,326
Korea	1983	56.4	71.5	4,209.6	11	5.66	39,910
Korea	1984	56.9	70.3	5,336.9	11	3.97	40,406
Korea	1985	57	70.65	5,950.7	10	4.22	40,806
Korea	1986	58.4	73	3,251.3	9	5.21	41,184
Korea	1987	60.6	82	1,871.2	9	12.06	41,575
Korea	1988	63.7	83	1,532.8	8	10.03	41,975
Korea	1989	67.6	79	1,322.4	5	2.23	42,380
Korea	1990	68.7	82	3,981.7	5	4.15	42,869

(*continued*)

TABLE B1.—*Continued*

Nation	Year	Institutional Investor	Euromoney	Borrowing (mil. 1994 $)	Participatory State	Uncertainty	Population (thousands)
Korea	1991	68.1	76.7	6,436.8	5	0.56	43,268
Kuwait	1982	68.1	80	730	8	2.74	1,524
Kuwait	1983	66.1	83.6	325	8	8.29	1,593
Kuwait	1984	63.6	76.2	160	8	3.33	1,655
Kuwait	1985	64.1	81.05	0	8	7.69	1,712
Kuwait	1986	62.3	63	50	8	8.6	1,791
Kuwait	1987	58.3	56	26.5	11	11.7	1,873
Kuwait	1988	59.1	64	80	11	4.48	1,958
Kuwait	1989	60.2	59	75	11	10.55	2,048
Kuwait	1990	60.8	27.9	0	10	42.24	
Kuwait	1991	41.8	36.9	5,500	14	14.69	
Liberia	1982	11	29.9	103.2	12	8.37	2,001
Liberia	1983	11.2	9.9	18.2	12	11.82	2,066
Liberia	1984	11	12.5	27.5	10	9.03	2,132
Liberia	1985	11.1	15.05	16.2	11	6.57	2,199
Liberia	1986	11	19	0	10	2.53	2,268
Liberia	1987	10.5	18	0	10	3.04	
Liberia	1988	10.7	21	0	10	0.23	
Liberia	1989	9.1	21	0	10	1.33	
Liberia	1990	9	17.3	0	11	2.27	
Liberia	1991	8.5	8.5	0	14	10.59	
Malawi	1982	19	23.7	0	13	5.64	6,527
Malawi	1983	16.4	26.2	0	13	0.6	6,737
Malawi	1984	15.7	11.3	0	13	14.81	6,957

Malawi	1985	18.3	15.45	0	13	13.2	7,188
Malawi	1986	18.1	24	2.5	13	4.46	7,430
Malawi	1987	16.8	18	0	13	9.19	7,682
Malawi	1988	15.1	24	0	13	1.53	7,945
Malawi	1989	15.6	37	0	13	10.98	8,220
Malawi	1990	15.6	40	0	13	13.98	8,507
Malawi	1991	16.5	31.7	0	13	4.81	8,796
Malaysia	1982	71.8	74	3,244.8	7	6.87	14,510
Malaysia	1983	69.1	83.8	2,468.5	7	5.56	14,887
Malaysia	1984	67.4	74.9	2,291.2	7	1.68	15,272
Malaysia	1985	63.7	78.35	2,178.5	8	5.38	15,682
Malaysia	1986	59.9	65	1,203.6	8	4.26	16,110
Malaysia	1987	54.6	65	489.2	8	0.92	16,526
Malaysia	1988	55.5	70	1,132.1	8	5.04	16,942
Malaysia	1989	57.4	68	540.6	9	1.18	17,353
Malaysia	1990	60.5	75.8	730	9	5.96	17,763
Malaysia	1991	62	76	512	9	4.69	18,178
Mauritius	1982	19.9	30	40	5	0.21	995
Mauritius	1983	17	15	0	4	12.38	1,006
Mauritius	1984	19.2	27.1	40	4	2.43	1,014
Mauritius	1985	24	21	0	4	13.22	1,020
Mauritius	1986	24.9	40	0	4	4.91	1,030
Mauritius	1987	24.2	35	0	4	0.59	1,040
Mauritius	1988	29.1	49	0	4	9.81	1,051
Mauritius	1989	31.4	59	0	4	17.56	1,063
Mauritius	1990	35.2	66.5	0	4	21.35	1,075
Mauritius	1991	33.4	40.2	0	4	3.19	1,087

(*continued*)

TABLE B1.— *Continued*

Nation	Year	Institutional Investor	Euromoney	Borrowing (mil. 1994 $)	Participatory State	Uncertainty	Population (thousands)
Mexico	1982	54.8	41.9	8,797.4	7	22.38	70,225
Mexico	1983	33.9	43.5	5,095.3	7	0.38	71,791
Mexico	1984	38.1	56.3	8,110	7	8.32	73,309
Mexico	1985	36.4	45.55	109	7	0.77	74,766
Mexico	1986	30.8	31	313.3	8	9.85	76,178
Mexico	1987	27.1	42	7,700	8	4.76	77,562
Mexico	1988	28.9	43	0	8	4	78,933
Mexico	1989	30.3	44	310	7	3.64	80,312
Mexico	1990	35	58.6	2,350	7	13.65	81,724
Mexico	1991	38.7	55.8	5,573.9	8	7.24	83,306
Morocco	1982	31.6	47.2	200.2	9	5.57	20,378
Morocco	1983	29.5	41.1	69.3	9	1.52	20,916
Morocco	1984	24.4	33.2	0	9	1.41	21,478
Morocco	1985	23.1	20.2	107.4	9	13.14	22,061
Morocco	1986	23.1	29	0	9	4.34	22,706
Morocco	1987	22.5	38	25	9	5.25	23,376
Morocco	1988	23.9	48	130	9	13.88	23,960
Morocco	1989	26.3	50	6.3	9	13.54	24,520
Morocco	1990	28.8	42.6	52	8	3.7	25,091
Morocco	1991	28.3	40	0	8	1.59	25,668
Mozambique	1982		27	0	14		12,756
Mozambique	1983		28.7	0	14		13,093
Mozambique	1984		38.1	0	13		13,438
Mozambique	1985		27.7	0	13		13,791

Country	Year						
Mozambique	1986		26	0	13		14,153
Mozambique	1987			0	13	0.79	14,525
Mozambique	1988	7.6	19	0	13	8.09	14,907
Mozambique	1989	7.3	26	0	13	4.02	15,301
Mozambique	1990	7	13.6	0	13	2.68	15,707
Mozambique	1991	7	20.3	0	12		16,128
Nicaragua	1982	6.7		0	11		2,969
Nicaragua	1983	5.5		0	11		3,056
Nicaragua	1984	4.7		0	11		3,143
Nicaragua	1985			0	10		3,229
Nicaragua	1986	5.5		0	10		3,314
Nicaragua	1987	5.3		0	11		3,401
Nicaragua	1988	5.2		0	10		3,489
Nicaragua	1989	4.5		0	9		3,580
Nicaragua	1990	5.9	14.5	0	10	2.05	3,676
Nicaragua	1991	7.1	22.2	0	6	4.48	
Nigeria	1982	48.1	59.2	396.2	5	1.46	75,774
Nigeria	1983	36.3	43.4	223	5	2.82	78,217
Nigeria	1984	29.9	38.7	0	5	1.27	80,699
Nigeria	1985	24	10.45	0	12	23.77	83,196
Nigeria	1986	22.8	17	0	12	16.04	85,718
Nigeria	1987	20.8	22	0	12	9.09	88,273
Nigeria	1988	19.2	28	0	11	1.53	90,866
Nigeria	1989	17.8	36	0	10	7.84	93,505
Nigeria	1990	18.2	33	0	11	4.45	96,203
Nigeria	1991	19.5	31	0	10	1.18	98,983
Oman	1982	45.4		0	12		1,096

(continued)

TABLE B1.—*Continued*

Nation	Year	Institutional Investor	Euromoney	Borrowing (mil. 1994 $)	Participatory State	Uncertainty	Population (thousands)
Oman	1983	47.7		343.5	12		1,153
Oman	1984	50		0	12		1,209
Oman	1985	53.4	63.15	400	12	0.24	1,263
Oman	1986	52.7	52	500	12	10.23	1,316
Oman	1987	50.3	41	0	12	18.89	1,368
Oman	1988	50.8	61	100	12	0.63	1,419
Oman	1989	53.2	57	400	12	5.72	1,471
Oman	1990	52.1	59	0	12	2.64	
Oman	1991	47.8	49.8	300	12	7.65	
Pakistan	1982	22.2	43.5	290.8	12	11.04	87,736
Pakistan	1983	20.4	40.5	267	12	9.8	90,452
Pakistan	1984	23.8	42	131	12	7.98	93,265
Pakistan	1985	28	26.55	281.9	12	11.57	96,180
Pakistan	1986	29.8	50	167.9	9	10.12	99,199
Pakistan	1987	30	43	167.3	9	2.93	102,324
Pakistan	1988	31.1	53	113.3	9	11.85	105,558
Pakistan	1989	31.1	49	350	6	7.85	108,900
Pakistan	1990	30	52.7	350	6	12.63	112,351
Pakistan	1991	27	41.3	96	8	4.16	115,844
Panama	1982	40.6	71	465.7	8	20.58	2,043
Panama	1983	36.3	40.4	329	10	5.82	2,088
Panama	1984	33.1	47.1	0	9	4	2,134
Panama	1985	30.9	27.9	80	7	13.05	2,180
Panama	1986	31	43	0	9	1.95	2,227

Country	Year						
Panama	1987	29.9	49	0	9	9.03	2,274
Panama	1988	24.8	30	0	10	5	2,322
Panama	1989	18	34	237.5	11	5.64	2,370
Panama	1990	18	50.2	0	13	21.84	2,418
Panama	1991	17.1	30.2	0	6	2.72	2,466
Papua New Guinea	1982	42.6		377	4		3,225
Papua New Guinea	1983	40.7	49.9	100	4	0.62	3,302
Papua New Guinea	1984	40.7	53.5	220.6	4	2.98	3,380
Papua New Guinea	1985	39.5	40.65	72.7	4	8.69	3,460
Papua New Guinea	1986	39.2	57	115	4	7.95	3,541
Papua New Guinea	1987	38.4		0	4		3,622
Papua New Guinea	1988	37.7	55	49.5	4	7.41	3,704
Papua New Guinea	1989	38.3	46	25	5	2.17	3,788
Papua New Guinea	1990	34.3	48.5	115	4	4.23	3,875
Papua New Guinea	1991	32.9	37.8	255	5	5.1	3,964
Paraguay	1982	42.3	53.2	74.7	10	1.12	3,359
Paraguay	1983	37.6	55.9	66.7	10	8.41	3,468
Paraguay	1984	33.3	48.7	0	10	5.41	3,580
Paraguay	1985	31.7	37.45	0	10	4.28	3,693
Paraguay	1986	31	31	0	10	10.05	3,807
Paraguay	1987	29.2	32	0	11	7.29	3,923
Paraguay	1988	26.9	32	0	11	5.05	4,040
Paraguay	1989	25.7	35	0	12	0.87	4,158
Paraguay	1990	27	53	0	7	15.86	4,277
Paraguay	1991	26.6	37	0	7	0.25	4,397
Peru	1982	37.6	54	1,066	5	6.51	18,134
Peru	1983	28.9	43.4	450	5	4.4	18,549

(continued)

TABLE B1.—*Continued*

Nation	Year	Institutional Investor	Euromoney	Borrowing (mil. 1994 $)	Participatory State	Uncertainty	Population (thousands)
Peru	1984	23.3	32.8	0	5	0.73	18,964
Peru	1985	15.9	10.35	0	5	15.96	19,383
Peru	1986	14.9	21	0	5	4.33	19,804
Peru	1987	13.5	20	0	5	3.97	20,228
Peru	1988	12.9	20	0	5	3.38	20,654
Peru	1989	10.2	25	0	5	4.25	21,082
Peru	1990	11.1	28.9	0	6	7.28	21,512
Peru	1991	12.2	27	0	7	4.3	21,945
Philippines	1982	38.8	69	1,234.6	10	20.34	50,800
Philippines	1983	32.6	65.4	650.5	9	22.79	52,055
Philippines	1984	22.2	39.6	0	10	4.44	53,351
Philippines	1985	18.7	22.3	925	8	6.74	54,700
Philippines	1986	21.4	25	0	7	6.68	56,004
Philippines	1987	23.3	39	0	6	5.47	57,356
Philippines	1988	24	34	0	4	0.22	58,721
Philippines	1989	25.2	38	0	5	2.61	60,097
Philippines	1990	25.9	41.4	715	5	5.33	61,480
Philippines	1991	24.5	33.9	0	6	0.8	62,868
Saudi Arabia	1982	73.3		1,040.6	12		10,510
Saudi Arabia	1983	72.2	90.6	535.1	12	9.34	11,122
Saudi Arabia	1984	71.2	87.7	1,017.6	13	7.41	11,750
Saudi Arabia	1985	68.3	85.95	560.5	13	8.49	12,379
Saudi Arabia	1986	64.9	65	148.7	13	9.14	12,991
Saudi Arabia	1987	60.6	56	0	13	13.94	13,612

Saudi Arabia	1988	60.4	70	0	13	0.26	14,016
Saudi Arabia	1989	61.2	65	660	13	5.53	14,435
Saudi Arabia	1990	59.8	60	76	13	9.16	
Saudi Arabia	1991	54.9	53.9	4,500	13	10.48	
Senegal	1982	19.3	23.7	0	8	5.93	5,855
Senegal	1983	16.3	9.9	0	8	16.8	6,019
Senegal	1984	16.4	9.1	0	8	17.7	6,192
Senegal	1985	18.2	23.75	0	7	4.8	6,375
Senegal	1986	18.6	23	0	7	5.94	6,565
Senegal	1987	18.2	19	0	7	9.55	6,762
Senegal	1988	19.3	29	0	7	0.63	6,968
Senegal	1989	19.2	33	0	7	3.47	7,182
Senegal	1990	19.5	37.8	0	7	7.98	7,404
Senegal	1991	17.9	33.1	0	7	4.84	7,625
Sierra Leone	1982	10.3			10		3,411
Sierra Leone	1983	8.5			10		3,488
Sierra Leone	1984	7.4			10		3,569
Sierra Leone	1985	7			9		3,654
Sierra Leone	1986	7.2			10		3,743
Sierra Leone	1987	6			10		3,835
Sierra Leone	1988	8.2			10		3,932
Sierra Leone	1989	7.3			10		4,032
Sierra Leone	1990	7.2	28.9		11	11.08	4,136
Sierra Leone	1991	6.9	27.2		11	9.68	4,243
Singapore	1982	78.5	86.2	372.1	9	1.21	2,366
Singapore	1983	78.1	86.8	174.5	9	0.22	2,406
Singapore	1984	79.6	83.7	417.5	9	4.79	2,444

(*continued*)

TABLE B1.—Continued

Nation	Year	Institutional Investor	Euromoney	Borrowing (mil. 1994 $)	Participatory State	Uncertainty	Population (thousands)
Singapore	1985	76.7	84.25	505.1	9	1.4	2,483
Singapore	1986	74.5	68	462.6	9	15.51	2,519
Singapore	1987	73.8	83	499.1	9	0.18	2,554
Singapore	1988	74.8	83	142	9	0.8	2,599
Singapore	1989	77	84	711	9	1.95	2,648
Singapore	1990	77.7	84.8	561.5	8	1.83	2,705
Singapore	1991	77.8	86.2	535.6	8	0.53	2,763
South Africa	1982	60.4	74.4	1,333.4	11	4.66	31,113
South Africa	1983	57.3	75.6	768.5	11	8.88	31,928
South Africa	1984	57.1	72.5	1,233	11	5.98	32,757
South Africa	1985	43.5	70.95	849.5	11	17.7	33,597
South Africa	1986	40.6	41	0	11	9.42	34,449
South Africa	1987	31.3	19	0	11	22.34	35,312
South Africa	1988	32.4	42	37.6	11	0.41	36,185
South Africa	1989	32.2	46	0	11	3.78	37,068
South Africa	1990	35.8	55	0	11	9.27	37,959
South Africa	1991	37.1	54	338.3	9	7	38,858
Sri Lanka	1982	30.4	69	122.2	5	28.54	15,189
Sri Lanka	1983	29.7	16	31.5	5	23.78	15,417
Sri Lanka	1984	26.3	41.8	42.5	7	5.34	15,599
Sri Lanka	1985	24.9	33	0	7	2.09	15,837
Sri Lanka	1986	24.6	39	20.9	7	4.2	16,117
Sri Lanka	1987	23.5	27	0	7	6.73	16,361
Sri Lanka	1988	22.7	30	0	7	2.95	16,587

Sri Lanka	1989	22.6	32	0	7	0.85	16,806
Sri Lanka	1990	23.3	42.4	0	9	8.87	16,993
Sri Lanka	1991	21.9	37.6	0	9	5.43	17,190
Sudan	1982	10	23.7	36	11	3.15	20,236
Sudan	1983	8.2	16	0	10	2.79	20,774
Sudan	1984	6.7	8.5	0	10	8.83	21,352
Sudan	1985	7.2	10	0	12	7.82	21,931
Sudan	1986	7.3	6	0	12	11.91	22,526
Sudan	1987	5.9	14	0	9	2.55	23,140
Sudan	1988	5.6	18	0	9	1.74	23,774
Sudan	1989	5	18	0	9	2.33	24,433
Sudan	1990	5.6	14.5	0	14	1.76	25,118
Sudan	1991	6.1	16.8	0	14	0.06	25,836
Swaziland	1982		25	0	10		600
Swaziland	1983		9.8	0	10		617
Swaziland	1984		32.1	0	10		637
Swaziland	1985		19.65	0	11		659
Swaziland	1986		36	0	11		683
Swaziland	1987		11	0	11		709
Swaziland	1988	18.6	32	0	11	3.06	737
Swaziland	1989	17.2	44	0	11	16.42	766
Swaziland	1990	18.4	45	0	11	16.25	
Swaziland	1991	18.4	0	0	11	28.75	
Syria	1982	21.3	33.5	0	11	1.92	9,318
Syria	1983	18.3	39.4	12	12	10.75	9,649
Syria	1984	17.5	42.1	0	13	14.23	9,993
Syria	1985	19.8	30.95	0	13	0.83	10,348

(continued)

TABLE B1.—*Continued*

Nation	Year	Institutional Investor	Euromoney	Borrowing (mil. 1994 $)	Participatory State	Uncertainty	Population (thousands)
Syria	1986	19.7	38	0	13	7.98	10,654
Syria	1987	16.8	20	0	13	7.19	10,969
Syria	1988	19.2	27	0	13	2.53	11,338
Syria	1989	17.8	30	0	13	1.84	11,719
Syria	1990	18.5	22.3	0	14	6.55	12,116
Syria	1991	19.5	25.2	0	14	4.62	12,529
Taiwan	1982	67.9	66	1,026	10	11.07	18,458
Taiwan	1983	68.3	80.9	326.6	10	3.44	18,733
Taiwan	1984	69.5	72.8	32.6	10	5.83	19,013
Taiwan	1985	72.6	72	0	10	9.65	19,258
Taiwan	1986	73.9	68	82.8	10	14.92	19,455
Taiwan	1987	74.8	76	74	10	7.8	19,673
Taiwan	1988	76.8	86	0	9	0.25	19,904
Taiwan	1989	77.9	72	865.3	8	14.83	20,101
Taiwan	1990	77.6	79.2	825	7	7.33	20,353
Taiwan	1991	77.1	83.8	884	6	2.25	
Tanzania	1982	10.6	25.2	0	12	4.06	19,298
Tanzania	1983	9.8	9.8	0	12	10.56	19,912
Tanzania	1984	8.2	14.5	0	12	4.29	20,533
Tanzania	1985	10.4	11.2	0	12	9.74	21,161
Tanzania	1986	10.8	27	0	12	5.67	21,751
Tanzania	1987	9.4	19	0	12	0.96	22,370
Tanzania	1988	9.8	23	40	12	2.64	23,020
Tanzania	1989	9.2	30	40	12	10.23	

Country	Year					
Tanzania	1990	10.7	33.7	0	12	12.47	
Tanzania	1991	12	31.4	30	11	8.9	
Thailand	1982	51.3	56	434.9	7	4.86	48,740
Thailand	1983	52.2	69.1	641.1	7	7.36	49,739
Thailand	1984	53.4	70.3	1,074.6	7	7.39	50,720
Thailand	1985	52.8	70.6	1,781.1	7	8.27	51,683
Thailand	1986	53.3	62	1,676.3	6	0.81	52,654
Thailand	1987	53.8	75	348	6	11.7	53,605
Thailand	1988	56	77	1,020.1	6	11.55	54,536
Thailand	1989	59.8	72	1,058.5	5	2.84	55,448
Thailand	1990	62.3	72.2	1,465.5	5	0.6	56,303
Thailand	1991	62.5	73.3	1,907.2	5	1.51	57,151
Trinidad & Tobago	1982	55	65.9	102.5	4	1.43	1,113
Trinidad & Tobago	1983	52.2	49.5	304.9	3	12.24	1,129
Trinidad & Tobago	1984	49.5	57.9	262.9	3	1.21	1,144
Trinidad & Tobago	1985	44.4	46.55	171.7	3	7.58	1,160
Trinidad & Tobago	1986	43.3	38	236.7	3	15.05	1,176
Trinidad & Tobago	1987	40	49	105.3	3	0.83	1,191
Trinidad & Tobago	1988	36.3	58	78.9	2	11.78	1,206
Trinidad & Tobago	1989	31.3	52	0	2	10.66	1,221
Trinidad & Tobago	1990	30.7	47.3	0	2	6.54	1,236
Trinidad & Tobago	1991	29.8	42.8	0	2	2.92	1,253
Tunisia	1982	46.8	54.1	0	10	2.37	6,732
Tunisia	1983	46.3	73.3	265	10	17.32	6,909
Tunisia	1984	44.8	73	130	10	18.48	7,086
Tunisia	1985	41.3	65.95	89.3	10	14.85	7,261
Tunisia	1986	39.7	52	136.3	10	2.46	7,465

(continued)

TABLE B1.—*Continued*

Nation	Year	Institutional Investor	Euromoney	Borrowing (mil. 1994 $)	Participatory State	Uncertainty	Population (thousands)
Tunisia	1987	34.1	46	0	11	1.93	7,639
Tunisia	1988	33.5	58	0	11	14.51	7,770
Tunisia	1989	36.7	58	0	10	11.39	7,910
Tunisia	1990	38.5		0	8		8,074
Tunisia	1991	37.5	39.1	0	9	8.29	8,237
Turkey	1982	20.2	45.4	307.8	10	14.89	46,657
Turkey	1983	26	58.2	262.5	9	22.03	47,877
Turkey	1984	30.6	59.9	516.6	9	19.24	49,105
Turkey	1985	37.3	43.2	1,658.5	8	4	50,306
Turkey	1986	38.6	54	2,754.2	8	5.53	51,475
Turkey	1987	40.1	45	3,187.4	7	4.93	52,622
Turkey	1988	41.1	57	3,186.5	6	6.09	53,764
Turkey	1989	41.1	62	3,011.7	6	11.09	54,916
Turkey	1990	41.4	54	2,498.4	6	2.8	56,098
Turkey	1991	42.7	53.1	2,279.5	6	0.63	57,326
Uganda	1982	4.7	23.1	0	10	7.72	13,340
Uganda	1983	4.1	9	0	10	5.79	13,596
Uganda	1984	4.3	5	0	9	9.99	13,857
Uganda	1985	5	10	0	9	5.67	14,134
Uganda	1986	5.1		0	9		14,460
Uganda	1987	5.2	11	0	9	4.87	14,839
Uganda	1988	5.6	14	0	9	2.26	15,274
Uganda	1989	4.5	25	0	10	9.82	15,769
Uganda	1990	5.8		0	10		16,330

Country	Year						
Uganda	1991	5.3	23.1	0	11	7.14	16,899
Uruguay	1982	39.4	43	30	10	6.25	2,951
Uruguay	1983	32.4	41.8	240	9	0.61	2,970
Uruguay	1984	28.8	19	0	9	19.9	2,989
Uruguay	1985	27.5	13.55	0	9	24.08	3,008
Uruguay	1986	27.8	28	45	4	9.92	3,025
Uruguay	1987	27.9	24	0	4	14.02	3,042
Uruguay	1988	28.4	36	12	4	2.51	3,060
Uruguay	1989	28.8	42	0	4	3.1	3,077
Uruguay	1990	30.9	60.1	11.5	3	19.15	3,094
Uruguay	1991	31.2	39.8	104	3	1.44	3,112
Venezuela	1982	60.3	55.2	4,329.1	3	14.45	15,744
Venezuela	1983	43.4	38.5	220	3	14.65	16,184
Venezuela	1984	37.4	48.4	0	3	1.11	16,630
Venezuela	1985	39.7	20.65	47.5	3	28.89	17,077
Venezuela	1986	38.1	31	0	3	16.98	17,526
Venezuela	1987	36.1	50	30	3	3.97	17,974
Venezuela	1988	36	49	827.4	3	3.07	18,422
Venezuela	1989	32.1	47	0	3	4.88	18,872
Venezuela	1990	32.2	46	1,595.1	4	3.78	19,325
Venezuela	1991	37.2	51.8	581.3	4	4.7	19,787
Zaire	1982	6.2		0	12		28,723
Zaire	1983	5.9		0	13		29,662
Zaire	1984	6		0	13		30,645
Zaire	1985	8.8	20.1	0	13	0.72	31,667
Zaire	1986	9.9	21	0	14	0.55	32,731
Zaire	1987	9.9		0	14		33,843

(continued)

TABLE B1.—*Continued*

Nation	Year	Institutional Investor	Euromoney	Borrowing (mil. 1994 $)	Participatory State	Uncertainty	Population (thousands)
Zaire	1988	10.2	21	0	13	0.25	34,995
Zaire	1989	9	20	0	13	0.43	36,180
Zaire	1990	10.1	21.5	0	13	0.85	
Zaire	1991	10.1	15.2	0	12	5.45	
Zambia	1982	11.7	27.3	25	11	5.09	6,056
Zambia	1983	9.1	16	0	11	3.67	6,279
Zambia	1984	9.8	9.4	0	11	10.96	6,512
Zambia	1985	10.8	11.8	0	10	9.53	6,753
Zambia	1986	11	20	0	10	1.53	7,001
Zambia	1987	10.1	18	0	10	2.65	7,256
Zambia	1988	10.1	21	0	10	0.35	7,517
Zambia	1989	9.2	25	0	11	5.23	7,782
Zambia	1990	9.9	23	0	11	2.55	8,050
Zambia	1991	9.8	23.8	0	11	3.44	8,319
Zimbabwe	1982	26.2	27.2	63.7	8	9.16	7,531
Zimbabwe	1983	20.7	43.5	27.9	8	12.51	7,822
Zimbabwe	1984	19.1	38.6	0	9	9.17	8,116
Zimbabwe	1985	21.2	25.15	0	9	6.33	8,406
Zimbabwe	1986	23.1	34	40	10	0.66	8,692
Zimbabwe	1987	21.4	26	45	10	5.68	8,976
Zimbabwe	1988	24.2	42	120.2	11	7.59	9,256
Zimbabwe	1989	28.1	41	105.8	11	2.78	9,532
Zimbabwe	1990	29.1	46	156	10	6.81	9,805
Zimbabwe	1991	28.7	44	170	10	5.2	10,079

TABLE B2.   Least Trimmed Squares Robust Regressions: Economic and Political
Determinants of Log of Nonzero Borrowing, Developing Nations

Variable	Linear Model	Quadratic Model
Intercept	−.369	1.719
Ecovector[a]	.996	.097
Participatory	.019	.008
Regulatory	.013	.000
Scale estimate of residuals	.999	1.019
Robust multiple R^2	.436	.445
N	273	273
Number of observations determining		
LTS estimate	139	139

[a]Ecovector is the predicted values of the log of nonzero borrowing derived from a loess model using the economic predictors of country credit risk, uncertainty, year, and population. This reflects the information contained in the full economic model of table 19.

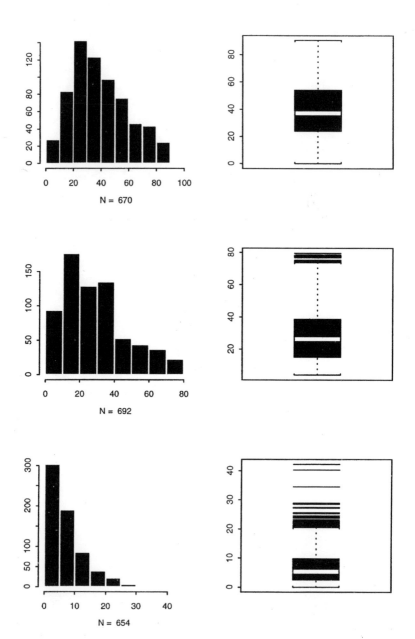

Fig. B1a. Predictor variables: *Euromoney, Institutional Investor,* and uncertainty

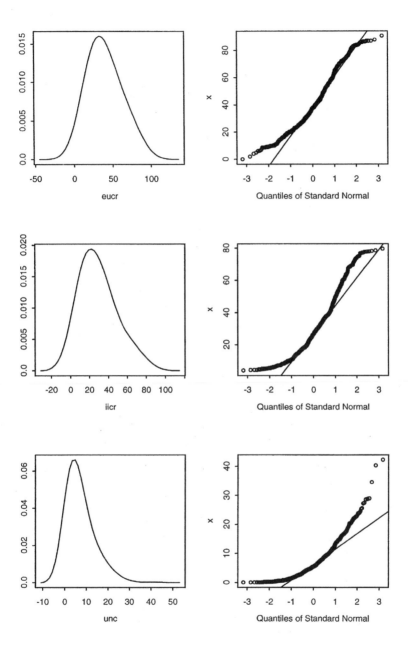

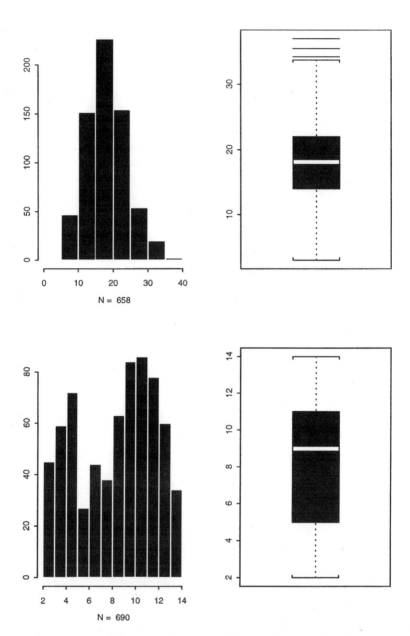

Fig. B1b. Predictor variables: the regulatory and participatory states

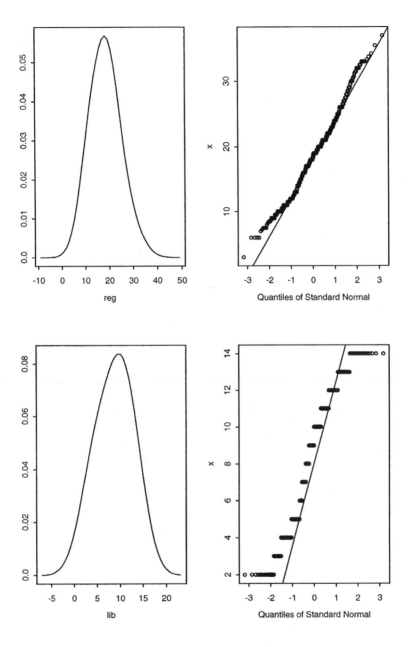

Notes

Chapter 1

1. With intermediation, savers invest in obligations of intermediaries, who lend those funds to borrowers. The intermediary stands between the saver and borrower, reducing the risk to the saver. With disintermediation, investors and borrowers bypass intermediaries such as commercial banks, which accept part of the lending risk. They conduct business directly. Financial institutions may act as brokers or go-betweens, but savers are directly "confronted with the credit risk of the issuer" (Dufey and Giddy 1978, 6).

2. J. M. Keynes argued that finance should be primarily national, as unrestrained international financial flows would severely handicap governments' abilities to stabilize their national economies ("National Self-Sufficiency," *Yale Review*, Summer 1933).

3. National governments have three basic financing mechanisms available: taxes, borrowing, and seignorage.

4. *Securitization* refers to the disintermediation of the banking system (see note 1).

5. Schattschneider (1935) noted the success of the U.S. political system in enshrining bad economic policy due to such pressures when he labeled import protections as "politically invincible." Although he was writing about tariffs and was proven wrong in this specific case, his conclusions are descriptive of the tensions politicians face when trying to balance short- and long-term interests.

6. Weingast labels such governments limited. Limited governments enforce "political, individual, and economic rights against intrusions by others, but also respect these rights as limits on its own action" (1995, 1). Limited government does not mean that less is necessarily better than more. Rather, it addresses the type of intervention. Some types promote exchange (i.e., disclosure and reporting requirements).

Chapter 2

1. Traditionally, investment banks enjoyed near monopolistic relationships with their industry clients. Industries were locked into relationships with specific financial service firms. Unwritten rules discouraged investment banks from preying upon the clients of other investment banks. This essentially constrained price competition. Fi-

nancial firms avoided bidding against one another to represent a particular borrower. IBM's break with Morgan Stanley in 1979 was the watershed event that marked the decline of exclusive investment bank and industry client relations and a shift toward competitive bids to provide investment banking services.

2. Of course, the size of the loan makes a difference for the borrower and the lender. There is some truth to the adage that if you owe the bank a thousand dollars it is your problem, but if you owe the bank, say, five hundred million dollars it is the bank's problem.

3. Individuals have borrowed in disintermediated markets, but such events are rare and limited to such unusual cases as David Bowie's issue of Bowie bonds in 1996–97.

4. Private placements are a notable exception.

5. The distinction between commercial and investment banking is mandated by regulation in some nations, but in nations with universal banking the distinction breaks down.

6. In recent years, commercial banks have diversified their income streams. Securities holdings, interbank lending, trading of government securities, underwriting public securities, foreign exchange trading, and the provision of other financial services have supplemented earnings from commercial lending.

7. Time limits on debt obligations in bond markets do exist, but they are not as confining as those limits in the intermediated lending markets. It is hard to find bond issues in the European markets with maturities beyond fifteen years. Most issues in the European markets mature in less than ten (Smith 1989, 59).

8. I sidestep differences across nations and those between debt and equity issues. Governments and market organizations establish, oversee, and enforce the laws and regulations that provide the institutional basis for capital markets. These rules establish responsibilities, disclosure requirements, accounting standards, and other guidelines for issuing a security. Differences in these areas matter to borrowers when they are deciding among instruments and where to issue a security, but the fundamental process of issuing a security remains similar.

9. At this stage, the primary underwriter acts as the agent of the issuer.

10. Of course, these are highly correlated.

11. A tombstone is an advertisement in the financial pages of the newspaper, which provides the reader with basic information about a securities offering on the day of the offering. The tombstone lists the names of the all the members of the underwriting syndicate.

12. For example, corporate goodwill is hard to value, yet it regularly shows up on accounting sheets as firms estimate the value of their assets.

13. There has been an explosion in such rating agencies. Prior to the 1980s, they were primarily an American phenomenon. U.S. institutional investors' interests in European markets prompted the growth of rating agencies in Europe. These institutional investors face regulatory constraints on their overseas purchases. This prompted many issuers to file U.S. Securities and Exchange Commission (SEC) disclosure documents even though they were issuing their securities outside the United States. Another response has been the emergence of more international and local rating agencies. In the 1980s, several American banking consortiums established ranking agencies for European issues. Several European banking consortiums soon followed. As of November 1994, there were at

least ten international and twenty local rating agencies evaluating securities issues from the emerging markets.

14. This is consistent with expectations about the role of a dominant actor, or a dictator, in overcoming barriers to collective action (Arrow 1951; Kindleberger 1986; Miller 1992; Olson 1965).

15. This is also the logic behind minimum winning coalitions.

16. Most IPOs do not offer the full number of shares listed in the disclosure statement. An issuer usually retains some shares to sell in the future, to distribute among employees as part of their compensation, or to ensure that management retains a block of shares to thwart shareholder challenges.

17. The exception constitutes complete "market failure." Here investors stay home, no deals are concluded, savers do not transfer their surpluses to borrowers, and the market collapses.

18. Accounting firms, investment institutions, private rating services, government agencies, and international organizations devote significant resources and expertise to evaluate creditworthiness and risk. Moody's, Standard & Poors, Duff & Phelps, and Fitch IBCA assess borrowers and rate securities. Accounting firms such as Coopers & Lybrand, Arthur Anderson, and KPMG Peat Marwick assess firm balance sheets. U.S. authorities established the Interagency Country Exposure Review Committee (ICERC) to identify countries that face potential problems in servicing external obligations. The U.S. comptroller of the currency issues a summary of such country risk assessments in its *Annual Report*. The World Bank issues an *International Country Risk Guide*. Publications such as *Euromoney* and *Institutional Investor* produce risk assessments annually.

19. Investors can diversify their portfolios along multiple dimensions—by industry sector, geography, time, market, type of financial instrument, and so on. Levels of risk acceptance vary by investor depending upon their objectives. Institutional investors want to include risks that may fail in their portfolios. Otherwise, the investor is carrying too little risk in the portfolio and is obtaining suboptimal performance.

20. I thank an anonymous reviewer for emphasizing this important point.

21. This amounts to enlarging the confidence intervals around the central tendency, but the central tendency remains the same.

22. A market failure is simply a suboptimal equilibrium.

23. Gresham's Law was initially a commentary on practices that debased the value of a currency. One practice involved shaving gold coins to produce additional coins. Traders assumed with a positive probability that the coins they were receiving were shaved and would discount their value. Those with unshaved coins would withhold their currency because it was undervalued. Economic history is replete with rich examples of Gresham's Law. The Dutch tulip mania of 1636–37, for instance, precipitated a rapid increase in the price of tulip bulbs. One variety peaked at a price of twenty thousand pounds (Kindleberger 1993, 209). As some investors began to worry about the market's stability, they withdrew. Prices temporarily leveled off and then tottered. More investors exited and took their profits. Investors refused to reenter the increasingly uncertain market. Prices collapsed, and the speculative bubble burst. Other, more reasonable, Dutch investment ventures suffered as a consequence. In another instance, the bursting of the British South Sea bubble in the early 1700s drove capital away from more than just the South Sea Company and constrained the formation of unincorporated joint stock companies in En-

gland for the next hundred years. The end of the Mississippi bubble in France in 1720 led to the demise of John Law as minister of finance and limited the development of paper currency in France for a hundred years. Keynes, commenting upon the collapse of financial markets during the interwar years, noted that individuals hoarded money at the very time the economy needed increased consumption and spending and when good investment opportunities were severely undervalued due to the downturn in markets. Bad money drove good capital into hoarding and away from good risks that could have stemmed the downward spiral of the 1930s—the foundation of Keynes's call for countercyclical economic statesmanship and intervention by governments (1933, 1936). As good investment opportunities, which would have stimulated economic growth, encountered huge difficulties in borrowing capital, economies sank further into depression.

24. I thank Jim Morrow for raising this possibility.

25. For example, the United States, France, and Italy score fairly high on measures of political strikes, regime change, or labor unrest; whereas many developing nations witness a change in political leadership infrequently and have underdeveloped and placid labor movements. Yet American, French, and Italian borrowers find capital far more accessible, and at lower costs, in the global markets. Political violence and unrest influence social accountability investment funds but not due to fears about returns on investments. Rather, social accountability funds follow an explicit policy of rewarding borrowers in industries or nations that meet specified standards of social accountability and penalizing borrowers that do not.

26. North (1990) and Knight (1993) distinguish between formal and informal institutions. Third-party enforcement mechanisms separate informal from formal institutions. Informal institutions are self-enforcing. I find this problematic, as states are usually interested parties in many exchanges. Recognizing the biased role of the state makes all institutions informal by the North and Knight definition.

27. In the limiting case, an institution may produce a specific equilibrium or category of equilibria (Calvert 1992, 1995).

28. This is not a motivational (causal) claim about the origin of such institutions but a statement about their function.

29. The shift from the Bretton Woods fixed exchange rate regime to a flexible exchange rate mechanism affords national policymakers greater latitude to employ monetary policy to address short-term political and economic pressures.

30. For example, the first post–World War II Labor government in the United Kingdom nationalized a slew of private industries, as did labor governments in other Western industrialized nations. A binge of national expropriations in developing nations during the 1960s targeted the property rights of overseas investors and owners. In the early 1980s, the incoming French government of François Mitterrand nationalized the bank Paribas to fulfill a campaign promise to his supporters.

31. This is a claim about the relation of institutions to order, not about whether order is preferable or a particular order produced by a set of institutional arrangements is preferable.

32. I use discrete categories for simplification, but one can easily conceive of a continuous distribution.

33. If Cap means capital, Acc means access, Exp means expectations, and Cos means costs, then:

(1) Borrowers who are evaluated positively and with less uncertainty enjoy greater capital access than borrowers with greater uncertainty, who, in turn, enjoy greater capital access than borrowers evaluated negatively and with less uncertainty. In other words,

CapAcc(PosExp·LowUncert) > CapAcc(HighUncert)

> CapAcc(LowExp·LowUncert).

(2) Borrowers who are evaluated positively and with less uncertainty pay less than borrowers with greater uncertainty, who, in turn, pay less than borrowers evaluated negatively and with less uncertainty. In other words,

CapCos(PosExp·LowUncert) < CapCos(HighUncert)

< CapCos(LowExp·LowUncert).

Chapter 3

1. In this chapter, I limit globalization to the domain of borrowing in international and foreign bond and commercial banking markets. Globalization is not necessarily synonymous with interdependence. The vast majority of economic activity in all states is financed by local capital.

2. Waltz (1989) used "outside-in and inside-out" classifications to distinguish among international and foreign policy phenomena. Sobel (1994) borrowed the terminology to analyze international outcomes and domestic causes.

3. It may be possible to sidestep this criticism by resorting to "anticipated or expected" causal pressures that will emerge. This requires national policymakers to have long time horizons and be proactive instead of reactive—empirically, an unlikely scenario.

4. I thank an anonymous reviewer for clarifying this point. Cohen makes a similar one (1996).

5. Both my approach and Garrett and Lange's (1995) describe dialectic processes.

6. With intermediation, savers invest in the obligations of intermediaries, who lend those funds to borrowers. The intermediary stands between the saver and borrower, reducing the risk to the saver. With disintermediation, financial institutions may act as brokers or go-betweens, but savers are directly "confronted with the credit risk of the issuer" (Dufey and Giddy 1978, 6). Investors and borrowers conduct business via securitized financial instruments, accepting the risks of lending directly instead of limiting that risk through financial intermediaries. Securitization involves the borrower issuing a security, debt, or equity, which a lender buys.

7. This is a best-case scenario for intermediated loans. It reflects the prime rate, which is reserved for the best customers. Bond yields, the costs to a borrower, constitute a

weighted average of annual yields from a sample for which there is an active domestic secondary market (see *Methodological Supplement to the OECD Financial Statistics Monthly*). These may include bonds rated from Aaa to Bbb.

8. Time limits on debt obligations in bond markets do exist, but they are less confining than limits in the intermediated lending markets. It is hard to find bond issues in the European markets with maturities beyond fifteen years. Most issues in the European markets mature in less than ten (Smith 1989, 59).

9. This is not completely true for this entire period. The Federal Reserve's Regulation Q imposed a ceiling on the interest rates U.S. commercial banks could pay on bank deposits. In 1966 and 1968–69, market interest rates exceeded the Regulation Q ceiling. During these periods, U.S. banks found depositors moving money from their deposits into disintermediated instruments. As a means of defending against such capital flight, U.S. commercial banks opened European branches, which avoided Regulation Q ceilings.

10. A warrant gives the right to purchase securities at a specified price within a specified time. Financial futures are commodity contracts based upon financial instruments. They entail the buying and selling of contracts that contain commitments to purchase or sell a particular financial commodity at a prearranged price on a specified date. Index funds involve a basket of futures representing the makeup of a stock price index. Index funds provide hedging and diversification opportunities between identical baskets of futures and stocks. Options are the right to buy or sell a specified quantity of a security at a specified price within a determined time. Futures markets tend to require low margins or a small amount of capital to purchase a disproportionately large amount of a commodity future. Investors can hedge a position in stocks by taking an offsetting position in futures, speculating on future price movements, or taking advantage of arbitrage opportunities between the futures price and the price of those stocks.

11. For example, lower margin requirements in derivatives markets can encourage speculation in derivatives, as participants can purchase more for less down. A margin requirement is the amount of cash or securities required to purchase a security in a market. This is a potential source of instability if investors are called to cover more of the cost of the instrument during a pinch and they have insufficient capital. This can spill over to other markets through the explicit linkages across instruments. Recent history provides examples of such risks. The great British merchant banking house Barings collapsed due to such unbalanced speculation. In another instance, linkages between financial instruments in the Chicago futures markets and the NYSE fed the October 1987 meltdown in financial markets.

12. Milgrom, North, and Weingast (1990) provide a nice example of the importance of an institutional infrastructure, private or public, for nurturing exchange relations.

Chapter 4

1. West Germany exempted the Soviet Union from this policy.

2. Hard currencies are those that are convertible and accepted for payment of international obligations.

3. "The Rising Soviet and Eastern European Debt to the West," U.S. Cong., Senate,

Permanent Subcommittee on Investigations, Committee on Government Affairs, S. Doc. 77-S 402-16, April 1977.

4. "The Rising Debt of East Bloc Countries," *International Herald Tribune,* November 8, 1976.

5. Ibid.

6. Ibid.; Ensor and Ohiles 1977.

7. Ensor and Ohiles 1977.

8. During the late 1990s, China began using domestic financial markets to impose discipline upon public corporations.

Chapter 5

1. This is different from most open economy approaches, which make globalization exogenous.

2. IOs raise capital predominantly for projects in developing nations. For example, no Western advanced industrialized nation has borrowed from the IMF or any other international development organization to cover balance of payments shortfalls since the mid-1970s. Industrialized borrowers find private capital mechanisms more flexible and autonomous.

3. One Wall Street guru, Irving Friedman (1987), argued that the contraction in global lending to developing borrowers exacerbated the Third World debt crisis. A bad situation turned worse as healthy enterprises were strangled by a lack of capital.

4. Paradoxically, this is the very time when investors might find great deals. Flight leads to large price declines, and the market becomes a buyers' market with potentially great deals as good opportunities become undervalued. Economically, this may be an opportune time to enter the markets, yet the opposite generally occurs.

5. The Japanese market displayed different behavior, as new public offerings increased in Japan by 36 percent during the first nine months of 1988 (U.S. Securities and Exchange Commission 1989, 41–44).

6. This is the logic that underpins the GINI index. Barber uses a similar logic to consider energy usage (1996, 301–6).

Chapter 6

I thank John Sprague for help with particularly perverse and obstinate data problems, which complicated the analyses in this chapter and the next. His assistance and insight were critical.

1. This suboptimal equilibrium constitutes a market failure, however small or large.

2. This choice depends partly upon the risk acceptance or adverseness of the investor.

3. Institutional investors do not seek to completely eliminate risk from their portfolios but to manage risk at levels acceptable to them. If an institutional investor does not have investments that fail, this probably indicates that the investor is carrying too little risk in the portfolio and is obtaining suboptimal performance. Levels of risk acceptance vary among investors depending upon their objectives.

4. One could substitute either measure of country credit risk without significantly changing the results.

5. Chapter 4 notes that this absence of accounting in Eastern bloc nations concerned public and private actors in the West and led to at least a temporary decrease in lending to borrowers from those nations.

6. S-Plus, a statistical package originally developed at Bell Labs in the 1970s and now commercially available from MathSoft, was an enormous help in managing these ill-tempered data.

7. Some chance always exists for minute random variation due to clerical errors in building the measures of risk, rounding errors in the statistical algorithms, and so on.

8. For example, in 1990 one of the surveys rated Kuwait as an extremely good credit risk, while the other evaluated it as extremely poor. During the time between surveys, Iraq had invaded and annexed Kuwait. The change in the measure was due not to uncertainty about Kuwait's country credit risk but to a fundamental change in the country's status in the global arena.

9. Taking the absolute value of the difference between the *Institutional Investor* and *Euromoney* rankings, differences in standard deviation, or differences in confidence intervals after controlling for sample size, provide alternative strategies for assessing differences across evaluations.

10. The analysis reports large and extremely significant F and t ratios for each category.

11. Market bubbles such as overinflated real estate markets and the Dutch tulip craze reflect such a dynamic in the extreme.

12. This list also includes a handful of nations that are without a doubt stunningly good risks but have no need of international capital (e.g., Kuwait).

13. Comparable visualizations of the independent variables are included in appendix B.

Chapter 7

Doug North, Art Denzau, and Lee Benham, of the Economics Departments at Washington University and Claremont Colleges, suggested that I contact Philip Keefer at the World Bank. Keefer and his coauthors examine the effects of state institutional arrangements upon economic growth. Keefer's data and recommendations proved to be particularly useful. I employ many of the same independent variables to account for variations on nominally different, but causally similar, dependent variables. This tests the replicability, generalizability, and robustness of theoretical claims across multiple frames.

1. Hans Belcsak, of Political Risk Consultants, quoted in *Euromoney*, September 1992, 61.

2. Brian Gendreau, of Developing Markets at J. P. Morgan, quoted in *Euromoney*, September 1992, 61.

3. Initially, I approached these as competing approaches to how the state affects risk, uncertainty, and borrowing.

4. The Center for Institutional Reform and the Informal Sector (IRIS) at the University of Maryland produced the ICRG. It uses data originally collected by Political Risk Services.

5. An excellent example of such design is the 1934 Reciprocal Trade Agreements Act (RTAA) passed by the U.S. Congress. Bhagwati (1988) and Destler (1997) note that the RTAA shifted power over many trade issues away from the legislative branch and to the executive branch, which enjoyed greater insulation from protectionist pressures arising from domestic society. Cukierman et al. (1992) advance similar arguments about the independence of central banks.

6. LTS proved to be far more successful than a linear parametric regression, but it fell far short of the loess regressions in dealing with the structure of the data.

7. This is the last model presented in table 14. The model results differ marginally due to differences in the number of observations.

8. This would be particularly true if the OECD nations were included.

9. If the data were skewed in the other direction, results from a linear parametric regression would overestimate effects.

10. I want to emphasize that these conclusions and results are based upon developing nations. I intentionally omitted developed nations due to the lack of variation on key variables of interest. The lack of appropriate data excluded transitional, former Eastern bloc political economies from this analysis.

Chapter 8

1. Cerny (1993), Sobel (1994), and Simmons (1996) note that what passes for financial deregulation is often reregulation.

2. Capital controls intended to prevent capital flight are good examples of this phenomenon. Meant to restrain the outflow of domestic capital, they impose limitations on international investors' desire for liquidity in their investments.

3. The marriage of offspring from two feudal kingdoms represents an early form of a joint venture. Alliances by marriage constitute attempts to overcome contractual and commitment problems.

Appendix A

This appendix draws heavily from Sobel 1994.

1. I provide a broad summary here. Other researchers provide a more detailed description of many of these changes. See Auerbach and Hayes 1986; Bagehot [1917] 1978; Dufey and Giddy 1978; Goldberg and White 1979; Hayes 1987; Hayes et al. 1990; Helleiner 1994; Horne 1985; Hultman 1990; Kerr 1986; Kindleberger 1993, 1974; Rosenbluth 1989; Seligman 1982; Sobel 1975, 1994; Suzuki 1987; Thomas 1986; Walter 1985; and Welles 1975).

2. A similar shakeout and consolidation occurred in the mid-1990s. Relaxed interpretations by federal regulators of the boundaries separating financial services resulted in a flurry of merger and acquisitions activity.

3. See U. S. Department of the Treasury 1979.

4. Japanese Law 25 of 1948, which was modeled after the U.S. legislation, established disclosure requirements and definitions of stock exchanges, securities companies, securities, and financial instruments.

5. A repo is a bond purchase in which the purchaser (or seller) retains the privilege of reselling (or repurchasing) those bonds at the end of a specified time.

6. These are bond trusts that pay no interest until maturity.

7. The United States is the exception in terms of capital controls.

Appendix B

1. A ninth question dealing with decentralization of power was on the Political Rights checklist, but it was eliminated beginning with the 1995–96 survey.

Bibliography

Agarwal, Jamuna P. 1980. "Determinants of Foreign Direct Investment: A Survey." *Weltgwirtshaftliches Archiv* 116:4

Akerlof, George. 1970. "The Market for Lemons: Quality Uncertainty and the Market Mechanism." *Quarterly Journal of Economics* 89:488–500.

Alesina, Alberto, and Dani Rodrik. 1994. "Distributive Politics and Economic Growth." *Quarterly Journal of Economics* 108:465–90.

Alt, James E., Fredrik Carlsen, Per Heum, and Kåre Johansen. 1996. "Collective Action, Institutions, and Asset Specificity: Evidence from Norway." Paper presented at the annual meeting of the American Political Science Association, San Francisco, August.

Andrews, D. 1994. "Capital Mobility and State Autonomy: Toward a Structural Theory of International Monetary Relations." *International Studies Quarterly* 38 (June): 193–218.

Arbetman, Marina. 1990. "The Political Economy of Exchange Rate Fluctuations." Ph.D. diss., Vanderbilt University.

Aronson, Jonathan David. 1977. *Money and Power: Banks and the World Monetary System.* Beverly Hills: Sage Publications.

Arrow, Kenneth. 1951. *Social Choice and Individual Values.* New Haven: Yale University Press.

Arthur, Brian. 1990. "Positive Feedbacks in the Economy." *Scientific American* 262, no. 2: 92–99.

Auerbach, Joseph, and Samuel L. Hayes. 1986. *Investment Banking and Diligence: What Price Deregulation?* Boston: Harvard Business School Press.

Bagehot, Walter. [1917] 1978. *Lombard Street: Description of the Money Market.* Salem, NH: Ayer.

Balkan, Erol. 1992. "Political Instability, Country Risk, and Probability of Default." *Applied Economics* 24:999–1008.

Bank of International Settlements. 1986. *Recent Innovations in International Banking.* April. Basel, Switzerland.

Banks, Jeffrey. 1991. *Signaling Games in Political Science*. Chur, Switzerland: Harwood Academic Publishers.

Barber, Benjamin R. 1996. *Jihad vs. McWorld*. New York: Ballantine Books.

Barro, Robert. 1991. "Economic Growth in a Cross Section of Countries." *Quarterly Journal of Economics* 106:407–44.

Barro, Robert. 1994. *Democracy and Growth*. Working Papers, no. 4,909. Cambridge, MA: National Bureau of Economic Research.

Berkson, J. 1942. "Tests of Significance Considered as Evidence." *Journal of the American Statistical Association* 37:325–35.

Bhagwati, Jagdish. 1988. *Protectionism*. Cambridge: MIT Press.

Bollen, Kenneth A. 1993. "Liberal Democracy: Validity and Method Factors in Cross-National Methods." *American Journal of Political Science* 37:1207–30.

Boudon, Raymond. 1982. *The Unintended Consequences of Social Action*. New York: St. Martin's Press.

Bryant, Ralph. 1987. *International Financial Intermediation*. Washington, DC: Brookings Institution.

Buchanan, James M., and Richard E. Wagner. 1977. *Democracy in Deficit: the Political Legacy of Lord Keynes*. New York: Academic Press.

Burkhart, R. E., and M. S. Lewis-Beck. 1994. "Comparative Democracy—The Economic Development Thesis." *American Political Science Review* 88:903–10.

Calvert, Randall. 1992. "Rational Actors, Equilibrium, and Social Institutions." Manuscript.

Calvert, Randall. 1995. "The Rational Choice Theory of Social Institutions: Cooperation, Coordination, and Communication." In *Modern Political Economy: Old Topics, New Directions*, edited by J. Banks and E. Hanushek. New York: Cambridge University Press.

Carr, Edward Hallett. 1946. *The Twenth Years' Crisis*. New York: St. Martin's Press.

Cerny, Philip G., ed. 1993. *Finance and World Politics*. Aldershot, England: Edward Elgar.

Clague, Christopher, Philip Keefer, Stephen Knack, and Mancur Olson. 1996. "Property and Contract Rights in Autocracies and Democracies." *Journal of Economic Growth* 1, no. 2: 243–76.

Clark, William, and Sylvia Maxfield. 1996. "Credible Commitments, International Investment Flows, and Central Bank Independence in Developing Countries: A Signalling Model." Paper presented at the annual meeting of the American Political Science Association, San Francisco, August.

Cleveland, William S. 1979. "Robust Locally Weighted Regression and Smoothing Scatterplots." *Journal of the American Statistical Association* 74:829–36.

Cleveland, William S. 1985. *The Elements of Graphing Data*. Summit, NJ: Hobart Press.

Cleveland, William S. 1993. *Visualizing Data*. Summit, NJ: Hobart Press.

Cohen, Benjamin J. 1996. "Phoenix Risen: The Resurrection of Global Finance." *World Politics* 48, no. 2: 268–96.

Cooper, S. Kerry, and Donald R. Fraser. 1993. *The Financial Marketplace.* 4th ed. Reading, MA: Addison-Wesley.

Cukierman, Alex, Steven Webb, and Bilin Neyapti. 1992. "Measuring the Independence of Central Banks and Its Effect on Policy Outcomes." *World Bank Economic Review* 6, no. 1: 353–98.

Destler, I. M. 1997. *American Trade Politics.* 3d ed. Washington, DC: Institute of International Economics.

Dufey, Gunter, and Ian H. Giddy. 1978. *The International Money Market.* Englewood Cliffs, NJ: Prentice-Hall.

Edwards, S., and Guido Tabellini. 1991. "Explaining Fiscal Policies and Inflation in Developing Countries." *Journal of International Money and Finance* 10: S16–48.

Eichengreen, Barry. 1994. *International Monetary Arrangements for the 21st Century.* Washington, DC: Brookings Institution.

Ensor, Richard and Frances Ohiles. 1977. "CMEA Debt May be $45 Billion. But the Loans Have Kept Flowing" in *Euromoney* January.

Fan, J. 1992. "Design-Adaptive Nonparametric Regression." *Journal of the American Statistical Association* 87:998–1004.

Feldstein, Martin, and Philippe Bacchetta. 1991. "National Savings and International Investment." In *National Saving and Economic Performance,* edited by D. Bernheim and J. Shoven. Chicago: University of Chicago Press.

Feldstein, Martin, and Charles Horioka. 1980. "Domestic Savings and International Capital Flows." *Economic Journal* 90, no. 358: 314–29.

Frankel, Jeffrey. 1992. "Measuring International Capital Mobility: A Review." *American Economic Review* 82, no. 2: 197–202.

Freedom House. 1995–96. Survey Methodology. www.freedomhouse.org on the World Wide Web.

Freeman, John. 1992. "Banking on Democracy? International Finance and the Possibilities for Popular Sovereignty." University of Minnesota. Mimeo.

Frieden, Jeffry A. 1989. *Banking on the World: The Politics of International Finance.* New York: Basil Blackwell.

Frieden, Jeffry A. 1991. "Invested Interests: The Politics of National Economic Policies in a World of Global Finance." *International Organization* 45:425–51.

Frieden, Jeffry A., and Ronald Rogowski. 1996. "The Impact of the International Economy on National Policies: An Analytic Overview." In *Internationalization and Domestic Politics,* edited by Robert O. Keohane and Helen V. Milner. New York: Cambridge University Press.

Friedman, Irving S. 1987. *Toward World Prosperity: Reshaping the Global Money System.* Lexington, MA: Lexington Books.

Garrett, Geoffrey. 1998. *Partisan Politics in a Global Economy.* New York: Cambridge University Press.

Garrett, Geoffrey, and Peter Lange. 1995. "Internationalization, Institutions, and Political Change." *International Organization* 49, no. 4: 627–55.

Gastil, Raymond D. [1983] 1987. *Freedom in the World.* Westport, CT: Greenwood.

Gerschenkron, Alexander. 1962. *Economic Backwardness in Historical Perspective.* Cambridge, MA: Belknap.

Gilligan, Michael. 1996. "An Examination of Party/Interest Group Coalitions." Paper presented at the annual meeting of the American Political Science Association, San Francisco, August.

Gilpin, Robert. 1981. *War and Change in World Politics.* Cambridge: Cambridge University Press.

Goldberg, Lawrence G., and Lawrence J. White, eds. 1979. *The Deregulation of the Banking and Securities Industries.* Lexington, MA: Lexington Books.

Goldstein, Morris, and Michael Mussa. 1993. "The Integration of World Capital Markets." Paper presented at the conference Changing Capital Markets: Implications for Monetary Policy, Jackson Hole, Wyoming, sponsored by the Federal Reserve Bank of Kansas City.

Goodhart, Charles. 1988. *The Evolution of Central Banks.* Cambridge, MA: MIT Press.

Goodman, John B., and Louis W. Pauly. 1993. "The Obsolescence of Capital Controls? Economic Management in an Age of Global Markets." *World Politics* 46:50–82.

Grabbe, J. Orlin. 1996 *International Financial Markets.* 3d ed. Englewood Cliffs, NJ: Prentice Hall.

Grier, Kevin B., and Gordon Tullock. 1989. "An Empirical Analysis of Cross-National Growth, 1951–80." *Journal of Monetary Economics* 24, no. 2: 259–76.

Haas, Ernst. 1953. "The Balance of Power: Prescription, Concept or Propaganda." *World Politics* 5:442–77.

Harding, Henry. 1987. *China's Second Revolution: Reform after Mao.* Washington, DC: Brookings Institution.

Hayes, Samuel L., ed. 1987. *Wall Street and Regulation.* Boston: Harvard Business School Press.

Hayes, Samuel L., A. Michael Spence, and David Van Praag Marks. 1990. *Investment Banking: A Tale of Three Cities.* Cambridge: Harvard Business School Press.

Helleiner, Eric. 1994. *States and the ʌeemergence of Global Finance: From Bretton Woods to the 1990s.* Ithaca: Cornell University Press.

Helliwell, John F. 1994. *Empirical Linkages between Democracy and Economic Growth.* Working Papers, No. 4,066. National Bureau of Economic Research, Cambridge, MA.

Horne, James. 1985. *Japan's Financial Markets.* Boston: George Allen & Unwin.

Hultman, Charles W. 1990. *The Environment of International Banking.* Englewood Cliffs, NJ: Prentice-Hall.

Jackman, Robert. 1993. *Power without Force: The Political Capacity of Nation-States.* Ann Arbor: University of Michigan Press.

Jaggers, Keith, and Ted Robert Gurr. 1996. *Polity III: Regime Type and Political Authority, 1800–1994.* Inter-University Consortium for Political and Social Research, study no. 6,695.

Kapstein, Ethan B. 1989. "International Coordination of Banking Regulation." *International Organization* 43, no. 2: 323–47.

Kapstein, Ethan B. 1994. *Governing the Global Economy: International Finance and the State.* Cambridge: Harvard University Press.

Katzenstein, Peter J., ed. 1978. *Between Power and Plenty: Foreign Economic Policies of Advanced Industrial States.* Madison: University of Wisconsin Press.

Keech, William R. 1995. *Economic Politics: The Costs of Democracy.* New York: Cambridge University Press.

Keefer, Philip. 1994. "The Dilemma of Credibility: Institutional Difficulties in Guaranteeing Property Rights and Reducing Rent-Seeking." World Bank. Mimeo.

Keefer, Philip, and Stephen Knack. 1997. "Why Don't Poor Countries Catch Up? A Cross-national Test of an Institutional Explanation." *Economic Inquiry* 35, no. 3: 590–602.

Keohane, Robert O., and Helen V. Milner, eds. 1996. *Internationalization and Domestic Politics.* New York: Cambridge University Press.

Keohane, Robert O., and Joseph S. Nye. 1977. *Power and Interdependence: World Politics in Transition.* Boston: Little, Brown.

Kerr, Ian M. 1986. *Big Bang.* London: Euromoney Publications.

Keylor, William R. 1996. *The Twentieth Century World: An International History,* 3d ed. New York: Oxford University Press.

Kindleberger, Charles P. 1974. *The Formation of Financial Centers: A Study in Comparative Economic History.* Princeton Studies in International Finances, no. 36. Princeton: Princeton University Press.

Kindleberger, Charles P. 1986. *The World in Depression, 1929–1939.* Rev. ed. Berkeley: University of California Press.

Kindleberger, Charles P. 1993. *A Financial History of Western Europe.* 2d ed. Oxford: Oxford University Press.

Kitschelt, Herbert, Peter Lange, Gary Marks, and John D. Stephens. (forthcoming). *Continuity and Change in Contemporary Capitalism.* Cambridge: Cambridge University Press.

Knack, Stephen, and Philip Keefer. 1995. "Institutions and Economic Performance: Cross-Country Tests Using Alternative Institutional Measures." *Economics and Politics* 7, no. 3: 207–27.

Knight, Jack. 1992. *Institutions and Social Conflict.* Cambridge: Cambridge University Press.

Kormendi, R. C., and P. G. Meguire. 1985. "Macroeconomic Determinants of Growth: Cross-Country Evidence." *Journal of Monetary Economics* 16:141–63.

Krasner, Stephen D. 1985. *Structural Conflict: The Third World against Global Liberalism.* Berkeley: University of California Press.

Kreps, David. 1990. *A Course in Microeconomic Theory.* Princeton: Princeton University Press.

Kugler, Jacek, and Marina Arbetman. 1989. "Choosing among Measures of Power." In

Power in World Politics, edited by Richard J. Stoll and Michael D. Ward. Boulder: Rienner.

Kugler, Jacek, and William Domke. 1986. "Comparing the Strength of Nations." *Comparative Political Studies* 19:39–69.

Kurtzman, Joel. 1993. *The Death of Money: How the Electronic Economy Has Destabilized the World's Markets and Created Financial Chaos.* New York: Simon and Schuster.

Leblang, David. 1995. "If the Dutch Boy Removes His Finger, Is He Forced to Float?" Paper presented at the annual meeting of the Midwest Political Science Association, Chicago, April.

Leblang, David. 1997. "Political Democracy and Economic Growth: Pooled Cross-Sectional and Time-Series Evidence." *British Journal of Political Science* 27:453–66.

Lipset, Seymour Martin. 1960. *Political Man.* New York: Doubleday.

Lizondo, J. Saúl. 1991. *Determinants and Systemic Consequences of International Capital Flows.* Washington, DC: International Monetary Fund.

McKenzie, Richard B., and Dwight R. Lee. 1991. *Quicksilver Capital: How the Rapid Movement of Wealth Has Changed the World.* New York: Free Press.

McKinnon, Ronald. 1973. *Money and Capital in Economic Development.* Washington, DC: Brookings Institution

MathSoft. 1997. *S-Plus Guide to Statistics.* Seattle: MathSoft, Data Analysis Division.

Maxfield, Sylvia. 1990. *Governing Capital: International Finance and Mexican Politics.* Ithaca: Cornell University Press.

Maxfield, Sylvia. 1997. *Gatekeepers of Growth.* Princeton: Princeton University Press.

Methodological Supplement to the OECD Financial Statistics Monthly. Various issues.

Milgrom, Paul R., Douglass C. North, and Barry R. Weingast. 1990. "The Role of Institutions in the Revival of Trade: The Law Merchant, Private Judges, and the Champagne Fairs." *Economics and Politics* 2:1–23.

Miller, Gary J. 1992. *Managerial Dilemmas: The Political Economy of Hierarchy.* Cambridge: Cambridge University Press.

Milner, Helen. 1988. *Resisting Protectionism.* Princeton: Princeton University Press.

Milner, Helen. 1997. *Bargaining and Cooperation: Domestic Politics and International Relations.* Princeton: Princeton University Press.

Moran, Michael. 1991. *The Politics of the Financial Services Revolution: The U.S.A., U.K., and Japan.* London: Macmillan.

Nomura Research Institute. 1986. *The World Economy and Financial Markets in 1995: Japan's Role and Challenges.* Tokyo: Nomura Research Institute.

Nordhaus, William. 1975. "The Political Business Cycle." *Review of Economic Studies* 42:169–90.

North, Douglass C. 1990. *Institutions, Institutional Change, and Economic Performance.* Cambridge: Cambridge University Press.

North, Douglass C., and Barry R. Weingast. 1989. "Constitutions and Commitment: Evolution of Institutions Governing Public Choice in 17th Century England." *Journal of Economic History* 49:803–32.

Obstfeld, M. 1995. "International Capital Mobility in the 1990s." In *Understanding Interdependence: The Macroeconomics of the Open Economy,* edited by Peter Kenen. Princeton: Princeton University Press.

OECD Financial Statistics Monthly. Various issues.

Okun, Arthur. 1975. *Equality and Efficiency: The Big Tradeoff.* Washington, DC: Brookings Institution.

Olson, Mancur. 1965. *The Logic of Collective Action.* Cambridge: Harvard University Press.

Olson, Mancur. 1982. *The Rise and Decline of Nations.* New Haven: Yale University Press.

Olson, Mancur. 1993. "Dictatorship, Democracy, and Development." *American Political Science Review* 87, no. 3: 567–76.

Organski, A. F. K. 1968. *World Politics.* 2d ed. New York: Knopf.

Organski, A. F. K., and Jacek Kugler. 1980. *The War Ledger.* Chicago: University of Chicago Press.

Organski, A. F. K., Jacek Kugler, Timothy Johnson, and Youssef Cohen. 1984. *Births, Deaths, and Taxes.* Chicago: University of Chicago Press.

Pastor, Manuel, and Jae Ho Sung. 1995. "Private Investment and Democracy in the Developing World." *Journal of Economic Issues* 29:223–43.

Pauly, Louis W. 1988. *Opening Financial Markets: Banking Politics on the Pacific Rim.* Ithaca: Cornell University Press.

Pauly, Louis W. 1997. *Who Elected the Bankers? Surveillance and Control in the World Economy.* Ithaca: Cornell University Press.

Persson, Torsten. 1988. "Credibility of Macroeconomic Policy: An Introduction and a Broad Survey." *European Economic Review* 32:519–32.

Persson, Torsten, and Guido Tabellini. 1994. "Is Inequality Harmful for Growth?" *American Economic Review* 84:600–21.

Pierson, Paul. 1996. "The Path to European Integration: A Historical Institutionalist Analysis." *Comparative Political Studies* 29, no. 2: 123–63.

Polanyi, Karl. 1957. *The Great Transformation.* Boston: Beacon.

Przeworski, Adam. 1991. *Democracy and the Market.* New York: Cambridge University Press.

Przeworski, Adam, Michael Alvarez, Jose Antonio Cheibub, and Fernando Limongi. 1996. "What Makes Democracies Endure?" *Journal of Democracy* 7:39–55.

Przeworski, Adam., and Fernando Limongi. 1993. "Political Regimes and Economic Growth." *Journal of Economic Perspectives* 7:51–69.

Rama, M. 1993. "Rent-Seeking and Economic Growth: A Theoretical Model and Some Empirical Evidence. *Journal of Development Economics* 42:35–50.

Reich, Robert B. 1997. *Locked in the Cabinet.* New York: Knopf.

Rodrik, Dani. 1989. "Promises, Promises: Credible Policy Reform via Signalling." *Economic Journal* 99:756–72.

Rodrik, Dani. 1997. *Has Globalization Gone Too Far?* Washington, DC: Institute for International Economics.

Rogowski, Ronald. 1989. *Commerce and Coalitions*. Princeton: Princeton University Press.

Roosevelt, Franklin D. 1938. *The Public Papers and Addresses of Franklin D. Roosevelt, with a Special Introduction and Explanatory Notes by President Roosevelt*. Vol. 1, *The Genesis of the New Deal, 1928–1932*. New York: Random House.

Rosenbluth, Francis. 1989. *Financial Politics in Contemporary Japan*. Ithaca: Cornell University Press.

Rostow, W. W. 1960. *The Stages of Economic Growth*. New York: Cambridge University Press.

Rothschild, M., and J. Stiglitz. 1976. "Equilibrium in Competitive Insurance Markets: An Essay on the Economics of Imperfect Information." *Quarterly Journal of Economics* 80:629–49.

Schotter, Andrew, 1981. *The Economic Theory of Social Institutions*. Cambridge: Cambridge University Press.

Scully, Gerald W. 1988. "The Institutional Framework and Economic Development." *Journal of Political Economy* 96:52–62.

Scully, Gerald W. 1992. *Constitutional Environments and Economic Growth*. Princeton: Princeton University Press.

Seligman, Joel. 1982. *The Transformation of Wall Street: A History of the Securities Exchange Commission and Modern Corporate Finance*. Boston: Houghton Mifflin.

Shaw, Edward. 1973. *Financial Deepening in Economic Development*. New York: Oxford University Press.

Simmons, Beth. 1996. "Capital Regimes: The International Politics of Financial Regulation." Paper presented at the annual meeting of the American Political Science Association, San Francisco, August.

Sirowy, Larry, and Alex Inkeles. 1990. "The Effects of Democracy on Economic Growth and Inequality: A Review." *Studies in Comparative International Development* 25:126–57.

Smith, Roy C. 1989. *The Global Bankers*. New York: Truman Talley Books/Plume.

Sobel, Robert. 1975. *N.Y.S.E.: A History of the New York Stock Exchange*. New York: Weybright and Talley.

Sobel, Andrew. 1994. *Domestic Choices, International Markets: Dismantling National Barriers and Liberalizing Securities Markets*. Ann Arbor: University of Michigan Press.

Sobel, Andrew. 1995. "The Capital Pool, Sink or Swim? Political Institutions and International Capital Markets." Paper presented at the meetings of the Midwest Political Science Association, Chicago, April.

Spence, A. Michael, 1974. *Market Signaling*. Cambridge: Harvard University Press.

Strange, Susan. 1986. *Casino Capitalism*. Oxford: Blackwell.

Strange, Susan. 1988. *States and Markets*. London: Pinter.

Suzuki, Yoshio, ed. 1987. *The Japanese Financial System*. Oxford: Oxford University Press.

Swank, Duane. 1996. "Funding the Welfare State: Globalization and the Taxation of Business in Advanced Market Economies." Paper presented at the annual meeting of the American Political Science Association, San Francisco, August.

Taylor, Alan. 1997. *International Capital Mobility in History: The Savings-Investment Relationship.* Working Papers, no. 5,743. Cambridge, MA: National Bureau of Economic Research.

Thomas, W. A. 1986. *The Big Bang.* Oxford: Philip Allan.

Tobin, James. 1958. "Estimation of Relationships for Limited Dependent Variables." *Econometrica* 26:24–36.

Triffin, Robert. 1961. *Gold and the Dollar Crisis: The Future of Convertibility.* Rev. ed. New Haven: Yale University Press.

Tukey, J. W. 1977. *Exploratory Data Analysis.* Reading, MA: Addison-Wesley.

UNCTAD. 1995. *World Investment Report: Transnational Corporations and Competitiveness.* New York: Random House.

U.S. Department of Treasury. 1979. *Report to Congress on Foreign Government Treatment of U.S. Commercial Banking Organizations.* Washington, D.C.: U.S. Government Printing Office.

U.S. General Accounting Office. 1988. *Financial Markets: Preliminary Observations on the October 1987 Crash.* Washington, DC: General Accounting Office.

U.S. Presidential Task Force. 1988. *Report of the Presidential Task Force on Market Mechanisms.* Washington, DC: Government Printing Office.

U.S. Securities and Exchange Commission. 1988. *October Market Break Study.* Washington, DC: Government Printing Office.

U.S. Securities and Exchange Commission. 1989. *The Securities Markets in the 1980s: A Global Perspective.* Washington, DC: Government Printing Office.

Vietor, Richard H. K. 1987. "Regulation-Defined Financial Markets: Fragmentation and Integration in Financial Services." In *Wall Street and Regulation,* edited by Samuel L. Hayes III. Boston: Harvard Business School Press.

Volcker, Paul, and Toyoo Gyohten. 1992. *Changing Fortunes.* New York: Times Books.

Walter, Ingo, ed. 1985. *Deregulating Wall Street.* New York: John Wiley.

Waltz, Kenneth N. 1959. *Man, the State and War.* New York: Columbia University Press.

Waltz, Kenneth. 1979. *Theory of International Politics.* New York: Random House.

Weingast, Barry R. 1993. "The Political Foundations of Democracy and the Rule of Law." Institutional Reform and the Informal Sector (IRIS) Working Papers, no. 54. Mimeo.

Weingast, Barry R. 1995 "The Political Foundations of Limited Government: Parliament and Sovereign Debt in 17th and 18th Century England." Paper presented at the conference The Frontiers of Institutional Economics, Washington University, St. Louis, March 17–19.

Welles, Chris. 1975. *The Last Days of the Club.* New York: E. P. Dutton.

Wittman, Donald. 1989. "Why Democracies Produce Efficient Results." *Journal of Political Economy* 97:1395–1424.

Wittman, Donald. 1995. *The Myth of Democratic Failure: Why Political Institutions Are Efficient.* Chicago: University of Chicago Press.

Wriston, Walter. 1988. "Technology and Sovereignty." *Foreign Affairs* 67:63–75.

Zevin, Robert. 1992. "Are World Financial Markets More Open? If So, Why and With What Effects?" In *Financial Openness and National Autonomy: Opportunities and Constraints,* edited by Tariq Banuri and Juliet B. Schor. Oxford: Clarendon Press.

Zysman, John. 1983. *Governments, Markets, and Growth: Financial Systems and the Politics of International Change.* Ithaca: Cornell University Press.

Author Index

Subject Index

ordinary least square (OLS), 157
parametric function, 156
parametric linear model, 158, 180, 183, 190, 191
robust estimator, 178
standard linear model, 132, 140–43, 147, 148, 150, 156, 157, 175, 176, 180, 188
Tobit procedure, 150
Strategic Arms Limitation Talks (SALT I and II), 78
stock market crash (1987), 37, 119, 121, 122

Test Ban Treaty, 78
Third World debt crisis, 25, 89, 101, 119, 120–22, 124, 126, 138, 141
transaction costs, 64, 123, 132

uncertainty, 14, 16, 17, 19, 33–46, 68, 69, 88, 93, 115, 119–21, 129–31, 133, 134, 138–43, 151, 152, 158, 198, 200, 202, 204, 205
measure of, 132–39
political, 70
premium, 35–37
United Kingdom, 57
London International Financial Futures Exchange, 68, 121
United Nations Development Program (UNDP), 89, 101
United States, 55, 57, 196
capital, 55
capital controls, 9, 53

Carter doctrine, 88
Chicago Board Options Exchange, 68
Chicago International Monetary Market, 68
Chicago Mercantile Exchange, 68
"China card," 84
foreign exchange restrictions, 9
hierarchy, 13
New York, 51, 55, 57
New York Futures Exchange, 68
New York Stock Exchange (NYSE), 121
NYSE Composite Index, 68
NYSE Composite Index Futures, 68
savings and loan crisis, 37
Standard and Poors Composite Indices, 68
supremacy, 78

Vietnam, 77, 81–82, 84
visualization
density function, 150, 153
histogram, 148, 150, 153
normal q-q plots, 150, 153
outliers, 147–50
probability density curve, 150
scatterplot, 143, 147
Tukey's box plot, 148, 149
Voluntary Foreign Credit Restraint Act (VFCR, 1965), 55, 56

Warsaw Pact, 90
World Bank, 89, 101, 117, 125
World War I, 51
World War II, 55, 77, 80, 82, 88